SOCIOLOGICAL THEORY
Its Development and Major Paradigms

SOCIOLOGICAL THEORY
Its Development and Major Paradigms

GRAHAM C. KINLOCH
Florida State University

McGRAW-HILL BOOK COMPANY

New York   St. Louis   San Francisco   Auckland   Bogota   Düsseldorf
Johannesburg   London   Madrid   Mexico   Montreal   New Delhi
Panama   Paris   São Paulo   Singapore   Sydney   Tokyo   Toronto

Library of Congress Cataloging in Publication Data

Kinloch, Graham Charles.
   Sociological theory.

   Bibliography: p.
   Includes index.
   1. Sociology. I. Title.
HM24.K54   301'.01   76-14963
ISBN 0-07-034738-7

SOCIOLOGICAL THEORY
Its Development and Major Paradigms

  34567890 DODO 7832109

This book was set in Helvetica Light by Creative Book Services,
subsidiary of McGregor & Werner, Inc.
The editors were Lyle Linder and David Dunham;
the designer was Nicholas Krenitsky;
the production supervisor was Robert C. Pedersen.
R. R. Donnelley & Sons Company was printer and binder.

For Marc and Andrew,
two practical individualists.

CONTENTS

CONTENTS

PREFACE

Sociological theory has occupied a prominent position within the discipline from its very foundation. However, as a major subfield it has been hampered by at least two major problems: (1) theory, particularly within the context of a pragmatic culture, has often been viewed as separate from and irrelevant to research and empirical reality while (2) theory texts have tended to be descriptive, historical, and philosophical compendiums of large numbers of theorists rather than analyses of the evolution, structure, and forms of sociological theory.

In reaction to such problems, this work attempts to analyze the *emergence, context (i.e., social, intellectual, and biographical conditions), and evolution of the major types of theory in sociology.* Such an approach views sociological theory as a dynamic, situational, and changing process—a systemic reaction to particular social situations by intellectuals thinking in particular philosophical traditions. These approaches result in three major paradigms or definitions of social reality: the organic-structure-functional, conflict-radical, and social-behaviorist–social-psychological paradigms. The result is an assessment of the basis, development, and structure of sociological theory and its possible alternatives.

Such an approach offers a number of advantages. It highlights the major types of explanations in sociological theory as well as associated situational factors, revealing the explanatory basis of each type. Instead of viewing theorists in relative isolation, it examines the particular type of theory each exemplifies and contributes to. The result is a set of portraits of the major paradigms implicit within sociological theory and, indeed, with sociology as a whole. The reader is thus able to assess the relative strengths and weaknesses of each theory and to draw analytical conclusions regarding theory in general.

As with *any* analytical perspective, however, this approach is subject to a number of limitations of which I am readily aware: it overemphasizes the similarities between theorists, does not examine their work in detail, focuses on one major dimension of theory only (i.e., its paradigmatic foundation), and views sociological theory as a set of general paradigms, compressing their longitudinal differences. There will also be those who disagree with the choice and categorization of particular theorists as well as the *interpretation* of their works—a constant problem in the field. It should be emphasized, then, that this volume does *not* represent a history of social ideas, a detailed sociology of knowledge model, a detailed analysis of all dimensions of theory's historical and social contexts, an in-depth examination of each theorist's total work, or a full-scale analysis of all the dimensions of sociological theory and its development. Rather, it represents a limited analysis of a particular aspect of theory in the attempt to *abstract the major types of explanation in sociological theory and factors associated with their evolution*. This approach reflects the contemporary trend toward a more formal analysis of sociological theory and attempts to make a modest contribution in this direction, aiming to develop a more objective view of theory and its structural analysis. Finally, it should be noted that in order to obviate the problems of extensive footnoting, each theorist's background, major aims, assumptions, methodology, and typology have been abstracted from the works listed at the end of each chapter, "Specific Works by Theorists."

I am most grateful to the following individuals for their help in the completion of this work: David Edwards, my former editor, for enthusiasm and encouragement from the beginning of this project; Lyle Linder, my present editor, for ongoing interest and help; Beverley, for encouragement and tolerance; and Denise, for patient and painstaking typing of the manuscript. I owe thanks to them all.

Graham C. Kinloch

SOCIOLOGICAL THEORY
Its Development and Major Paradigms

INTRODUCTION

1

THE RELEVANCE OF THEORY TO KNOWLEDGE

THE RELATIONSHIP BETWEEN THEORY AND KNOWLEDGE

It is often assumed that a vast gulf exists between theory and reality: the former is viewed as abstract, obscure, the domain of intellectuals, and largely irrelevant to the latter which, in contrast, is regarded as practical and part of real, everyday affairs.

Such a view, however, is uninformed and distorted. Contrary to popular opinion, theory is an intimate part of practical reality and everyday life, representing the implicit foundation of all bodies of knowledge and each individual's everyday interpretation of social and physical phenomena. From the definition of theory as "a set of relations utilized to explain and interpret how particular phenomena operate," it is clear that such interpretations are involved in scientific and everyday observations alike. Theorizing (or the formulation and modification of interpretive explanations), then, is an ongoing process basic to formal, scientific knowledge *and* everyday social interaction. Thus, whether a physicist is attempting to explain (account for) a particular molecular structure or a parent is helping children understand why they should not lie or cheat, theory is involved insofar as "a set of relations" is implicit in each event.

Theory of one kind or another[1] is implicit in interpersonal relationships, the structure of human language, and human scientific endeavors as people attempt to account for their physical and social environment and to structure the latter through generalized interpretations (or social norms). In this way the individual relates to the physical universe and society through a complex set of assumptions which attempt to explain how these phenomena operate. Whether we are dealing with ideology, methodology, or technology, we are faced with a set of interpretive assumptions, defined within the context of a particular social setting, which account for what occurs. Thus theory is neither strictly abstract nor definitively practical; it is actually both in its attempt to explain what is viewed as real.

A number of different kinds of factors may be used in attempts at explanation: the structure of the physical universe, magic, astrology, mysticism, religion, a person's biological nature, the social system, and the effects of interaction are but a few examples. Furthermore, the structure of theory ranges from the very simple (e.g., X is related to Y) to the highly complex (e.g., X in conjunction

---

[1]We are not concerned with the various types of theory at this stage but will discuss them in the chapter to follow.

4

with a wide range of variables under a number of specific conditions is related to Y in a number of specific ways). Whatever the *type* of theory (the kinds of factors used) or its *structure* (level of complexity), its central importance rests on the manner in which it *defines reality for its adherents* and affects their views and behavior. Hence theory is dynamic in the way it constantly defines physical or social reality for its adherents.

THEORIZING AND SOCIOLOGICAL THEORY

In general, then, theorizing may be viewed as *the process by which individuals account for* (or explain and interpret) *their physical and social environments. Such a process occurs within the context of a specific social setting* (i.e., theorizing is ideologically, intellectually, and historically defined) *and defines the physical and social reality of this setting.* In this manner, theory represents an interpretation of reality.

Furthermore, the foundation of any theory is its paradigm or *model of reality.* This model consists of two major elements: (1) a *conceptualization* of the phenomenon being explained (e.g., society may be viewed as a "set of interdependent institutions") and (2) an assumed underlying *causal relationship* (e.g., the view that social structure represents, and evolves in response to, society's basic functions or system needs).

In sociology, these models appear to take one of three major forms: (1) general theory which conceptualizes society as a functioning, integrated system (the *organic-structure-functional* approach); (2) general theory which focuses on society as a dynamic, changing, conflict-ridden system based on competition and exploitation (*conflict-radical* theory); and (3) theories which deal with social phenomena at the microscopic or interpersonal level, focusing on processes such as socialization and role behavior (the *social-behaviorist-social-psychological* approach). We shall deal with all three types of theory within both traditional and contemporary sociology.

CENTRAL PROBLEMS

It is evident, then, that theorizing is socially significant, and it is important to understand this process in as much depth as possible. Accordingly, this volume, recognizing the central importance of sociological theory, attempts to answer four major questions:

1 What is theory?

2 What is sociological theory?

3 What is traditional sociological theory?

4 What is contemporary sociological theory?

OUR APPROACH

Section One of our discussion refers to the first two topics. Chapter 2 deals with what theory is in general—defining it formally and outlining its major types, its formal structure, the ways in which it may be constructed and the influence of the societal environment in which it develops. The next chapter discusses sociological theory in particular—its background, major types, development, and relationship to specific social contexts. We shall end this first section by developing a model of the most relevant societal and individual factors which result in the evolution of particular kinds of sociological theory.

Section Two introduces traditional sociological theory by discussing its sociohistorical setting and then delineating three major types of theory which these varying environments have created: organic theory, the conflict approach, and social behaviorism. As we discuss the theorists individually, we shall introduce six major facets of each one's work:

1 The *social* and *psychological context* in which the theorist works—i.e., the historical, ideological, and intellectual setting—as well as the theorist's particular experiences or personal biography.

2 The *major aims* of the theoretical work.

3 The *major assumptions* the individual makes concerning physical and social phenomena.

4 The *methods* advocated and used in the study of the theoretical system.

5 The *typology of assumed relationships* (conceptual model of society) which is either implicit or explicit in the theorist's work and used as the *explanation* system.

6 Finally we shall discuss the type or *structure* of each theory—that is, the type of explanation used and the issues this explanation raises for contemporary sociology.

At the end of Section Two, we shall (1) attempt to summarize how these factors relate to traditional sociological theory and (2) develop an appropriate typology.

Section Three represents a consideration of contemporary theory in American sociology. Here the same format used in the above discussion is applied to an analysis of three kinds of theory which, in some respects, parallel the types in Section Two: structure functionalism, modern conflict theory, and theory in social psychology. This section also concludes with a summary typology.

The analysis is concluded in Section Four with a discussion of major types of theory, an explanation of these types, and an outline of theoretical problems in sociological theory. The focus is on the three types of explanation discussed above and on sociology's emphasis on the questions of social order and change at individual and societal levels of analysis. This final chapter will relate the implications of the above conclusions to the kinds of theoretical development most needed in sociology.

CONCLUSIONS

This introductory discussion has attempted to highlight the relevance of theory to knowledge by pointing out that the former is neither strictly abstract nor totally practical. Rather, theory represents the attempt to explain reality in both scientific and everyday settings. Theorizing, therefore, represents an attempt to account for physical and social environments and defines an individual's physical and social reality accordingly. Theory is primarily a "social definition of a person's situation," representing an important link between patterns of thought and actual behavior.

Having introduced the three basic kinds of theory in sociology and the procedure we shall use in applying them to traditional and contemporary sociology, we turn now to answer our first basic question: What is theory?

EXERCISES

1 Obtain the following material and analyze its content in regard to the major kinds of assumptions involved:

   a The introductory chapter in a biology textbook

   b A religious sermon

   c A political speech

   d The American Declaration of Independence

   e A contemporary novel

   f A local newspaper editorial

   g An introductory geometry textbook

2 Analyze the major kinds of assumptions which occur in the following types of conversation:

   a Parent-child interaction over discipline

   b Student-faculty interaction concerning grades

   c Customer-clerk sales interaction

   d Interaction in dating

   e Husband-wife interaction over child-rearing practices

   f Interaction with friends concerning recreation activities

   g Lawyer-judge interaction in court

READINGS

Collins, R., and M. Makowsky: "Introduction," *The Discovery of Society,* Random House, New York, 1972.

Garfinkel, H.: *Studies in Ethnomethodology,* Prentice-Hall, Englewood Cliffs, N.J., 1967, chaps. 2 and 7.

Klapp, O. E.: *Models of Social Order,* National Press Books, Palo Alto, Calif., 1973, chap. 1.

Larson, C. J.: *Major Themes in Sociological Theory,* McKay, New York, 1973, chap. 1.

Martindale, D.: *The Nature and Types of Sociological Theory,* Houghton Mifflin, Boston, 1960, chap. 1

Timasheff, N. S.: *Sociological Theory, Its Nature and Growth,* 3d ed., Random House, New York, 1967, chap. 1.

Truzzi, M. (ed.): *Sociology and Everyday Life,* Prentice-Hall, Englewood Cliffs, N.J., 1968.

2

WHAT IS THEORY?

MAJOR TOPICS:

Theory defined

Major types of theory

The process of theory construction

The social context of theorizing

Since *theory* is defined differently by so many writers, it is important to define this term exactly before proceeding to an analysis of sociological theory. Accordingly, in this chapter, four major aspects of theory are examined: (1) its definition and structural characteristics, (2) major types of theory, (3) the process of theory construction, and (4) major influences exerted by the social context in which theory construction takes place.

THEORY DEFINED

The term *theory* tends to be confused with a wide variety of terms designating concepts that lack explanatory power. Examples of these include *description, typology, model, prediction,* and *conceptual framework.* It is also difficult to find widespread consensus regarding the definition of *theory* among writers on the subject. We shall proceed, then, by distinguishing between *theory* and these other concepts before turning to examine the way in which it is defined by a number of authors. We shall conclude by developing our own definition of *theory* and outlining the major characteristics of its formal structure.

The primary function of a theory is to attempt to explain or account for a particular phenomenon in terms of some other phenomenon which is viewed as explanatory. It is this *explanatory function* which distinguishes a theory from related but nonexplanatory concepts. Thus a *description* refers to the delineation or listing of a particular phenomenon's characteristics without accounting for its existence or change. A *typology* also represents a set of characteristics assumed to refer to (or be typical of) a particular phenomenon. *Models,* while sometimes viewed as typologies, are based on less empirical observation and define interrelationships between characteristics as well. Once again, however, they tend to lack explanatory power. *Prediction* involves the ability to predict where an individual will stand with respect to variable Y by knowing his or her position on variable X, this prediction being based on previous empirical *correlations* which have been observed between these two variables. However, an investigator may be able to develop high levels of predictability without understanding or being able to account for these relationships. Thus we may have high predictability with low explanation and vice versa. Prediction, then, in no way provides theory or explanation ipso facto. The facts will not speak for themselves and have to be explained or accounted for. Finally, *conceptual frameworks,* while often viewed as theories, represent ways of conceptualizing phenomena within the context of a specific viewpoint which specifies major relevant variables. Such a framework, however, neglects to explain the internal relationships among variables within it.

The above distinctions may be illustrated as follows: describing the characteristics of a particular subculture such as that of the hippies does not account for the evolution and change in that group. A typology of the nuclear family similarly explains or accounts for nothing within such a unit. A model of an advanced industrialized society of the future may be useful and be based on a certain amount of empirical data, but it does not explain the evolution or the structure and internal processes of such a projected society. Furthermore, an educator may be able to predict a student's college grades from his or her performance in high school with a high degree of accuracy without being able to explain the relationship. Thus, although empirical correlations may be very high, the researcher's ability to *account for* these relationships may be extremely low. Finally, a conceptual framework such as the symbolic interactionist approach to the family may be very useful in highlighting specific theoretical and research problems as well as relevant variables without being able to account for them. While all these terms, concepts, and frameworks are part of the structure of theory, they do not explain the phenomena they refer to; it is this function that is basic to a theory.

In order to highlight the central characteristics of a theory, we turn to some of the major authors who have dealt with the subject.

With regard to formal scientific theory (in contrast to the informal, ideological, and untestable kind), a number of writers on the subject have developed the following definitions:[1]

H. M. Blalock: "It has been noted that theories do not consist entirely of conceptual schemes or typologies but must contain law-

---

[1]H. M. Blalock, *Theory Construction, From Verbal to Mathematical Formulations,* Prentice-Hall, Englewood Cliffs, N.J., 1969, p. 2; J. Gibbs, *Sociological Theory Construction,* Dryden Press, New York, 1972, p. 5; J. Hage, *Techniques and Problems of Theory Construction in Sociology,* Wiley, New York, 1972, p. 172; P. D. Reynolds, *A Primer in Theory Construction,* Bobbs-Merrill, Indianapolis, 1971, p. 11; A. L. Stinchcombe, *Constructing Social Theories,* Harcourt, Brace & World, New York, 1968, p. 3; D. Willer, *Scientific Sociology, Theory and Method,* Prentice-Hall, Englewood Cliffs, N.J., 1967, p. 9.

like propositions that interrelate the concepts or variables two or more at a time."

J. Gibbs: "A theory is a set of logically interrelated statements in the form of empirical assertions about properties of infinite classes of events or things."

J. Hage: "There is general agreement that a theory is a set of propositions or theoretical statements. . . ."

P. D. Reynolds: ". . . the use of the term *theory* will refer to abstract statements that are considered part of scientific knowledge in either the set-of-laws, the axiomatic, or the casual process forms."

A. L. Stinchcombe: "Theory ought to create the *capacity* to *invent explanations."*

D. Willer: "A theory is an integrated set of relationships with a certain level of validity."

While these authors emphasize different aspects of formal theory, it is possible to perceive a number of common characteristics: abstractness, logic, propositions, explanations, relationships, and acceptance by the scientific community. At this preliminary point in our discussion, then, it is possible to say that a theory is "a set of abstract and logical propositions which attempts to explain relationships between phenomena."

The above definition, however, does not indicate the *structure* of a *formal* theory. While various sociologists may differ on the kind and number of elements involved in the structure of a theory, it appears reasonable to summarize them as follows:

1 The foundation of any theory is its underlying *paradigm,* defined in Chapter 1 as consisting of a particular conceptualization of the phenomena being explained and the underlying explanatory relationships which account for the manner in which these phenomena operate. Thus the particular phenomena in question are conceptually defined while an underlying causal relationship is assumed to exist; the implications of this relationship are used to explain the particular phenomena in question. If a paradigm is highly developed beyond the simplistic, general hypothesis level, it may become a model of assumed relationships which represents the foundation of the theory's formal structure. The following are examples of theoretical paradigms: the structure-functional framework, the conflict orientation, Sigmund Freud's personality theory,[2] and symbolic interactionism.

2 Any paradigm implies certain *concepts*—a label or name given to a class of phenomena (e.g., *personality, social class, social system, institution, social mobility, social change*). These concepts need to be carefully defined and their relationship to the underlying paradigm demonstrated.

3 The *logical relationships* between these concepts need to be stated; that is, they have to be linked theoretically. The level and form of these relationships tend to vary: they may be *axioms* (propositions that are assumed to be true in and of themselves), *propositions* (statements of relationship that may be derived from axioms), or *hypotheses* (statements of relationship between concepts in their operationalized form, that is, their empirical indexes). Furthermore, these relationships may be positive, negative, or independent of one another.

Finally, the *structure* of a theory depends on the kinds of relationship statements it contains and their relationship to one another. Thus, a theory may be *axiomatic* in structure (a set of definitive propositions), *propositional* in form (a set of propositions derived from an axiom), or *axiomatic-deductive-inductive* (a set of related axioms and derived propositions). On a more informal level, a set of linked hypotheses may be viewed as a theory but tends to be incomplete in the absence of its basic axioms and propositions.

4 The concepts and statements of relationships then need to be defined empirically or *operationalized* in the form of variables (as personality tests, social class scales, demographic measures of a social system, the organizational structure of institutions, measures of rates of social mobility, and socioeconomic measures of social change). Each variable also contains a number of empirical indexes defined by the kind of research instrument (e.g., scores on specific items of a questionnaire) the theorist concerned has selected. A major difference between scientific and nonscientific theories, then, is the extent to which they are empirically testable rather than ideological or closed systems of thought.

[2]For discussion of Freud's paradigm, see Reynolds, *A Primer in Theory Construction*, pp. 23–26.

5 The next stage consists of an empirical *methodology* to test the hypothesized relationships between the variables and indexes. This may consist of an opinion survey, participant observation, interview data, the mathematical manipulation of demographic data, or a small group experiment in a laboratory. This methodology is dictated in large measure by the kinds of variables derived from the theory's structure and is defined by that structure rather than developed prior to it. Whatever methodology is used, it is constrained by characteristics of the sample available, sampling error, the investigator's level of control, and measurement error as well as error in the data analysis.

6 Once the data are gathered, they have to be *analyzed* in reference to the theory's major hypotheses. Such analysis often consists of the application of statistical techniques to indicate levels of association and statistical significance. If applied naïvely or abused, these tests may be entirely misleading. Furthermore, they are entirely dependent on the quality of the sample and data concerned.

7 Upon completion of the data analysis, the theorist must proceed to *interpret* data results in reference to the structure of his or her theory—its basic paradigm, axioms, propositions, and hypotheses. Since empirical methodologies, tests, and data analysis provide only indirect tests of a theory's basic structure, an investigator needs to be extremely cautious in drawing conclusions from (necessarily) limited data. It is most naïve to overestimate the theoretical significance of any set of empirical data, no matter how broad their scope.

8 Finally, the theorist seeks to *evaluate* the theory in terms of two major criteria: (a) the efficiency, scope, and logic of its theoretical structure and (b) its level of testability, prediction, and accuracy when submitted to empirical examination. A number of possible alternatives are open at this point: scrap the theory entirely, modify its underlying paradigm, or develop further axioms, propositions, hypotheses, and/or new methodologies. Whatever the case, the individual is forced to make some decision concerning the theory he or she has developed and tested. Theorizing is an ongoing, dynamic process and consists of continuous change and modification.

14   To summarize, we have defined *formal theory* as "a set of

accepted, abstract, and logical propositions which attempts to explain relationships between phenomena." Second, the structure of formal theory consists of eight major elements: (1) a paradigm, (2) a set of concepts, (3) statements (axioms, propositions, and hypotheses) concerning the logical relationships between these concepts are operationalized, (5) the methodology used to test the hypothesized relationships, (6) data analysis, (7) interpretation of the results, and, finally, (8) evaluation of the theory's logical and empirical structure in view of the data analysis and interpretation.

These elements are outlined in Figure 2.1, which illustrates the structure of formal theory and the ongoing dynamics of the

FIGURE 2.1

THE STRUCTURAL CHARACTERISTICS OF FORMAL THEORY AS AN EXPLANATION SYSTEM

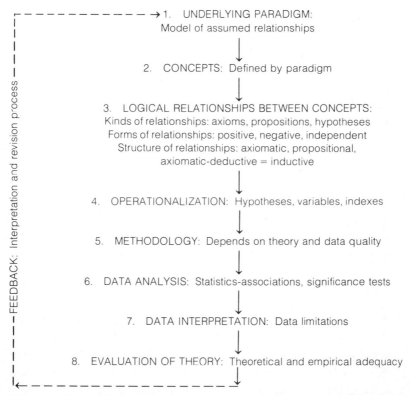

process of theorizing. We conclude this section, then, with the view that *theory is an explanation system,* and that *formal theory consists of the eight major elements outlined above.* Furthermore, this system is based on its underlying paradigm, which can only be tested indirectly and is assumed to exist theoretically for purposes of useful explanation.

MAJOR TYPES OF THEORY

The kind of theory we have discussed so far is the formal, scientific type which we introduced in order to highlight the characteristics of explanation. Theories, however, obviously differ in a number of characteristics, as follows:

1 Informal-Formal   Theory may be of the formal, scientific type described above, structured by assumptions underlying the scientific method, or it may be informal and relatively unstructured, typified by assumptions relating to everyday life. Mathematical theory and theory in the physical sciences tend to conform to the former type, while single hypotheses, ideology, or research hunches fall into the latter category.

2 Descriptive-Explanatory   Similarly, theories may be predominantly descriptive, lacking an underlying explanatory paradigm, or they may focus on the explanatory function and be structured accordingly. While descriptive theory may be implicitly explanatory, it fails to represent an explanation when its basic paradigm is either absent or invisible.

3 Ideological-Scientific   The context of a theory may be predominantly ideological or guided by the scientific method, with its emphasis on the formulation of assumptions which are empirically testable. While this distinction is a matter of degree rather than form—the scientific method contains ideological elements also—it is important to define a theorist's major aims in order to appreciate the values behind the work. Thus no theory is completely objective: no matter how objective it appears to be, it *always* possesses certain ideological implications.

4 Intuitive-Objective   Theories also differ in the extent to which they argue that knowledge is intuitive and subjective as opposed to external and objective. Thus phenomenologists and mystics would argue the former, while scientists hold more to the latter.

In sociology, the distinction is exemplified by the ethnomethodologists on the one hand and structure functionalists on the other.

5 Inductive-Deductive   Theories may be one of two major types: they may attempt to move from the specific to the general or vice versa. The former are inductive and the latter deductive in structure. In sociology, as we shall see, most theories are deductive, using the general (e.g., the social system) as the independent variable in their explanation system. Psychological and social-psychological theories, on the other hand, tend to be inductive in form.

6 Microscopic-Macroscopic   Theories also differ in their level of analysis: they may focus on the specific and individual level (the microscopic) or the general and societal (the macroscopic). In sociology, they tend to be predominantly of the latter kind; while psychological explanations focus more on the other level. Each level has its own advantages and problems. However, the macroscopic tends to become too general to explain individual phenomena adequately, while the microscopic suffers from the opposite problem.

7 Structure-Functional   Theories also differ in focus: some concentrate on explaining the structure of phenomena, while others are more concerned with the manner in which these phenomena are evolving and changing. In sociology, for example, structure-functional theory is concerned with the structure of a particular society in terms of its underlying functions, while conflict theory focuses more on the dynamics of a society.

8 Naturalistic-Social   Finally, theories vary in the kinds of phenomena they use as explanatory factors: some use biological and naturalistic variables while others concentrate on social phenomena. Thus a social scientist may attempt to explain social behavior in terms of humanity's biological instincts (a naturalistic approach) *or* in terms of characteristics of the social system, such as its division of labor, level of industrialization, and degree of institutionalization (a systemic orientation). These are two very different kinds of explanation with varying implications.

From our discussion here, then, it is evident that theories may differ in a wide range of characteristics; we shall illustrate these differences with respect to sociological theory in the chapter to

17

follow. A general distinction runs through these eight dimensions, however: theories tend to be formal, explanatory, scientific, deductive, and objective *or* informal, descriptive, ideological, inductive, and intuitive.

While these differences may be ranged on a continuum, it appears that most theories fall on one particular end. As far as we are concerned in this work, *theory* represents the former, explanatory type in contrast to the latter, informal type. In sociology, on the other hand, many, if not the majority, of theories are informal, descriptive, ideological, and nonexplanatory. We shall thus discuss both kinds in detail, with awareness of the limitations of nontheoretical arguments.

THE PROCESS OF THEORY CONSTRUCTION

How are theories developed? While this book is not specifically concerned with theory construction, it is important to discuss this process by way of introduction, and we shall do so in reference to our previous delineation of a formal theory's structure.

Since most theories in sociology represent little more than descriptive paradigms, they are predominantly the function of a specific historical, ideological, and intellectual situation—that is, they represent theoretical models developed by individuals (philosophers, academics, intellectuals, etc.) born and socialized within a particular social situation. Theory construction of this kind represents the formal reaction to and conceptualization of that social situation. Early theorizing involved little formal theory construction. However, with the evolution of the scientific method and empirical sociology, theory construction has gradually become a more formal process and may be outlined as follows:

1 The first step is delineation of the theory's underlying causal relationships. As we have pointed out, this explanatory framework is basic to the theory's explanatory structure. The paradigm should be made as explicit as possible, especially the causal relationships within it that are assumed to be explanatory. The delineation of this model of assumed relationships is the initial and major step in the theorizing process.

2 The next step involves definition of the concepts in the paradigm as clearly and as fully as possible. Meanings of concepts are often assumed rather than defined, leading to ambiguity and possible confusion.

3   The logical relationships between these concepts implied by the theory's paradigm then require definition in the form of axioms and/or propositions. Further propositions may be logically deduced if the method of axiomatic deduction is followed.[3]

4   The concepts are then operationalized in the form of variables and the logical relationships between these variables are deduced from the above axioms and propositions in the form of hypotheses.

5   The methodology implied by these variables is then developed in order to test these hypotheses through empirical indexes. This methodology is then applied as rigorously as possible to test the hypotheses empirically.

6   The data are then analyzed according to techniques, statistical or otherwise, derived from the theoretical system just developed.

7   Having analyzed the data, the theorist needs to interpret the significance of the results in reference to the theory he or she has developed. The theory may be interpreted on the basis of those results[4] or in reference to them,[5] depending on the approach to theory construction accepted.

8   Finally, having completed the above steps, the theorist attempts to evaluate the theory on theoretical and/or empirical grounds depending, once again, on the particular approach to theorizing accepted.

It should be evident from the above discussion that theory construction is a complex but unified process in which a basic paradigm is translated into theoretical and empirical form and evaluated on the grounds of both sets of criteria. Thus theory and methodology are *not* separate entities; the one implies the other, and they should be evaluated together.

---

[3]For a discussion of this method, see H. L. Zetterberg, *On Theory and Verification in Sociology,* Bedminster Press, Toronto, 1965.
[4]See Blalock, *Theory Construction, From Verbal to Mathematical Formulation.*
[5]See Gibbs, *Sociological Theory Construction.*

THE SOCIAL CONTEXT OF THEORIZING

Theorizing obviously does not take place in a vacuum; on the contrary, it is structured by the specific historical, ideological, and intellectual characteristics of the social situation in which it occurs. Furthermore, the theorist's biographical experiences define his or her intellectual and ideological orientations, which in turn affect this individual's conceptualization of reality. We shall relate these factors directly to sociology in the next chapter, but it is appropriate to introduce their general influence at this point as follows:

1 Societal Conditions   Theories tend to develop most markedly in reaction to society's changing development and needs. Thus sociology was founded during a period of marked unrest and revolution in Europe, and the discipline has continuously reacted to social developments such as industrialization, bureaucratization, welfare needs, the population explosion, and so on. Theory, then, may be viewed as a changing reaction to and conceptualization of society's ongoing physical and social problems as perceived by a particular group of academics or intellectuals. Depending on general societal conditions as well as the theorist's position in the social structure, particular kinds of theory tend to appear at various stages of a society's development, as we shall demonstrate. Thus, structure-functional theory tends to develop among particular intellectuals in the wake of social and/or economic disruption, while more radical approaches have reacted to the kinds of dominance that appear to accompany high levels of industrialization and bureaucratization. War conditions have also resulted in the development of technological theory and invention. Less formal theory also develops in reaction to particular societal situations. Theory may thus be viewed as the function of specific societal conditions.

2 Intellectual Conditions   Theory is also a function of predominant intellectual norms. Thus much of early sociological theory was influenced by particular branches of philosophy—naturalism, rationalism, the Renaissance, and the Reformation, for example—and reflects these particular views of humanity and society. As science developed in conjunction with pragmatism, however, they began to take on a rather different form, as is evident in the present focus on mathematical theory and the process of formal theory construction in the more empirical rather than metaphysical vein. The intellectual modes of thought which are prominent at a particular point of a society's development, then, tend to define the kind of theory which develops.[6] As a society's level of industrialization proceeds, these modes of thought move from the philosophical and ideological toward the empirical and scientific.

3 Biographical Conditions There are a number of specific aspects of a theorist's life which appear to influence the kind of perspective he or she develops. These include the individual's socio-economic status, academic training, intellectual peers, ideological views, and personal life. Thus, for example, sociologists with upper-class backgrounds and an elitist education tend to be conservative in ideology and to adhere to the more organic structure-functional kinds of theory. By contrast, those who come from more middle- and lower-class backgrounds and whose training is different generally tend toward a more radical ideology. Personal experiences also make theorists aware of particular aspects of social phenomena in contrast to others, and this affects their theorizing too. The influence and encouragement of intellectual peers is of considerable importance also. The academic community at large represents another important subculture, particularly in the matter of recognition and the evolution of an academic status hierarchy. Such reaction provides important feedback which may further or hinder the thinker's ongoing work.

From the above it should be clear that theorizing is affected by a wide range of factors—societal, intellectual, and biographical—representing a society's particular stage of social development as much as it does the thoughts of a particular individual. In this way, theorizing is a sociological rather than an individual process.

CONCLUSIONS

In this chapter we have attempted to define formal theory, present its major structural characteristics, outline its major types, delineate the process of theory construction, and reveal the influence of its societal context.

---

[6]See T. S. Kuhn, *The Structure of Scientific Revolutions,* University of Chicago Press, Chicago, 1962, for an excellent discussion of this.

We defined a theory as "a set of abstract and logical propositions which attempt to explain relationships between phenomena" and pointed out that it consists of eight structural elements: (1) a paradigm, (2) a set of concepts, (3) statements (axioms, propositions, and hypotheses) concerning the logical relationship between these concepts, (4) a set of operationalized variables and indexes, (5) a methodology designed to test these predicted relationships, (6) data analysis, (7) data interpretation, and, finally, (8) evaluation of the theory in light of all the above.

We distinguished broadly between theories which are formal, explanatory, scientific, deductive, and objective on the one hand and the more informal, descriptive, ideological, inductive, and intuitive theories on the other. Further, the process of theory construction consists of developing the eight structural features just described, beginning with the underlying paradigm. Finally, we attempted to show how theorizing is influenced by the particular societal, intellectual, and biographical conditions in which the theorist works.

Having outlined the major characteristics of theory as an explanatory system, along with relevant influencing factors, we shall go on to apply that discussion to the kind of theory which has developed in sociology.

EXERCISES

1 Consider the various definitions of *theory* presented in the theory texts suggested under "Readings," below, and develop your own definition.

2 Compare and contrast examples of what you view as theories with conceptual frameworks, descriptions, typologies, models and predictive correlations.

3 Select a particular concept and attempt to explain it (i.e., account for the phenomenon to which it refers) theoretically.

4 Outline the major societal, intellectual, and biographical influences which affected Marxism and Freudian theory.

5 Select a number of explanations in sociology and consider the extent to which you would regard them as theoretical.

READINGS

Blalock, H. M.: *Theory Construction, From Verbal to Mathematical Formulations,* Prentice-Hall, Englewood Cliffs, N.J., 1969, chap. 1.

Gibbs, J.: *Sociological Theory Construction,* Dryden Press, New York, 1972, chap. 1.

Hage, J.: *Techniques and Problems of Theory Construction in Sociology,* Wiley, New York, 1972, chap. 1.

Hill, R., and D. A. Hansen: "The Identification of Conceptual Frameworks Utilized in Family Study," *Marriage and Family Living,* **22**:299–311, 1960.

Kuhn, T. S.: *The Structure of Scientific Revolutions,* University of Chicago Press, Chicago, 1962, chaps. 7 and 8.

Reynolds, P. D.: *A Primer in Theory Construction,* Bobbs-Merrill, Indianapolis, 1971, chaps. 1–6.

Stinchcombe, A. L.: *Constructing Social Theories,* Harcourt, Brace & World, New York, 1968, chap. 1.

Willer, D.: *Scientific Sociology, Theory and Method,* Prentice-Hall, Englewood Cliffs, N.J., 1967, chap. 1.

Zetterberg, H. L.: *On Theory and Verification in Sociology,* Bedminster Press, Toronto, 1965, chap. 1.

3

WHAT IS SOCIOLOGICAL THEORY?

So far theory, both formal and informal, has been discussed as an explanation system in general. In this chapter we examine the kinds of theory which have developed in sociology in particular. Viewing sociological theory as the attempt to explain or account for social phenomena, we shall apply our discussion in the last chapter by dealing with the following aspects of sociological theory: (1) its definition and structural characteristics, (2) major types of sociological theory, (3) the historical development of sociological theory, (4) major influences exerted by the societal context in which sociological theory has evolved, and finally, (5) some major examples of sociological theory.

SOCIOLOGICAL THEORY DEFINED

People have conceptualized society and social phenomena from the time of Plato until today. These conceptualizations have obviously varied from Greek philosophical and metaphysical views of the world through theological definitions of reality, Enlightenment views of human nature, rationalism and the scientific method, to sociology's conceptualization of social phenomena in terms of societal and systemic variables. Sociological theory has been implicit in much human thought, in particular views of society and its relationship to the individual. However, as we shall emphasize later, it was not until the nineteenth century, when society was viewed as a "real" and separate entity—a unit of analysis in itself which could be used to explain social phenomena within it—that sociological theory actually developed. While earlier conceptualizations of society were metaphysical theological, and philosophical, they failed to be sociological in this respect.

Sociological theory, then, represents *a set of assumptions concerning society and social phenomena in reference to their separate societal reality*. Thus it stands in contrast to earlier systems of thought which emphasized mystical, theological, and naturalistic explanations of these phenomena. While clearly influenced by these foregoing cosmologies, particularly Enlightenment philosophy, sociological theory is based on *the assumed existence of the social system as an independent entity* in contrast to metaphysical or theological phenomena. In this manner the development of sociological theory represents the evolution of a new system of thought in which metaphysical and religious explanations were replaced by the notion of societal reality which was then conceptualized and used to explain social phenomena.

In general, then, sociological paradigms represent the conceptualization of the social order and the manner in which it changes—that is, social structure and social process. We defined theory as "a set of accepted, abstract, and logical propositions which attempt to explain relationships between phenomena." Sociological theory, accordingly, represents such propositions couched in sociological terms. These propositions attempt to explain relationships between social phenomena, with the underlying assumption that society and social phenomena possess an independent reality—that they are real in and of themselves.

While books on the subject are notable for their failure to define the term *sociological theory*, it is possible to illustrate the preceding discussion by examining definitions of *sociology* in these same texts. Don Martindale, for example, refers to sociology as "the science of man's interhuman life,"[1] while Nicholas S. Timasheff, in another well-known work, states that "sociology means the study of society on a highly generalized or abstract level."[2] From this it follows that sociological theory is a "set of assumptions which attempts to explain or account for society and 'man's interhuman life.' " In general, then, sociological theory is an explanation system of social phenomena.

From the above it may appear that there is general agreement concerning the structure of sociological theory. However, this is clearly *not* so. Depending on how sociologists view the nature of sociological phenomena (with regard to level of complexity and the corollary suitability of the scientific method), they tend to vary in the degree to which they view sociological theory as informal and essentially descriptive or formal and explanatory. Robert Nisbet, for example, views sociology as an "art form" which makes its major advances through creative processes and themes which it "largely shares with art."[3]

C. Wright Mills takes a similar view in his description of the classic craftsman who uses the "sociological imagination" while shuttling between "macroscopic conceptions and detailed expositions," focusing on the structure of a society as a whole, its

[1]D. Martindale, *The Nature and Types of Sociological Theory*, Houghton Mifflin, Boston, 1960, p. 3.
[2]N. S. Timasheff, *Sociological Theory, Its Nature and Growth*, 3d ed., Random House, New York, 1967, p. 4.
[3]R. A. Nisbet, "Sociology as an Art Form," *Pacific Sociological Review*: **5**:67–74, 1962.

historical development, and the types or "varieties" of people which prevail within it at a particular stage of its development.[4] In contrast to a focus on very general theory or highly specific empirical studies, Mills sees sociologists utilizing both in a flexible and classical tradition.

Robert K. Merton also attempts to bridge the gap between highly general and specific levels of analysis by using "middle-range theories"[5]—"limited sets of assumptions from which specific hypotheses are logically derived and confirmed by empirical investigation." Operating at the group level of analysis (e.g., reference group and role theory), middle-range theory attempts to link the individual to the social structure through the network of his or her social relationships. Sociological theory, according to this approach, focuses on the group rather than the societal or strictly individual level of analysis.

At the formal end of this continuum stand sociologists who accept a scientific definition of theory. Foremost among these are George C. Homans and Hans L. Zetterberg. Theory, according to the former, consists of a conceptual scheme and set of deductive propositions, some of which are contingent to experience and can thus be tested. Homans concludes that "There are few theories in sociology . . . that meet the definition . . . of what a theory ought to be,"[6] whether we are dealing with normative, nonnormative, structural, functional, or psychological theories. Sociological theory, according to this well-known writer, is too loose and requires formalization in order to qualify as theory in the scientific tradition.

Zetterberg also argues for a formal approach, emphasizing a systematic analysis of types of relations between variables and propositions in axiomatic-deductive form.[7] His axiomatic-deductive approach to sociological theory, along with specific rules for the logical derivation of propositions, represents one of the most formal approaches to theory and has been further elaborated by recent authors dealing with the process of theory construction in sociology.[8]

[4]C. W. Mills, The Sociological Imagination, Oxford University Press, New York, 1959.
[5]R. K. Merton, On Theoretical Sociology, Free Press, New York, 1967.
[6]G. C. Homans, "Contemporary Theory in Sociology," in R. E. L. Faris (ed.), Handbook of Modern Sociology, Rand McNally, Chicago, 1964, pp. 951–977.
[7]H. L. Zetterberg, On Theory and Verification in Sociology, Bedminster Press, Totowa, N.J., 1965.
[8]See, for example, the works by Blalock, Gibbs, Hage, Reynolds, Stinchcombe, and Willer cited in the previous chapter.

From the above discussion, a range of opinion concerning the characteristics of sociological theory is evident, highlighting a continuum of formality. On the more informal end we are confronted with Nisbet and Mills, who see sociology as a form of classic art and craftsmanship, while at the other extreme, Homans and Zetterberg argue for a formal, logical, and—in the case of the latter—axiomatic approach to sociological theory. Bridging the two extremes is Merton's notion of middle-range theory, which attempts to link the individual and the social structure at the group level. Sociological theory is thus viewed from a range of perspectives, depending on the theorist's definition of theory in general and sociological theory in particular. Thus these views imply very different theoretical aims, assumptions, and methodologies, as demonstrated in Figure 3.1. Sociological theory, then, represents a range of intellectual traditions—from the classical and philosophical to the logical and scientific—rather than a homogeneous perspective.

Whatever the theorist's perspective, most sociological theory, as Homans points out, fails to conform to the logical type

FIGURE 3.1
VIEWS OF SOCIOLOGICAL THEORY: A CONTINUUM OF FORMALITY

THEORIST ASPECT	NISBET	MILLS	MERTON	HOMANS	ZETTERBERG
1. Aims	Theory as creative art	The "sociological imagination" as classic craftsmanship	The development of middle-range theory	Theory as a set of deductive propositions	Sociology as science
2. Assumptions	Sociology and art are part of the same creative process	The importance of society's historical context	Middle-range theory links the macro-micro levels of analysis	Importance of the psychological element in sociological theory	Scientific theory in sociology is possible
3. Methodology	Informal, creative theorizing and the abstraction of themes	Application of macroscopic concepts to microscopic empirical studies	Utilize reference group theory and research	Logical structure and deduction	Axiomatic deduction process

that he delineates—that is the formal end of the continuum. Rather, most theory in sociology goes little beyond the paradigm stage (a particular conceptualization of the phenomenon being explained and the underlying explanatory relationships which are assumed to exist and thus account for the manner in which these phenomena operate). With their foundation in particular societal, intellectual, and biographical contexts, these paradigms are used to account for social phenomena. The heart of any paradigm or theoretical operation according to Jerald Hage is "the classes of variables of social phenomena that are its particular focus,"[9]—that is, its theoretical focus. Thus paradigms in sociology, as we shall see, vary in their focus on societies as organic, functional units, through an emphasis on social systems as sets of opposing forces, to the conceptualization of society as a set of interacting and communicating individuals. Whatever the focus, these theoretical orientations or paradigms represent the foundation of theoretical explanation in sociology.

From the above discussion, then, it is evident that sociological theory may be defined as "a set of paradigms (abstract assumptions) concerning society and social phenomena in reference to their separate societal reality that is used to account for a society's social structure and internal social processes." These paradigms vary in focus, level, and formality—characteristics we shall deal with next in our discussion of major types of sociological theory.

MAJOR TYPES AND CENTRAL
PROBLEMS OF SOCIOLOGICAL THEORY

In Chapter 2 we indicated that theory in general varies on a number of basic dimensions: level of formality, explanation, ideology, objectivity, kind of explanation (microscopic or macroscopic), focus (structure or process), and factors used (naturalistic or social). Most sociological theories as defined above tend to be informal, descriptive, ideological, intuitive, and deductive. However, they vary in *level* (macroscopic-microscopic), *factors used* (naturalistic-biological or systemic-social), and *focus* (social structure or process). Using these three dimensions, it is possible to develop a typology of major types of

[9]J. Hage, *Techniques and Problems of Theory Construction in Sociology,* Wiley, New York, 1972, p. 192

FIGURE 3.2
MAJOR TYPES OF SOCIOLOGICAL THEORY

LEVEL OF ANALYSIS	MACROSCOPIC		MICROSCOPIC	
TYPE OF EXPLANATION	NATURALISTIC	SYSTEMIC	NATURALISTIC	SYSTEMIC
FOCUS				
Structure	Organic theory	Structure functionalism	Social behaviorism	Social psychological theory
Process	Conflict theory	Radical sociology	Social behaviorism	Social psychological theory

sociological theory as illustrated in Figure 3.2. This typology encompasses a number of basic sociological paradigms as follows: the organic-structure-functional, conflict-radical, and social-behavorist–social psychological. Furthermore, macroscopic theory is deductive in form, while microscopic theory is generally inductive. Macroscopic theory which focuses on social structure also tends to be conservative in ideology, while other theory at this level which concentrates on social process (the conflict-radical paradigm) is generally more radical in its implications. Microscopic theory, on the other hand, is generally conservative in its emphasis on the scientific method and functionalistic phenomena at the interpersonal level of analysis.

The major characteristics of these paradigms may be outlined as follows.

The Organic-Structure-Functional Paradigm

This paradigm views society as a system of functionally interrelated parts. Its initial form—the organic approach—sees the operation of a number of natural laws in society in a mechanical and organic manner as the social system evolves.

A second form of the organic approach—that is, the view that society is like an organism—is evident in the writing of Emile Durkheim and Ferdinand Tönnies. These authors take more of a social-psychological or systemic approach, holding that society is an integrated organism dependent on its division of labor system which, in turn, is related to the kinds of norms or social will

31

binding the individual to his or her social setting. This approach emphasizes sociological or systemic rather than naturalistic phenomena, but it is equally organic in its view of society as an integrated organism.

Structure functionalism represents a contemporary version of the earlier organic approach. Focusing on the manner in which a social system represents a number of underlying functions or systemic problems, theorists of this school attempt to develop general theories of society in terms of basic underlying problems which are solved socially through the evolution of a number of societal subsystems.

In general, then, the organic-structure-functional paradigm conceptualizes society as an integrated, organic system at the microscopic and macroscopic level, a system evolving toward greater societal integration and internal efficiency. Having its roots in enlightenment philosophy and being further elaborated by reference to the biological analogy, this paradigm became basic to sociological theory. As can be seen from our typology, its major characteristics are its macroscopic focus on society's social structure and its utilization of both naturalistic and systemic modes of explanation.

The Conflict-Radical Paradigm

The conflict-radical paradigm is as systemic as the organic-structure-functional, but it views conflict rather than conformity and integration as central to the social system. As individuals struggle with nature to meet their primary needs, various forms of conflict and domination evolve, representing the basis of the social system. Thus society is in continuous conflict and evolution. The traditional conflict approach, of course, is evident in the work of Karl Marx, who applied the methodology of dialectical materialism to a historical analysis of humanity's struggle with nature and itself. A similar societal problem approach is taken by Robert Park, who applies the ecological framework to society's "natural" evolution. A more naturalistic approach is taken by Vilfredo Pareto and Thorstein Veblen, who utilize notions such as *residues* and human *traits* to explain social equilibrium and conflict.

Modern conflict theory attempts to elaborate the Marxian approach in order to make it relevant to the understanding of modern industrial society. Here we shall discuss Ralph Dahrendorf's theory of group conflict and Lewis Coser's discussion of the functions of social conflict. Conflict theory has also been absorbed into contemporary sociology in the notion of a radical approach. C. Wright Mills is well known for the development of a more radical and applied sociology in the Marxist tradition, while David Riesman has delineated a demographic foundation of social conflict and change in the form of three types of social conformity.

The conflict-radical paradigm, then, views society as a system of competing forces evolving out of the individual's struggle to meet primary (physical) needs. Utilizing naturalistic as well as systemic explanations, this approach is similar to the organic-structure-functional paradigm in its conceptualization of society as a macroscopic system; however, it differs in its emphasis on conflict, in contrast to societal integration, as the underlying social process. Its ideological implications differ accordingly.

The Social-Behaviorist–Social-Psychological Paradigm

In contrast to the above two, this third paradigm conceptualizes society at the microscopic and interpersonal level. The form of its explanation is inductive rather than deductive, and it generally views society as the individual writ large rather than the system's underlying functional problems. Traditional social behaviorism includes both social and naturalistic explanations: Max Weber and George Mead, for example, study the individual as a social product, focusing on the meaning of social behavior and on social interaction processes; George Simmel and William Sumner, on the other hand, utilize assumed *instincts* or *wishes* to account for social structure and evolution.

Modern social psychological theory, in contrast, concentrates on the social environment and the individual's relation to it through socialization, roles, exchange, role playing, and his or her personal definition of reality. Here we shall discuss symbolic interactionism, role theory, exchange theory, and ethnomethodology.

The social-behaviorist–social-psychological paradigm differs markedly, then, from the other two in its microscopic approach to sociological phenomena. It is similar, however, in its use of naturalistic and systemic forms of explanation.

The Three Paradigms Compared

The three paradigms just discussed differ in a number of distinct ways: the organic-structure-functional concentrates on societal integration, in contrast to the conflict-radical's focus on conflict and the microscopic-inductive approach of the social-behavorist-social-psychological. Their mode of explanation also changes over time from both naturalistic and systemic arguments in the earlier fields (organicism, conflict theory, and social behavior) to a predominant emphasis on systemic-social explanations in contemporary theory. Such differences are outlined in Figure 3.3, which summarizes our introduction of these paradigms.

FIGURE 3.3
THE THREE PARADIGMS COMPARED

PARADIGM ASPECTS	ORGANIC-STRUCTURAL-FUNCTIONAL	CONFLICT-RADICAL	SOCIAL-BEHAVIORIST-SOCIAL-PSYCHOLOGICAL
1. Aims	1. Develop a general theory of society using a systemic approach	1. Develop a general theory of society using a systemic approach	1. Understand social individual as a product of society
2. Assumptions	1. Society is a system of functionally inter-related parts 2. The relevance of natural laws 3. The relevance of the division of labor 4. The relevance of underlying societal problems	1. Society is a system of competitive and conflicting parts 2. The relevance of natural laws 3. The relevance of industrialization and bureaucratization 4. The relevance of underlying primary needs	1. Society is social individual writ large 2. The relevance of wishes and instincts 3. Individual as a social product 4. The relevance of socialization as an underlying process
3. Methodology	1. Application of natural laws to society 2. Application of division of labor to society 3. Application of societal problems to society 4. Utilize both naturalistic and systemic arguments deductively	1. Apply natural conflict to society 2. Apply bureaucratization and industrialization to society 3. Apply primary needs to society 4. Utilize both naturalistic and systemic arguments deductively	1. Apply instincts and wishes to society 2. Apply human social nature to society 3. Apply the socialization process to society 4. Utilize both naturalistic and systemic arguments deductively

Despite the above differences, these paradigms are *not* mutually exclusive views of three different worlds and have at least two major features in common: (1) they focus on the conceptualization of social *order* and *change* and (2) all three include naturalistic and systemic kinds of explanations. Thus, at this point in our discussion, it is appropriate to redefine *sociological theory* as "a set of paradigms conceptualizing social order and change, utilizing naturalistic and systemic forms of explanation." We turn, at this point, to a discussion of these paradigms' historical development.

THE DEVELOPMENT OF SOCIOLOGICAL THEORY

Human thought has obviously progressed through a number of distinct stages: folk wisdom, theology, philosophy, naturalism, rationalism, and pragmatism are major examples.[10] Sociology and sociological theory evolved at a later stage of human intellectual development within a specific historical context—that is, during the late nineteenth and early twentieth centuries after the European political revolutions and acceleration of the process of industrialization. Robert Nisbet portrays this period as one of two major revolutions: the industrial and the French.[11] The former, according to this writer, highlighted the issues of labor conditions, property, the city, technology, and the factory system; while "revolutionary democracy" raised the themes of centralization, egalitarianism, nationalist collectivism, secularism, and bureaucracy. Thus economic and political problems came to the fore, highlighting the need to understand society as a unit of analysis in and of itself. Sociological theory, utilizing the philosophical heritage of the Renaissance and Enlightenment periods, began to apply this intellectual tradition to the study of the individual and society.

As further economic development took place and as pragmatism and the scientific method came into existence, this philosophical heritage was modified. Sociological theory changed its focus and assumptions accordingly, from the abstract and philosophical toward the more concrete and empirical. It is important to stress here, however, that *sociological theory arose in response to economic and political change in European society and attempted to deal with these social problems as a new*

[10]See D. Martindale, *The Nature and Types of Sociological Theory,* Houghton Mifflin, Boston, 1960, chap. 1.
[11]R. A. Nisbet, *The Sociological Tradition*, Basic Books, New York, 1966.

intellectual discipline. As society itself has changed, so has sociological theory in response to changing perceptions of social reality. In this manner, sociological theory developed within the context of nineteenth-century philosophy and has been further modified by society's general development of the scientific method, representing ongoing and changing conceptualizations of social order and progress.

The way in which sociological theory has changed is dealt with by a number of writers. Of particular interest, however, is William Catton's analysis entitled "The Development of Sociological Thought."[12] This author sees sociology's goals moving from the prescientific to the scientific and its methodology changing from the cosmic or general to the highly specific as the natural science method gains prominence. He sees the discipline as becoming less ethnocentric in content, adopting a more microscopic focus, and increasingly clarifying its central concepts. In general, then, Catton sees sociology as having moved from the philosophical, macroscopic, and ethnocentric to the scientific, microscopic, and objective as the scientific method became the dominant philosophy of science.

In his own analysis of the development of sociological theory, this author outlined the following major changes: (1) an increase in microscopic and specifically sociological aims; (2) increasing emphasis on microscopic interaction and definitions of social reality; (3) utilization of empirical observation in contrast to philosophical analysis; and (4) the development of typologies concentrating on microscopic processes rather than structural and societal change. In general, it can be seen that sociological theory has developed from the philosophical, descriptive, macroscopic, and ideological to the more scientific, explanatory, microscopic, and objective type in response to society's changing intellectual norms.

It should *not* be assumed, however, that the above development is strictly linear: as we have pointed out, the organic, conflict, and social-behaviorist paradigms reappear in contemporary sociology in the form of structure functionalism, modern conflict theory, and social psychology. Thus the organic, conflict, and social-behaviorist perspectives which developed earlier are

[12]W. R. Catton, "The Development of Sociological Thought," in R. E. L. Faris (ed.), *Handbook of Modern Sociology*, Rand McNally, Chicago, 1964, pp. 912–950.

reflected in contemporary theory as well, with greater emphasis on social rather than naturalistic explanation and application of the scientific method on the microscopic level. The development of sociological theory is thus *somewhat* cyclical in the resurgence of these earlier three paradigms but linear in the movement toward a more scientific and microscopic approach as the intellectual context of sociology is influenced by the development of a pragmatic-empirical philosophy. Closely related to this development is sociology's reaction to the norms and perceived needs of its social environment—a topic we turn to next.

THE SOCIAL CONTEXT OF SOCIOLOGICAL THEORY

In Chapter 2 we emphasized the relevance of particular societal, intellectual, and biographical conditions to the development of theory generally. Here we shall examine the relevance of these factors to sociological theory in particular.

Societal Conditions

Sociological theory arose, as we have pointed out, in reaction to specific societal conditions, in particular political revolution, economic change, the effects of industrialization, and the development of science. Thus the three paradigms just discussed developed in reaction to specific societal developments as follows: organic theory evolved in reaction to revolutions in Europe, with a major emphasis on the reestablishment of social order and social control, while structure functionalism represented a reaction to America's economic needs during the 1930s.[13] Macrosociological theory, in general, has developed in reaction to a society's economic and technological needs, the latest emphasis being placed on cybernetics and systems theory.[14] The organic-structure-functional paradigm, then, has evolved primarily in reaction to society's need for the reassertion or further elaboration of social, political, and economic order.

[13]For a useful discussion of the background to American functionalism, see A. W. Gouldner, *The Coming Crisis in Western Sociology*, Avon, New York, 1970, pp. 141–157.
[14]See the following, for example: A. Etzioni, *The Active Society, A Theory of Societal and Political Processes*, Free Press, New York, 1968; W. Buckley, *Sociology and Modern Systems Theory*, Prentice-Hall, Englewood Cliffs, N.J., 1967.

The conflict-radical paradigm was developed primarily by those who experienced and were most aware of political conflict and oppression. Early Marxian theory evolved under such conditions, while radical sociology and modern conflict theory developed in the 1960s in response to a greater awareness of the oppressive effects of industrialization and sociology's commitment to the status quo. Societal conditions of conflict and elite control thus result in a sociological perspective which highlights these processes as central to society and sociological theory. In contrast to the organic-structure-functional perspective, then, the conflict-radical paradigm reacts to an awareness of domination and the need to change society rather than to reassert social control in the face of perceived systemic needs.

The social-behaviorist–social-psychological paradigm may be viewed as reflecting the development of behaviorism in science, the rise of pragmatism, increasing emphasis on the scientific method, and a consequent focus on characteristics of the individual rather than of society. Reactions to the needs of an industrial technology in the form of industrial psychology and sociology—that is, the social and human problems created by increased economic development and specialization—also highlighted the importance of studying the individual in relation to the group context rather than the reverse. Thus sociology's increasing emphasis on microscopic and social-psychological theory may be seen as a reaction to society's increasing emphasis on pragmatism (that is, on the view that "truth" is knowledge which is useful), the scientific method (empiricism), and the individualistic effects of a bureaucratic, technological society (the individual effects of an increasingly impersonal, hierarchical, controlled, efficiency-oriented, and materialistic society).

From our discussion it can be seen that sociological theory represents the major reaction of sociology to specific societal needs, conditions, and normative emphases. As pointed out, these conditions include societal, political, and economic needs, the experience of oppression, and the development of science in a manner which highlights a movement toward the microscopic and social-psychological but in a somewhat cyclical fashion, revealing the reemergence of the earlier organic, conflict, and social-behaviorist paradigms in contemporary form. These trends are illustrated in Figure 3.4, where the relationship between societal context and type of sociological theory is illustrated.

FIGURE 3.4
THE HISTORICAL DEVELOPMENT OF SOCIOLOGY THEORY

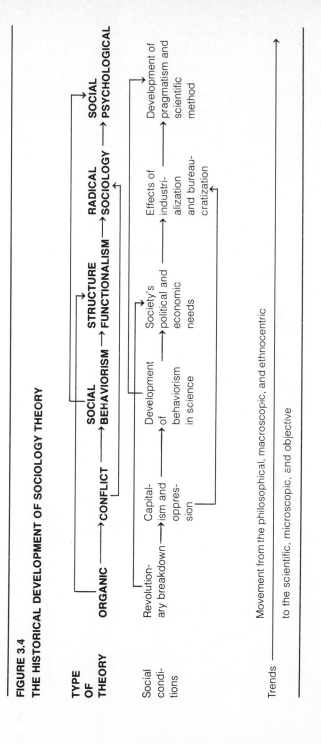

Intellectual Context

Sociological theory has also been closely defined by the intellectual values of the day, as we have pointed out above, particularly as these values reflect varying stages of a society's movement toward industrialization. Thus early theory was strongly influenced by Enlightenment philosophy emphasizing naturalism, rationalism, and the organic analogy. Assumptions concerning human nature were also basic to Marxian conflict theory. The relevance of earlier systems of thought such as utopianism and medieval theology to initial sociological theory is also evident. However, as the spirit of pragmatism and the consequent application of the scientific method came to dominate the intellectual scene, particularly in the United States, earlier philosophies such as rationalism became translated into scientific pragmatism, and the consequent movement was toward more social-psychological and microscopic theory.

A theorist's intellectual environment, then, has an obvious effect upon his or her work. Furthermore, the reaction of intellectual peers, particularly their encouragement and support, also affects that thinking as this environment is either reinforced or critiqued, resulting in new and changing patterns of thought. Collaboration with other thinkers as well as academic and/or economic support in the university setting are particularly important to the stimulation and proliferation of any theorist's work. The academic environment thus may help or hinder sociological theory in the measure and quality of its support. Thus, as sociology has become increasingly institutionalized in the university setting and is increasingly broadcast through academic journals, its development in general has been exponential. Ironically, however, in the wake of scientific pragmatism, its major emphasis has been more empirical than theoretical. Earlier theory, then, developed in an intellectual context apparently more conducive to abstract and philosophical theorizing, a context with low academic constraints.

Biographical Context

We previously emphasized that an individual's position in the social structure exerts a strong influence on his or her perception of society and consequently on the kind of sociological theory this person develops. Thus, it would appear that organic-structure-functional theorists generally came from upper-middle-class backgrounds, where social control and societal development represent central issues. Conflict theorists were more subject to oppression and consequently perceived society in more competitive and conflict terms; that is, their *societal experience* differed. Finally, since the pragmatic ethic is more typical of the middle classes, social-behavioral and social-psychological theorists may be broadly described as coming from this particular sector of society and, in fact, increasingly so, since contemporary sociology to a large degree tends to represent a white middle-class discipline.

A theorist's position in society, then, tends to define his or her sociological outlook in general. While other experiences such as personal relationships and contact with other scholars are also relevant to particular theorists, we are concerned here primarily with broad sociological factors; the individual's social-class background appears to be particularly relevant in this regard.

In this portion of our discussion, we have outlined a number of societal, intellectual, and biographical conditions and their relevance to the evolution of the three major sociological paradigms. We have seen that a paradigm represents a theorists reaction to particular combinations of these factors as follows: organic-structure-functionalism represents the reaction of generally upper-class individuals to society's political, economic, and social needs in the spirit of Enlightenment philosophy. The conflict-radical paradigm, on the other hand, tended to evolve from the experience of more lower-class individuals who experienced political and economic oppression. Finally, social-behaviorist–social-psychological theory may be viewed as the response of more middle-class pragmatists to the perceived needs of an industrialized society at the microscopic level.

It should be emphasized here that these delineations represent *very broad* trends only, since individual theorists represent, in part, unique sets of experiences and there are dramatic departures from these trends. However, it can be seen from this in general that *sociological theory represents the reaction of a particular set of academics* (not necessarily sociologists) *to society's perceived needs within the context of a particular set of intellectual values and societal experiences*. Therefore, as society and its perceived needs change, so also does sociological theory, especially as it is increasingly influenced by pragmatism and the scientific method. In this manner, sociological theory represents an individual's reaction to society at a particular stage of its development as he or she attempts to account for that development and to evolve solutions to its underlying problems. Far from being an abstract activity, then, sociological theory is an ongoing intellectual reaction to perceived social reality. This process is summarized in Figure 3.5.

FIGURE 3.5
MAJOR FACTORS DEFINING SOCIOLOGICAL THEORY

SOCIETAL CONTEXT

SOCIETAL CONDITIONS	INTELLECTUAL CONDITIONS	BIOGRAPHICAL CONDITIONS	TYPE OF THEORY
1. Systemic needs: political, social economic	1. Enlightenment philosophy: rationalism, naturalism	1. Upper class socio-economic background and socialization	Organic-Structure-Functional
2. Social conflict and oppression: class conflict and the effects of industrialization and bureaucratization	2. Enlightenment philosophy: rationalism, naturalism	2. Lower-middle and lower socio-economic background and socialization	Conflict-radical
3. Development of society's industrial needs: development of science and behaviorism	3. Pragmatism	3. Middle class socioeconomic background and socialization	Social-behaviorist–social-psychological

EXAMPLES OF SOCIOLOGICAL THEORY

In order to illustrate our discussion in this chapter, we shall conclude by presenting examples of the ways in which the three major paradigms conceptualize the social order as evident in the work of particular theorists.[15] These various views are presented in Figure 3.6. As it shows, society is conceptualized variously as a

[15]E. Durkheim, *The Rules of Sociological Method*, Macmillan, New York, 1938, edited by G. E. G. Catlin, and translated by S. A. Solovay and J. H. Muller; T. Parsons, *The System of Modern Societies*, Prentice-Hall, Englewood Cliffs, N.J. 1971, p. 4; K. Marx and F. Engels, *Manifesto of the Communist Party*, Kerr,

FIGURE 3.6

EXAMPLES OF SOCIOLOGICAL THEORY

PARADIGM	THEORIST	CONCEPTUALIZATION OF SOCIAL ORDER
1. Organic-structure-functional	1. Durkheim	"It is . . . the collective aspects of the beliefs, tendencies, and practices of a group that characterize truly social phenomena." *(The Rules of Sociological Method)*
	2. Parsons	"We consider social systems to be constitutents of the more general system of action, the other primary constituents being cultural systems, personality systems, and behavioral organisms . . ." *(The System of Modern Societies)*
2. Conflict-radical	1. Marx	"The history of all hitherto existing society is the history of class struggles." *(The Manifesto)*
	2. C. W. Mills	". . . in this particular epoch a conjunction of historical circumstances had led to the rise of an elite of power . . ." and ". . . the decisions that they make and fail to make carry more consequences for more people than has ever been the case . . ." *(The Power Elite)*
3. Social-behaviorist–social-psychological	1. Simmel	". . . society is conceived as interaction among individuals . . ." *(The Sociology of George Simmel)*
	2. Garfinkel	"I use the term "ethnomethodology" to refer to the investigation of the rational properties of . . . practical actions as contingent ongoing accomplishments of organized artful practices of everyday life." *(Studies in Ethnomethodology)*

set of norms, a functionally integrated social system, a set of forces in opposition, a system dominated by a power elite, the institutionalization of mankind's basic wishes, or the operation of the "moral order" in everyday life. Whatever the differences here, it can be clearly seen that sociological theory is basically concerned with the conceptualization of social order and process within the context of three basic paradigms.

CONCLUSIONS
In this chapter we have attempted to define sociological theory, present varying views of its structure, describe its major types,

Chicago, 1888; C. W. Mills, *The Power Elite*, Oxford University Press, New York, p. 28; G. Simmel, *The Sociology of George Simmel*, Free Press, New York, 1950, edited and translated by Kurt H. Wolff; H. Garfinkle, *Studies in Ethnomethodology*, Prentice-Hall, Englewood Cliffs, N.J., 1967, p. 11.

outline its historical development, reveal the influence of the social context, and provide major examples of conceptualizations of the social order. We defined sociological theory as a "set of paradigms concerning society and social phenomena in reference to their separate societal reality that is used to account for a society's social structure and internal social processes." We also discussed a continuum of views on theory, ranging from the informal and artistic to the formal and scientific.

Using the dimensions of level of analysis, factors used, and focus, we described three major sociological paradigms: the organic-structure-functional, the conflict-radical, and the social-behaviorist–social-psychological. We then described these as arising in response to economic and political change in Europe and America as theorists attempted to deal with these social problems as a new intellectual discipline. We also showed that while theory's historical development revealed a movement toward the scientific and microscopic, these three paradigms reemerged in contemporary sociology with an added emphasis on sociological rather than naturalistic explanation.

Finally, in discussing the influence of theory's social context, we concluded that sociological theory represents the reaction of a particular set of academics to society's perceived needs within the context of a particular set of intellectual values and societal experiences.

In general, then, sociological theory represents the emergence of three rather different but not mutually exclusive explanatory paradigms in response to society's changing political, economic, and social needs within specific societal, intellectual, and biographical contexts. The remainder of this text will discuss the characteristics of these paradigms as we analyze the context and structure of sociological theory.

EXERCISES

1 Consider the various definitions of *sociology* and *theory* presented in the theory texts listed under "Readings," below, and develop your own definition of sociological theory.

2 Compare and contrast the three paradigms discussed in this chapter with regard to the differing kinds of explanation they represent.

3 Select a particular concept and attempt to explain it differently with the three paradigms.

4 Delineate the major societal, intellectual, and biographical influences which affected the development of organic and social-behaviorist theory.

5 Compare the structure-functional and social-psychological paradigms as differing explanation systems.

READINGS

Barnes, H. E., and H. Becker: *Social Thought from Lore to Science*, 2nd ed., Harren Press, Washington, 1952.

Becker, H., and A. Boskoff (eds.): *Modern Sociological Theory*, Dryden Press, New York, 1957.

Catton, W. R.: "The Development of Sociological Thought," in R. E. L. Faris (ed.), *Handbook of Modern Sociology*, Rand McNally, Chicago, 1964, pp. 912–950.

Gouldner, A. W.: *The Coming Crisis of Western Sociology*, Avon, New York, 1970.

Larson, C. J.: *Major Themes in Sociological Theory*, McKay, New York, 1973, chap. 1.

Martindale, D.: *The Nature and Types of Sociological Theory*, Houghton Mifflin, Boston, 1960, chap. 1.

Nisbet, R. A.: *The Sociological Tradition*, Basic Books, New York, 1966, chaps. 1 and 2.

Timasheff, N.S.: *Sociological Theory, Its Nature and Growth,* 3d ed., Random House, New York, 1967, chap. 1.

TOWARD A MODEL OF THE THEORIZING PROCESS:

SUMMARY OF SECTION ONE

In this introductory discussion we have attempted to outline the relevance of theory to knowledge, characteristics of theory in general, and the nature of sociological theory in particular. We made the following major points:

1 Theorizing is the process by which people account for their physical and social environments within the context of a specific social setting, thereby defining their physical and social reality. This process applies to both science and everyday life; the perceived gulf between theory and reality is thus more apparent than real.

2 We defined *formal theory* as a set of abstract, logical propositions which attempts to explain relationships between phenomena and consists of eight structural elements; a paradigm, a set of concepts, logical relationships between these concepts, a set of operationalized variables and indexes, a methodology designed to test these predicted relationships, data analysis, data interpretation, and, finally, evaluation of the theory in light of all the above. Furthermore, we distinguished generally between theories which are formal, explanatory, scientific, deductive, and objective and others which are more informal, descriptive, ideological, inductive, and intuitive. Finally, we attempted to show how theory is influenced by the particular societal, intellectual, and biographical context in which the theorist operates.

3 Applying the above discussion to sociology, we defined *sociological theory* as a set of paradigms concerning society and social phenomena in reference to their separate societal reality, paradigms that are used to account for a society's social structure and internal social processes. We also discussed a continuum of views on theory, ranging from the informal and artistic to the formal and scientific. Then—using the dimensions of level, factors used, and focus—we delineated three major paradigms: the organic-structure-functional, the conflict-radical, and the social-behaviorist–social-psychological, viewing them as arising in response to political and economic change in Europe and the United States. This historical development also revealed a movement toward a scientific, microscopic, and sociological emphasis in contrast to earlier philosophical, macroscopic, and naturalistic kinds of explanation. Finally, we attempted to show that sociological theory represents the reaction of a particular set

FIGURE 4.1

A MODEL OF THE THEORIZING PROCESS

SOCIAL CONTEXT:	TYPE OF THEORY:	DEFINITIONS OF REALITY:	SOCIETAL CHANGE:	CHANGE IN THEORY:
Societal, intellectual, and biographical conditions	→ Organic-function conflict-radical Behaviorist-social-psychological = variation in scope, ideology, and type of explanation	→ The manner in which these paradigms dominate academic and social definitions of reality	→ Change in societal economic conditions, philosophy, and the structure of the academic scene	→ Increasingly microscopic, scientific, and sociological, with reemergence of earlier paradigms in modern terminology

of academics to society's perceived needs within the context of a particular set of intellectual values and societal experiences.

From the above, we conclude that theory is neither abstract nor divorced from reality; rather, it represents an individual's attempt to account for his or her physical and social environment within specific societal, intellectual, and biographical conditions. As such, theory defines the individual's physical and social reality. Furthermore, theory represents a response to perceived societal needs. It follows, then, that as these needs and conditions change, so does the theory defining them. We conclude, therefore, that theory is a dynamic sociological process relevant to formal and everyday reality rather than a static set of abstract ideas which are divorced from the real world. This general process is illustrated in Figure 4.1.

Having completed our introductory discussion of theory, we turn now to the main task of this book: the analysis of sociology's major theoretical paradigms.

TRADITIONAL SOCIOLOGICAL THEORY

5

INTRODUCTION TO TRADITIONAL SOCIOLOGICAL THEORY

MAJOR TOPICS:

Presociological paradigms

The context of sociological theory

We have emphasized the manner in which theory represents a reaction to specific societal, intellectual, and biographical conditions. In this chapter we shall introduce traditional sociological theory by discussing, first, the paradigms that were developed before sociology was conceived and, second, the specific contexts in which the major three sociological paradigms evolved. The remainder of Section Two will be devoted to detailed analysis of these paradigms—organic, conflict, and social-behaviorist.

PRESOCIOLOGICAL PARADIGMS

Each major period of human history may be viewed as a series of particular paradigms or belief systems—that is, the predominant definition of physical and social reality of the day. Thus particular kinds of theory or explanations defined social reality at particular points in society's development. These differed primarily in terms of which particular variables were viewed as *causal* in the explanation of reality. They ranged, for example, from the external, mystical, and irrational; through the religious and Christian; to the more internal (subject to human control), rational, and scientific. Each paradigm represents a particular view of reality as society progresses from the metaphysical, through the theological and philosophical, to the positivistic and scientific. We shall examine each of these preliminary paradigms by way of introduction to the emergence of sociology.

The Metaphysical Paradigm

Mankind's initial and formal definition of reality may be viewed as metaphysical. Emerging with the development of Greek civilization, this view, in contrast to the primitive paganism which preceded it, represented a projection of the human self into the mystical and unknown. Thus the Greek gods were supernatural but possessed human qualities as well. The natural universe operated in a relatively uniform order which was subject to the desires and control of the gods. The latter, in turn, were—if only in a limited fashion—accessible to interaction with humans. According to this view of reality, the universe was ordered and subject to the control of supernatural gods with humanlike qualities. The gods, in turn, related to people.

54
        Such a paradigm represents a projection of the human self

into the supernatural as a means of explaining the perceived structure of the universe. This external projection of the human into the mystical and supernatural may be viewed as an important preliminary to the theological and Christian paradigm which developed next, particularly in its depiction of the human element in the supernatural, the conceptualization of gods with humanlike qualities, and the linking of these gods to the natural order.

The Theological Paradigm
Society's medieval development may be seen as an institutionalization of the mystical and irrational in Christian form. Many gods became one God with three major subdivisions in the Trinity, which controlled the entire universe but related to mankind in human form. Access to this Supreme Being was institutionalized in the form of the church—a political and economic bureaucracy which governed people's relations as well as their knowledge. In this way, an earlier view of reality was modified to conform with a theological explanation of the universe. However, it is clear that there was great continuity between the two: an informal, humanistic, and mystical explanation of the universe became formalized, sanctified, and institutionalized in the form of the church, which controlled access to this unified and supreme God and proceded to rule social life in general. A sacred and essentially irrational view of reality (little subject to human control) thus became institutionalized in Christian form, reinforcing the locus of control as external to society and mankind.

The Philosophical Paradigm
The third major stage in the development of human thought may be summarized as philosophical in content. With the decline of the European church's power came the development of the more secular political state. Beliefs began to turn more toward the individual as the locus of control, in contrast to a mystical and external universe. With an increasing emphasis upon nature and the natural order came an increase in rationalism and materialism, along with the beginnings of science. While Christianity obviously remained an important set of beliefs, Enlightenment philosophy placed the individual and humanity's apparent rationality, rather than God and His universe, at the center of knowledge. The

55

eighteenth century thus saw the development from religion to rationalism, the latter representing a secular faith in human nature.

Believing in the existence of a "natural order," Enlightenment philosophers focused on the understanding of this order as it applied to human beings in order to maximize happiness, freedom, material development, and general social progress. Knowledge during this era, then, was of the applied kind, designed to aid ongoing social evolution. Thus, while philosophers such as Thomas Hobbes, Niccolò Machiavelli, John Locke, François Voltaire, David Hume, and Henri Rousseau represent strikingly different points of view, they are centrally concerned with the application of philosophy and knowledge to matters of political and social concern. Social paradigms move from a belief in the sacred (in order to control individuals) to a belief in understanding people and nature (in order to contribute toward general social evolution—that is, movement from a sacred to a secular belief system).

In this manner, the dominant paradigm moved from the institutionalization of the irrational in Christian and theological form toward the establishment of the rational in the form of Enlightenment philosophy. In general, this implied movement away from a sacred and irrational conceptualization of physical and social reality toward the secular and rational—an essential ingredient for the evolution of science and the scientific method. Beliefs moved from the definition of reality as an external, sacred, and mystical system under the control of a Supreme Being to belief in an internal, secular, and rational system with the potential for the individual's understanding and control. The latter belief was carried through to the nineteenth century, where it was further elaborated and institutionalized in the form of the scientific method.

The Positivistic Paradigm

Since Enlightenment philosophy involved belief in the existence of a natural order as well as human rationality, it was logical that these thinkers should develop a methodology in order to understand and control these phenomena. Thus, with Francis Bacon as a forerunner, nineteenth-century thinkers evolved a positivistic paradigm as an extension of Enlightenment philosophy. This paradigm suggested the scientific method as a means of discovering this underlying order and thus maximizing social progress—an evolution that these thinkers held to be inevitable.

As we shall see, Auguste Comte, for example, believed strongly that application of the scientific method in the positivistic tradition (i.e., knowledge restricted to data obtained through use of the scientific method) would contribute to humanity's social evolution toward greater happiness and "moral unity." The positivistic or scientific method—with its emphasis on the derivation of general laws through experiment, comparison, and historical deduction—was simply a means of maximizing social development in face of the general belief in an underlying physical and social order based on rationality. While the eighteenth century provided a secularized *paradigm*, then, the following century developed a *methodology* designed to translate that paradigm into scientific knowledge and, thereby, greater social control.

Summary

Our brief discussion of the paradigms preceding sociology has highlighted the movement from a metaphysical and mystical view of reality, through the institutionalization of such a view in theological and Christian form in the concept of the church, to a secular belief in the natural order, human rationality, and the scientific method as defined by Enlightenment philosophy and nineteenth-century positivism.

These developments reveal a number of distinct trends: an increase in secular views of reality; a belief in humanity rather than a Supreme Being as the locus of control; and a change in focus from an emphasis on the universe to society and the individual. Since these paradigms changed as the structure of society was modified, particularly its economic system, it is evident that humanity's changing definition of reality, particularly its movement from the physical to the social, is primarily a function of ongoing societal development, emphasizing once again that theory and explanation represent people's reactions to particular societal conditions.

While our discussion of the above paradigms is extremely brief and generally crude, it serves to introduce the evolution of sociology. It shows how societal awareness was achieved at a particular stage of social evolution, when definitions of reality had become secularized and a secular methodology was used to discover an underlying natural order. At this point, awareness of social as opposed to physical reality evolved within the context of secularized knowledge. As we shall see, the sociological paradigm emerged within the context of secular and scientific values.

Sociology, then, may be viewed as a function of the discovery of society as a separate dimension of reality, along with the development of the scientific method to understand and control it. With this in mind, we turn to a discussion of the general contexts in which sociology's major paradigms developed.

THE CONTEXT OF SOCIOLOGICAL THEORY

In this section we shall continue our discussion of sociology's historical background by outlining major characteristics of the contexts in which organic, conflict, and social-behaviorist theory developed.

The Context of Organic Theory

Organic theory in sociology originated during the positivistic era just described, under certain important nineteenth-century conditions which may be summarized as follows:

1 Political revolution and social breakdown in Europe had been a predominant condition for some time, accentuating the perceived need to rebuild the political and social order.

2 Industrial development was also beginning to accelerate, highlighting the importance of society's economic as well as political needs. The resultant emphasis on societal political and economic needs was high.

3 Philosophical orientations toward the problems of social breakdown and industrial development represented a synthesis of eighteenth-century Enlightenment philosophy and nineteenth-century positivism. That is, these philosophical orientations emphasized:

   a Naturalism—the assumption that nature is causal

   b Rationalism—the assumption that human beings are rational

   c Social evolution—the assumption that there is an evolutionary drive in society

   d Social reform—the assumption that social progress is humanity's major aim

   e The importance of conformity to society's general will (an essentially conservative view)

   f Application of the positivistic (or scientific) method to achieve these ends

4 Finally, these orientations tended to reflect an intellectual elite of upper-class origins whose views of society were essentially systemic and conservative.

     Organic theory may thus be summarized as a positivistic, rational, social philosophy, representing a synthesis of philosophical ideas of the day and reaction to society's perceived economic and political needs. The continuity between foregoing systems of thought and this particular paradigm is evident, highlighting the manner in which sociological theory represents the application of previous ideas to later societal needs.

The Context of Conflict Theory

Conflict theory developed under similar societal conditions but was defined by thinkers whose social experience tended to be rather different. The specific context behind conflict theory may be delineated as follows:

1 A strong emphasis on those aspects of Enlightenment philosophy emphasizing social progress, social evolution, the importance of human nature and mankind's rationality, and faith in the possibility of changing society in order to maximize freedom and happiness (i.e., "idealism")

2 The influence of Social Darwinism—the application of the concept of biological evolution to society—whicn outlines conflict as part of human and social evolution

3 The experience of political conflict and change, particularly economic oppression by a political elite

     Conflict theory is far from homogeneous: some theorists are conservative in comparison with the more radical, while they differ in their emphasis on naturalistic or sociological types of explanation. In general, however, this kind of theory may be seen as

59

a function of the application of Enlightenment ideals concerning human nature to a historical analysis of social conflict, concluding with sociological suggestions concerning the new order in which human nature and that of society will be more closely aligned.

This trend, coupled with the social background of the thinkers concerned, especially their experience of oppression or bitter conflict, reveals the continuity as well as the differences between organic and conflict theory. Once again, the application of previous philosophical ideas to present societal conditions by a particular group of intellectuals is evident.

The Context of Social Behaviorism

Social behaviorist theory differs from the previous two approaches in its focus on the individual at the microscopic level of analysis and in its utilization of induction rather than deductive explanation. However, it is similar in its application of Enlightenment ideals to societal problems within an industrial-technological era, utilizing the scientific method. More specifically, the factors defining the emergence of social behaviorism may be delineated as follows:

1 Enlightenment idealism regarding human nature—a belief in the human being as a dynamic, free actor—as well as Social Darwinism in reference to society's general progress.

2 The individualistic emphasis of the Protestant ethic predominant in American culture (a belief in individualism, self-discipline, thrift, and hard work, based on Calvinistic doctrine), focusing sociology in the United States on the nature of the individual and his or her relationship to society.

3 The influence of American pragmatism—a philosophy which emphasized the experimental method as the basis for policy decisions. In this way a synthesis between philosophical values and the scientific method was achieved.

4 The increasing needs of an industrial-urban society. This made the application of the social sciences to the individual and his or her relationship to the social system an urgent need. It was a development which, along with the evolution of applied psychology, contributed to the development of a more microscopic sociology.

From the above factors it is evident that social behaviorism represented an extension of Enlightenment values, along with the scientific method, to the developing problems of an industrial-urban society within the context of American values such as pragmatism and the Protestant ethic. The continuity between earlier value systems and sociology's reaction to contemporary societal problems is evident once again, with an added emphasis, in this case, on understanding the individual scientifically.

Summary

A number of common themes in the above typologies are evident:

1 Enlightenment values concerning the natural order and human rationality

2 A belief in social evolution in the tradition of Social Darwinism

3 A concomitant belief in the inevitability of societal progress

4 Utilization of naturalistic explanations of social behavior

5 Idealism concerning human nature and society

6 Belief in positivism and the scientific method as methodologies for understanding and maximizing social progress

To this extent, then, traditional sociological theory represents a relatively homogeneous synthesis of Enlightenment philosophy, Social Darwinism, and belief in the scientific method. However, when these paradigms are examined in order, the following general trends do become evident:

1 A movement from societal to individual naturalism

2 A change in methodology from historical deduction to pragmatic use of the scientific method

3 A concomitant movement from Enlightenment philosophy to pragmatism

4 A change from conservatism to more radical definitions of humanity and society

5 A resultant movement from a perceived need for social control to the need for societal change

6 An increasing focus on individual in contrast to societal perfectability

7 A focus on individual rather than societal definitions of "reality"

8 Less elitist views on society and the individual in general

Such trends suggest the general development away from societal, philosophical, and elitist views of sociological reality toward more microscopic, scientific, and nonelitist orientations. Nevertheless, our general view of sociological theory still holds, that is, that *it represents the application of earlier philosophical ideas to a changing societal context*. In this manner sociological theory represents a reaction to this changing context as viewed from the perspective that society is "real."

CONCLUSIONS

In this introductory chapter we have discussed major presociological and sociological paradigms. Beginning with the *metaphysical* and its emphasis on mystical projections, we saw how the irrational became institutionalized in Christian form during the *theological* stage of human thought. An external and irrational orientation predominated until the eighteenth century, when Enlightenment *philosophy* developed a secular view of the individual and society. This was further developed during the *positivistic* era in the following century, when a synthesis of Enlightenment values and the scientific method emerged.

It was within the context of the positivistic paradigm that sociology began in the form of the *organic* paradigm—an Enlightenment-positivistic approach based on the assumption that society was "real" and part of the natural order. The *conflict* paradigm evolved next, concentraing on societal change in accordance with human needs. Finally, the *social-behaviorist* paradigm developed within the context of Enlightenment idealism, the Protestant ethic, and American pragmatism, in reaction to the ongoing needs of an industrial-technical society. The structure of this development of thought or belief systems is summarized in Figure 5.1.

FIGURE 5.1

THE EVOLUTION OF PRESOCIOLOGICAL AND TRADITIONAL SOCIOLOGICAL PARADIGMS

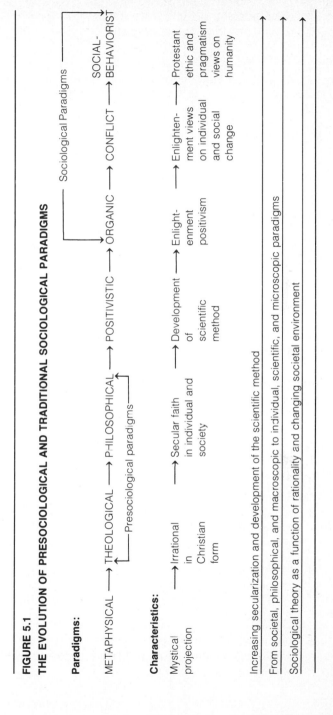

Paradigms:

METAPHYSICAL → THEOLOGICAL → PHILOSOPHICAL → POSITIVISTIC → ORGANIC → CONFLICT → SOCIAL-BEHAVIORIST

Presociological paradigms

Sociological Paradigms

Characteristics:

Mystical projection → Irrational in Christian form → Secular faith in individual and society → Development of scientific method → Enlightenment positivism → Enlightenment views on individual and social change → Protestant ethic and pragmatism views on humanity

Increasing secularization and development of the scientific method

From societal, philosophical, and macroscopic to individual, scientific, and microscopic paradigms

Sociological theory as a function of rationality and changing societal environment

It is possible to draw a number of conclusions regarding traditional sociological theory from the above analysis:

1 Sociological theory may be viewed as a function of increasing secularization in human thought and the evolution of the scientific method.

2 Sociological theory changes in reaction to its changing societal context.

3 Sociological theory has moved from the societal, philosophical, and macroscopic to the individual, scientific, and microscopic.

In general, sociological theory may be viewed as a function of an increasing level of rationality and reaction to a changing societal environment in the face of ongoing industrialization and urbanization. Having thus introduced the development and changing context of traditional sociological theory, we turn now to examine its three paradigms in detail.

EXERCISES

1 Compare and contrast the historical circumstances behind the evolution of presociological and traditional sociological paradigms. Delineate significant differences between the two.

2 Compare and contrast the historical circumstances behind the development of the three traditional sociological paradigms. Outline significant differences among the three of them.

3 What major factors—societal and philosophical—do you see behind the evolution of sociology as a "new" paradigm in the nineteenth century?

4 In what major respects does the social-behaviorist paradigm differ from the organic and conflict? What is the significance of these differences for the ongoing development of American sociology?

5 Demonstrate the extent to which both presociological and sociological paradigms are belief systems rather than statements of truth.

READINGS

Becker, C.: *The Heavenly City of the Eighteenth-Century Philosophers*, Yale University Press, New Haven, 1932.

Cantor, N. F.: *Medieval History: The Life and Death of a Civilization*, 2d ed., Macmillan, New York, 1969.

Cassirer, E.: *The Philosophy of the Enlightenment*, Princeton University Press, Princeton, N.J., 1951.

Gouldner, A. W.: *Enter Plato*, Basic Books, New York, 1965.

Martindale, D.: *The Nature and Types of Sociological Theory*, Houghton Mifflin, Boston, 1960, chaps. 1 and 2.

Nisbet, R. A.: *The Sociological Tradition*, Basic Books, New York, 1966, chaps. 1 and 2.

Zeitlin, I. M.: *Ideology and the Development of Sociological Theory*, Prentice-Hall, Englewood Cliffs, N.J., 1968, chap. 1.

6

THE ORGANIC PARADIGM

n this chapter we shall discuss the earliest form of sociological theory: the organic approach. By way of introduction we shall summarize the societal, intellectual, and biographical conditions under which this type of theory developed as well as discuss its major assumptions. We shall then discuss two major variants: the mechanical and systemic or social-psychological types as evident in the work of four major theorists: Auguste Comte, Herbert Spencer, Emile Durkheim, and Ferdinand Tönnies. We shall conclude our discussion by examining the organic paradigm as a whole.

INTRODUCTION

In our previous discussion we viewed sociological theory as a particular group's reaction to the perceived societal problems of the day. In the case of the organic approach, theorizing came from a group of upper-class intellectuals, educated in the tradition of Enlightenment philosophy, who were reacting to a societal context experiencing high levels of political revolution, social breakdown, and industrial development.

Utilizing the assumptions provided by naturalism, rationalism, social revolutionism, social reform, and the positivist method, these thinkers developed a view of society which concentrated on its systemic needs functioning in the tradition of natural laws as a system of functionally interrelated parts through the division of labor or role structure. According to this view, society represented a functional organism, part of the rest of the natural order, which evolved in reference to its underlying needs.

Emphasis was placed either on the mechanical structure of this social organism (as is the case with Comte and Spencer) or the type of normative system within it dependent upon the division of labor (the social-psychological type evident in the views of Durkheim and Tönnies). In both cases, however, society is viewed as a functionally integrated organism which is part of the natural order and operates through its division of labor system.

Such a paradigm is systemic in its view of society's "natural" needs as paramount and is ideologically conservative in its emphasis upon the adaptation of the individual to these needs rather than the reverse. Such a view, however, is explicable in light of an attempt by the intellectual community of the time to deal with the political, economic, and social disorder of the day. Systemic paradigms tend to arise in such circumstances, particularly among members of the elite. The chief function of sociology in such a situation is the discovery of underlying laws of the social order so that it may be better understood and thereby controlled more efficiently.

To summarize, the organic approach, the earliest type of formal sociological theory, evolved among a predominantly upper-class intellectual community, steeped in the tradition of Enlightenment philosophy, in response to political, economic, and social developments of the day. The major result of these factors is a type of sociological theory which is naturalistic and systemic, varying according to whether the particular theorist emphasizes society's mechanical or normative chracteristics. Such a process is summarized in Figure 6.1.

We turn now to examine the first major type of organic theory—the mechanical approach—as revealed in the work of Comte and Spencer. We shall examine each theorist's background, major aims, assumptions, methodology, and typology,

FIGURE 6.1
MAJOR FACTORS BEHIND ORGANIC THEORY

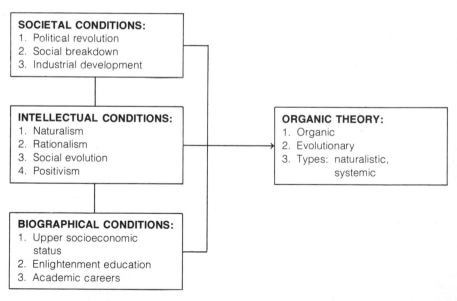

summarizing the work of each in a diagrammatic figure.[1] We shall also discuss the major theoretical issues each raises for contemporary sociology.

THE NATURALISTIC TYPE OF ORGANIC THEORY
Comte and Spencer are useful examples of this type of theory in that their backgrounds and systems of thought are highly similar.

Auguste Comte (1798–1857)

Background   Comte was born in France during 1798, the son of a Catholic, monarchist family. Educated in medicine and physiology at the Polytechnique, he later taught positivistic philosophy and founded the Positivist Society. Educated in the tradition of Enlightenment philosophy, he experienced many of France's political upheavals as well as the post-Revolution decline, the beginnings of the industrial revolution, and the increased conflict between science and religion. His major works include *The Positive Philosophy* (1830–1862) and *A General View of Positivism* (1848). Comte is best known for giving sociology its name.

Aims   Given the societal context in which Comte lived, it is understandable that the major aim of his sociology was to "eliminate the revolutionary construction of modern society" (i.e., prevent its "moral disorganization"). He was concerned with the reorganization of society in reference to his philosophy of positivistic humanism.

Since for Comte the foundation of society was its underlying *ideas*, his sociology was concerned with establishing those ideas which would reinforce moral order. Accordingly, he attempted to develop a kind of "social physics" which would establish social laws and the social reorganization of society in accordance with the kind of value system Comte valued most and viewed as most natural.

This thinker, then, attempted to apply principles of Enlightenment philosophy to the revolutionary problems of his day,

[1]Note that each theorist's major aims, assumptions, methodology, and typology have been abstracted from the works listed at the end of each chapter: Specific Works by Theorists.

resulting in a theory of social evolution which highlighted the central importance of the *mind* and dominant social values. Using the new science of sociology, he hoped to reestablish as well as bring about a new moral order in contrast to the apparent social chaos around him.

Assumptions   Having established the major aim of Comte's sociology, we may summarize his major assumptions as follows:

1   To Comte, the universe was ordered by "invisible natural laws," which lay behind the evolution and development of the *mind* or dominant social values.

2   Comte perceived this evolutionary process proceeding through three major stages: the *theological stage,* or first stage, in which there is a search for final causes attributed to the super-natural; the *metaphysical stage*, in which "personified abstractions" are viewed as causal; and the *positivistic stage*, in which there is the development of relative knowledge and study of the laws of phenomena. During this stage the positive method permits one to discover and understand natural laws of social phenomena, thereby developing intellectual unity and a moral order which will unify progress and order in contrast to the chaotic existing situation. Sociology was to be an integrative, unifying science, based on the positive method, contributing directly to the evolution of a natural moral order.

3   Accordingly, Comte perceived all knowledge as social insofar as it reflected the social context in which it had developed, in particular the context of one of the three intellectual stages.

4   Comte divided the social system into two main parts: *social statics*, comprising social and human nature and the "laws of human social existence," and *social dynamics*, or the "laws of social change."

5   Underlying this system are human instincts of three major types: the *instincts of preservation* (i.e., the sexual and material) *instincts of improvement* (the military and industrial), and *social instincts* (attachment, veneration, and universal love). Intermediary are the instincts of *pride* and *vanity*.

   Social progress is evident in the eventual preponderance of the social instincts—in contrast to those of preservation and improvement—as the interaction between theological and military elements results in a shift toward the positive mode of thought. This development is aided by problems or humanistic failings in the system as it progresses inevitably through the three stages of intellectual development.

Other contributing factors include the general level of ennui or boredom in the population, the average life span, the rate of population growth, and the rate of intellectual evolution in society as a whole. All these factors contribute to the evolution from low to high instincts in society as the process of civilization proceeds.

6 Finally, Comte posited a kind of sociological utopia—a sociocracy—as the end-point of social evolution in which a religion of humanity or positivism would predominate in the social order. This represents society at its most positivistic or evolved stage, in which there is a vital unity between the mind and the social order. All parts of the social structure would have become positivistic at this stage, and Comte discusses the kinds of contributions institutions such as education and art could make toward this evolution of "benevolence and love based on positivism."

To summarize: (1) Comte perceived the universe as ordered by natural laws. (2) These laws were evident in society in the relationship between human instincts and the mind or dominant social values within the context of the structure of social statistics and dynamics. (3) the social system as a whole evolves through three stages of intellectual development toward the positive stage—the most scientific and morally integrated. (4) Sociology's task as a positive science is to examine and understand this system in detail in order to contribute to the scientific solution of social problems.

Methodology According to Comte, the positive method would lead to the development of ultimate or organic truth. This involves the utilization of *observation, experiment*, and *comparison* in order to understand the details of social statics and dynamics. Such methods permit the abstraction of social laws, through direct and indirect experimentation, as well as the details of general societal evolution. In this manner Comte saw positivism as a methodology leading to greater elaboration of his theoretical model based on naturalistic and organic assumptions.

The Typology   As we have previously stated, Comte divided his model of the society into two main parts: social statics and social dynamics, representing society's institutional structure and the principles of social change. The former comprises *social nature* (religion, art, the family, property, and social organization) and *human nature* (instincts, emotions, action, and intelligence); whereas the latter (social dynamics) consists of the laws of social change and related factors (level of boredom, life span, population growth, and level of intellectual development). He saw this structure as a whole as progressing through the three stages of intellectual development toward positivism. This typology of the social system, along with its evolutionary trends, is summarized in Figure 6.2.

Summary and Conclusions   Comte's is a major example of the mechanical type of organic theory. Reacting to the political chaos of his day in the tradition of Enlightenment philosophy, he developed a naturalistic and conservative model of social reality based upon naturalistic and deterministic assumptions concerning social phenomena. According to this theorist, the social system consists of statics and dynamics based upon a particular kind of mind or set of social values which in turn are founded upon human instincts—the basis of the natural order. This social organism as a whole evolves through three major stages—the theological, metaphysical, and positivistic—as the process of civilization and the influence of specific factors such as boredom, the life span, population characteristics, etc., move the society's foundation from lower- to higher-order instincts in the direction of more intellectual and positivistic emphases.

We are thus presented with a naturalistic model of the social order—a social system which acts in a mechanical fashion as it proceeds through certain predetermined stages. Such a naturalistic-evolutionary theory represents the foundation of sociological theory, as we shall see, and should be viewed as basic to the sociological paradigm of social reality. In order to draw together Comte's contribution to sociology, the major elements of his theoretical framework are summarized in Figure 6.3.

Before turning to a consideration of Spencer, it is appropriate to sketch some of the major issues Comte raised for contemporary sociology. We have summarized these issues on page 76.

FIGURE 6.2
COMTE'S TYPOLOGY

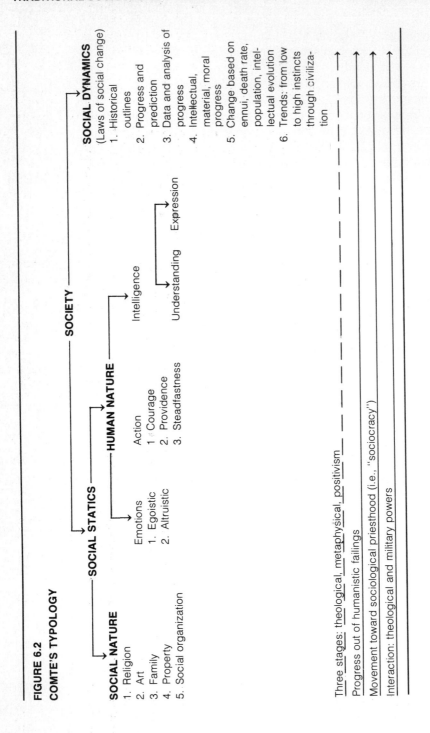

FIGURE 6.3

COMTE'S THEORETICAL FRAMEWORK SUMMARIZED

**AUGUSTE COMTE
(1789–1859)**

BACKGROUND:
1   Catholic, monarchist family
2   Educated in medicine and physiology
3   Taught positive philosophy
4   Enlightenment education
5   France's political and economic upheavals

AIM:
Eliminate the revolutionary construction of modern society, i.e., reorganize society according to positivism.

ASSUMPTIONS:
1   The universe is ordered by invariable natural laws.
2   Three stages of development—theological, metaphysical, and positivism.
3   All knowledge is social.
4   Society may be divided into social statics and social dynamics.
5   Underlying society are humanity's major instincts: preservation, improvement, and social instincts.
6   Social progress evolves out of humanity's failures.

METHODOLOGY:
1   *Positivism*—leads to development of organic truth
              —observation, comparison, experiments, analysis, determination,
                discovery, laws
              —theological, metaphysical, positivistic stages
2   Observation and comparison = social statics and social dynamics

TYPOLOGY:
Social statics and social dynamics

ISSUES:
1   Theoretical or practical sociology
2   Naturalistic explanations
3   Positive methodology
4   Structure and process

1 Comte's approach raises the issue of to what extent sociology's aims are theoretical, practical, or both, particularly within the context of modern empiricism.

2 His major assumptions raise the issues of naturalistic explanations (i.e., the relevance of instincts), deterministic models of social evolution, conceptualizations of society in terms of its dominant value system or view of reality (a somewhat social-psychological view with parallels in the works of other theorists such as Durkheim, Weber, and Mannheim), and his division of society into statics and dynamics (a forerunner of later concepts such as *structure* and *process*).

3 His positive methodology represents an early foundation of the more contemporary scientific method.

4 His typology delineates major elements of and processes within the social system, thereby anticipating later work by structure-functionalist and even conflict theorists.

From the above, then, it can be seen that Comte's views are neither simplistic nor irrelevant: his work represents the foundation of both sociology and sociological theory, and contains significant elements which remain relevant to the problems of this discipline in contemporary society. By conceptualizing society as he did, he laid the foundation for the development of a science of society. We turn now to a similar thinker, Herbert Spencer.

Herbert Spencer (1820–1903)

Background Spencer, an Englishman, was born the son of nonconformist Dissenters. He received a classical education at home and worked as a draftsman and, eventually, as editor of *The Economist*. An individualist in the Victorian tradition, Spencer viewed society, as it was influenced by the industrial revolution and economic expansion, from a Darwinian-evolutionary perspective. His theory is very much of an organic-evolutionary type, similar to Comte's in its division of society into social statics and dynamics. Spencer's major works include *Social Statics* (1850), *First Principles* (1862), and *The Study of Sociology* (1873).

Aims Spencer's major concern was "to trace the process of social evolution" throughout society historically and sociologically. In view of his strong background in Darwinism, his application of the principle of biological evolution to society is not surprising. Thus the organic analogy is applied to society directly in the evolutionary framework. Understanding of such organic evolution becomes relevant to the greater control of society in a manner which results in a closer correlation between individual and societal needs. As with Comte, we are presented with an organic, evolutionary, and essentially practical theory of society, based on paramount societal needs.

Assumptions

1 In the Victorian tradition, Spencer saw the universe in a constant state of evolution and dissolution. He held that it is sociology's task to trace these processes as they apply to society.

2 He assumed that evolution was a *universal process*, that is, a universally applicable natural law. Underlying his framework, then, is the principle of universal, naturalistic evolution.

3 With reference to sociology, Spencer viewed society as an organic and evolving whole, representing more than the sum of its parts and not subject to complete dissection. Relationships were similar to functional and sustaining relationships within biological organisms. In this manner, Spencer was a forerunner of contemporary structure functionalism.

4 As Comte had done, Spencer divided society into two main parts: social statics and social dynamics. Statics represented society's institutional structure and social systems, while dynamics involved the structure's ongoing evolution.

5 For Spencer, society's major institutions consisted of the family and ceremonial, political, ecclesiastical, professional (the division of labor), and industrial institutions. This structure he viewed as having evolved from a primitive, polygamous, military, tribal, and slavery system to a society based on monogamy, the state, professional occupations, and contract labor.

6 Further he divided society into two major systems: the inner (relating to sustaining and distribution functions) and the outer (concentrating on social control or regulation). These subsystems serve to maintain society as an organic whole in its ongoing evolution.

7 With reference to social dynamics, Spencer outlined a number of distinct processes: (*a*) continuity of motion, (*b*) movement from homogeneous to heterogeneous mass, (*c*) the accumulation of superorganic materials with evolution, and (*d*) society's continuous movement toward equilibrium—a state which breaks down and results in change once that equilibrium becomes too rigid.

To summarize, Spencer perceived society as an evolving, organic whole subject to the laws of universal evolution. This organic system consists of inner and outer subsystems and is constantly evolving toward and away from new levels of equilibrium as it develops from the primitive toward the modern and industrial. Sociology's major task is to understand these processes in depth in order to maximize societal harmony.

Methodology Spencer's methods are similar to those proposed by Comte: empirical observation, the comparative method, historical deduction, and induction. These methods are to be used in tracing the process of social evolution.

The Typology Spencer's major typology is his division of society into social statics and dynamics, as pointed out above. However, he also provided a detailed model of the ideal-type characteristics of two types of society: the military and the industrial. The former represents a society based on subjugation of the individual, high rigidity, regimentation, and regulation, with arbitrary distribution of rewards and a highly centralized form of government. The industrial society, on the other hand, is seen as providing the individual with higher status, as being much lower on regimentation and regulation, as decentralized, and as distributing rewards by contract. These societal types essentially represent stages of evolution from the primitive to the modern and are echoed in the typologies of Durkheim and Tönnies, as we shall see. Spencer's typology as a whole is summarized in Figure 6.4.

Summary and Conclusions We have attempted to describe Spencer's contribution to the "mechanical" type of organic theory

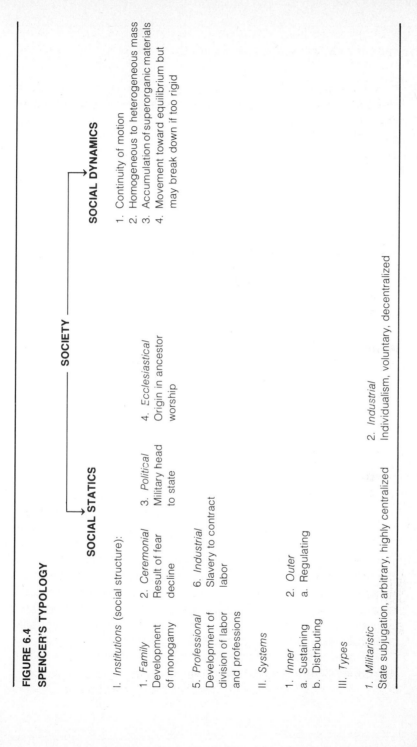

FIGURE 6.4
SPENCER'S TYPOLOGY

SOCIETY

SOCIAL STATICS

I. *Institutions* (social structure):

1. *Family*
Development
of monogamy

2. *Ceremonial*
Result of fear
decline

3. *Political*
Military head
to state

4. *Ecclesiastical*
Origin in ancestor
worship

5. *Professional*
Development of
division of labor
and professions

6. *Industrial*
Slavery to contract
labor

II. *Systems*

1. *Inner*
a. Sustaining
b. Distributing

2. *Outer*
a. Regulating

III. *Types*

1. *Militaristic*
State subjugation, arbitrary, highly centralized

2. *Industrial*
Individualism, voluntary, decentralized

SOCIAL DYNAMICS

1. Continuity of motion
2. Homogeneous to heterogeneous mass
3. Accumulation of superorganic materials
4. Movement toward equilibrium but
   may break down if too rigid

FIGURE 6.5
SPENCER'S THEORETICAL FRAMEWORK SUMMARIZED

HERBERT SPENCER
(1820–1903)

BACKGROUND:
1 Nonconformist English family
2 Classical education at home
3 Victorian background
4 British social and economic changes

AIM:
To trace the process of social evolution in order to maximize social harmony

ASSUMPTIONS:
1 Evolution is a universal process and a universally applicable natural law.
2 Organistic model of society.
3 Two divisions of society: Statics and Dynamics.
4 Universe is in a constant state of evolution and dissolution.
5 The organic whole of society is not subject to dissection.
6 Relationships within society are comparable to organic relations.

METHODOLOGY:
1 Positivism
2 Deduction, induction, and comparative method
3 Use of ethnological and historical data

TYPOLOGY:
Social statics and social dynamics

ISSUES:
1 Social evolutionary theory
2 Organic functionalism
3 Societal equilibrium notion
4 Types of society approach

in his naturalistic, evolutionary, organic conceptualization of society. In the context of Victorian individualism and Social Darwinism, he conceptualized the effects of industrialization within his organic-evolutionary framework, using biological-organic and evolutionary analogies directly applied to society. The major elements of his theoretical framework are summarized in Figure 6.5.

Spencer's naturalistic, evolutionary, organic approach raises a number of contemporary issues:

80

1 The application of evolutionary theory to sociology. A recent attempt was made to revive this in Parson's notion of *evolutionary universals.*[2]

2 Spencer's view of society as an organic whole with a number of specific subsystems relates to the contemporary issue of structure-functionalism as a form of explanation in sociology.[3]

3 The notion of societal equilibrum is basic to both sociology and structure-functionalism, and raises the issue of how to conceptualize such a state as well as the question of its general utility in sociological explanation.

4 Finally, Spencer's delineation of two types of society—the military and industrial—parallels Comte's *three stages,* Durkheim's *types of solidarity,* and Tönnie's notion of *gemeinschaft* and *gesellschaft.*

THE NATURALISTIC TYPE OF ORGANIC THEORY SUMMARIZED

Before turning to the more social-psychological type of organic theory, it is appropriate at this point to summarize the approaches of Comte and Spencer.

A number of basic similarities between these two thinkers is evident:

1 They both reacted to the economic and political problems of their time in the tradition of the Enlightenment and, in the case of Spencer, Victorian philosophy. The focus of their work is on understanding how natural laws operate in society as it evolves, in order to provide a scientific basis for social control, social policy, and happiness.

2 They both perceived society as ordered by natural laws.

3 Both perceived society as an evolving, organic whole, proceeding through a particular set of stages toward the more positive or industrial.

[2]See T. Parsons, "Evolutionary Universals in Society," *American Sociological Review*, **29:** 339–357, 1964.
[3]See D. Martindale, *The Nature and Types of Sociological Theory*, Houghton Mifflin, Boston, 1960, pp. 65–69 and 447.

4 Both described the structure of society as consisting of social statics and social dynamics.

5 Both emphasized empirical observation and the comparative method as appropriate methodologies.

6 Both delineated types of societies at particular stages of evolution as their basic typologies.

While Comte emphasized social values or "mind" and Spencer used the notion of organism as his paradigm of society, it can be seen from the above points that the views of both thinkers represent a naturalistic, evolutionary, and organic type of explanation in sociology—the foundation of the discipline itself as people attempted to understand society scientifically in order to guide its development and solve its social problems. The structure of this type of explanation is outlined in Figure 6.6. Having summarized this, we shall now move on to a consideration of a second kind of organic theory—the social-psychological.

THE SYSTEMIC TYPE OF ORGANIC THEORY

In contrast to the more mechanical-naturalistic kind of organic theorists, Durkheim and Tönnies emphasized a more *normative* or social-psychological dimension in the conceptualization of society as a social system. While not radically different from the ideas of Comte and Spencer, their ideas move us away from the strictly mechanical toward the more sociological kind of explanation. It is to these two thinkers that we turn now.

Emile Durkheim (1858–1917)

Background Durkheim was born in France, the son of a Jewish family. Trained in law and positive philosophy, he taught the latter at the university level and offered the first sociology course in France in 1896. Educated in the Enlightenment tradition, he reacted to the political revolution and social breakdown of his day and was concerned with the notion of "general will" and social solidarity. As a result, he conceptualized society in terms of its norms or kinds of *social integration* (that is, the manner in which the individual is sociologically related to the social structure through "social facts"). One of his major concerns in this regard

FIGURE 6.6
THE STRUCTURE OF NATURALISTIC ORGANIC THEORY

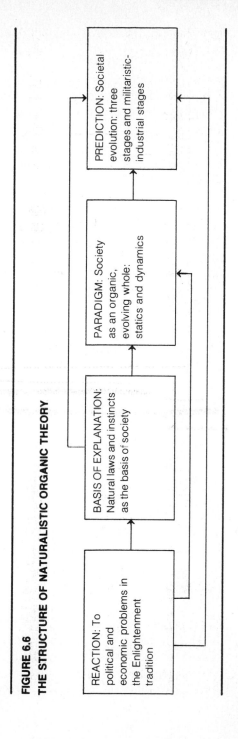

REACTION: To political and economic problems in the Enlightenment tradition

BASIS OF EXPLANATION: Natural laws and instincts as the basis of society

PARADIGM: Society as an organic, evolving whole: statics and dynamics

PREDICTION: Societal evolution: three stages and militaristic-industrial stages

was the kind of "social solidarity" characteristic of a particular society.

Aims Durkheim was primarily concerned with the understanding of "social phenomena" (social norms) and "their influence on social problems in contrast to psychologistic explanations." He saw sociology as focusing on "collective psychic phenomena" and "moral obligations," particularly in the manner these phenomena constrain the individual's behavior within the group context. Thus, in contrast to the predominantly internal and psychological explanations of his day, Durkheim posited an external and sociological framework as well as a methodology for studying these social data. In such a view, Durkheim contributed significantly to the founding and development of sociology as a new and unique science, concentrating on society as a "real" and independent phenomenon.

Assumptions

1. Durkheim's major assumption was that society as collective consciousness has an independent existence; that is, as did Spencer also, he felt that society represents more than the sum of its parts. Society, then, is an organic, collective whole, which operates primarily through the constraining influence of its *normative structure*.

2 It follows from this that social facts (i.e., collective norms) are real, as evident in the coercive power of norms and their related institutional structures. Accordingly, Durkheim was primarily concerned with the reality of norms and their coercive power.

3 "Social power" is based on "collective thought"; that is, various forms of dominance rest on the normative structure of the particular group insofar as control is exercised on group members through these norms. In general, in fact, all aspects of the social structure, including institutions, are founded upon a society's normative system.

4 Durkheim saw the evolution of social facts or norms as based on society's underlying needs. In this manner, social phenomena represent social needs—a correlation Durkheim felt sociologists should explore in greater depth. Such a view also anticipates the more contemporary approach of structure functionalism.

84

5   Durkheim's second major assumption is that social cohesion or integration is founded upon society's division of labor; that is, the more similar the division of labor (or the less complex the role structure), the higher the level of social cohesion.

6   Expanding this assumption, he linked population size with its social density and consequent level of division of labor and social cohesion; that is, the higher the population size, the greater the level of social density, resulting in an increase in the division of labor and a decline in social solidarity.

7   Furthermore, Durkheim perceived two major types of solidarity: mechanical solidarity and organic solidarity. The former is characteristic of traditional societies in which the division of labor is low, norms are repressive, and there is a high level of social integration. Organic solidarity, on the other hand, is characteristic of more advanced, industrialized societies with a complex (dissimilar) division of labor, increased contractual relationships, and lower levels of integration or cohesion. In such a setting control of the individual is low, leading to high levels of anomie or normlessness. It is at this stage that high levels of deviance, such as suicide occur, since the bond between individuals and the social structure has become weaker and their appetites are no longer adequately regulated.

8   Finally, Durkheim assumed that crime and other forms of deviance are functional for society to the extent that they reinforce goup norms as well as contribute to their ongoing change by modifying those norms.

To summarize, Durkheim perceived society as an organic, normative whole, representing society's underlying needs. As this system's population, social density, and division of labor increased, it moved from a society based on mechanical solidarity to one founded on organic solidarity. The resultant practical question is the reintegration of individuals and their social environment, i.e., the development of moral unity. Durkheim's suggestions include the use of education and a new social morality which transcends the individual, providing a harmonious link with society. As were Comte and Spencer, Durkheim is also concerned with the practical aspects of social harmony.

Methodology   Durkheim is particularly well known for his work *The Rules of Sociological Method*, which emphasizes that social facts are "things" requiring objective study. Focusing on these indexes of collective thought, sociology should attempt to determine the underlying societal needs they represent. It should utilize methods such as "concomitant variation" (correlation) and experimental and comparative techniques, paying particular attention to the changing development of social facts over time. Using these methods, it may be possible to abstract scientific laws concerning the operation and development of such social phenomena.

The Typology   As mentioned earlier, Durkheim's typology is based on a society's predominant form of social solidarity. Mechanical solidarity, on the one hand, consists of a low division of labor, a homogeneous traditional culture, repressive norms, communal property, totemic religion, and "altruistic" suicide (i.e., for the sake of the group). Organic solidarity, on the other hand, denotes a complex division of labor system with industrialization, increased individuality, restitutive norms, contractual relationships, private property, individualized forms of religion, and "egotistic" and "anomic" types of suicide. The former (egoistic suicide) is the result of a conflict between individual desires and group authority. The latter (anomic suicide) stems from social disintegration, particularly in times of economic crisis, when the gap between aspiration and reality is too great. Similar to Spencer's militaristic and industrial societies, this typology describes the sociological structure of society at particular stages of its development. It is summarized in Figure 6.7.

Summary and Conclusions   In contrast to Comte and Spencer, Durkheim conceptualized society in more normative terms. Nevertheless, his paradigm is equally organic and evolutionary: society represents a form of collective will which has evolved in reference to underlying social needs, defining and constraining the behavior of individuals within it. As those needs change with increasing population size, so does the division of labor and related norms, moving from the mechanical to the organic type of solidarity. Such a normative, organic, and evolutionary approach represents the very foundation of sociology, and Durkheim's contribution can be seen as highly important and lasting.

Some of the major issues raised by such a theory may be summarized as follows:

86

FIGURE 6.7
DURKHEIM'S TYPOLOGY

TYPES OF SOCIAL SOLIDARITY

FACTORS:	MECHANICAL	ORGANIC
1. Behavior	Dominated by tradition. Beliefs, opinions, etc., are similar	Increased individuality. Specialization of labor causes individuality
2. Laws, morals, social controls	Repressive punishment	Emphasis on restitutive law
3. Political structure	Public meetings	Contractual relationship of government to people
4. Economics	Sharing—communal property	Contractual and private property
5. Religion	Totemic—tribal and local patriotism	Individualization of God—monotheism and polytheism
6. Suicide	Altruistic	Egoistic and anomic

Division of labor increases proportionately to time passage because of increase in moral and dynamic density of population

Importance of moral unity—developed through education—habit, discipline, respect for authority

1 To what extent does a collective conscience possess an independent existence in reality? That is, is Durkheim simply identifying this *term* with *society* and then assuming that the term has an independent existence?

2 To what extent is the posited relationship between population size, division of labor, and social integration simplistic? The linking of such macroscopic factors involves the risk of oversimplification.

3 The problems of *measuring* social facts at individual, group, and societal levels would appear to be great.

4 To what extent do social facts represent elite rather than general societal needs? While Durkheim discussed the problem of social inequality, he still maintained a macroscopic and structure-functional explanation of society.

Despite the above problems, Durkheim's work remains among the foremost contributions to sociological thought, particularly his normative conceptualization of society. His framework as a whole is summarized in Figure 6.8.

87

FIGURE 6.8
DURKHEIM'S THEORETICAL FRAMEWORK SUMMARIZED

EMILE DURKHEIM
(1858–1917)

BACKGROUND:
1 Jewish family
2 Trained in law and positive philosophy
3 Enlightenment tradition
4 France's political, social, and economic disorder

AIM:
To understand social phenomena and their influence on social problems in contrast to psychologistic explanations.

ASSUMPTIONS:
1 A collective conscience (consciousness) exists; whole is more than sum
2 Social facts are real
3 Cohesion comes from similitude
4 Cohesion comes from division of labor
5 Power is based on collective thought
6 Social facts represent societal needs
7 Changes in population size, social density, and the division of labor
8 Deviance is functional for society

METHODOLOGY:
1 "Social facts" are "things" and can be measured
2 Propositions based on factual material (history)
3 Comparison
4 Proof through concomitant variation

TYPOLOGY:
Mechanical and organic solidarity

ISSUES:
1 Existence of "collective conscience"
2 Relevance of population effect
3 Measuring "social facts"
4 What do "social facts" represent?

Ferdinand Tönnies (1855–1936)

Background Tönnies was born in Eisenstadt, a farm community, and was educated in the tradition of Hobbes, Hegel, Comte, and Spencer at the University of Tübingen. He observed the economic and political upheaval of Germany during his time and was centrally concerned with understanding society as a product of human will. As with Durkheim, then, he added a social-psychological dimension to organic theory. His major works include *Gemeinschaft and Gesellschaft* (1887) and *Introduction to Sociology* (1931).

Aims For Tönnies, sociology was a study of social will as the basis of social reality—a "theory of human will" based on the attempt to understand human nature. He thus attempts to understand society as a function of human will.

Assumptions

1 Tönnies's major assumption was that society, including relationships and associations, is a product of human will.

2 This relationship consists of individual acts of will combining to form collective acts of will and, thereby, the social structure.

3 Interaction represents the expression of these acts of will in interchange.

4 This will may be one of two types: (*a*) natural will, the basis of gemeinschaft, and (*b*) rational will, the basis of gesellschaft. Natural will represents the foundation of traditional society, rational will the basis of modern industrial society. Societies thus differ according to their underlying norms and move from the natural to the rational.

5 Finally, society represents an organic whole founded upon a particular kind of will.

Methodology Tönnies divided sociology into three kinds: (*a*) pure sociology, concentrating on the development of conceptual models (*b*) applied sociology, involving the application of these concepts to sociological phenomena; and (*c*) empirical sociology, utilizing empirical methods and data in an inductive fashion. Using all three of these, Tönnies essentially employed the general method of historical induction to outline his gemeinschaft-gesellschaft model of the ideal-type forms of social will.

The Typology Tönnies's though is well-known for the dichotomous typology of the two major forms of social will—gemeinschaft and gesellschaft—that he developed. The former repre-

FIGURE 6.9
TONNIES' TYPOLOGY

TYPES OF "SOCIAL WILL"

FACTORS (Type of):	GEMEINSCHAFT	GESELLSCHAFT
Life	Communal	Public
Society	Traditional	Industrial
Relations	Family, close, instinctual	Economic, impersonal, artificial
Motives	Mutual aid and protection	Economic competition
Norms	Love, understanding, organization	Economic value, labor, consumption
Groups	Based on family structure	Based on economic classes
Possessions	Communal	Individual
Authority	Fatherhood	Power
Bonds	Common blood, place, mind	Economic contract exchange

sents a traditional, communal society based on close family relationships; the norms of love, understanding, and protection; and the social bonds of kinship, locality, and common language (i.e., the "natural" society). Gesellschaft, on the other hand, is typified in modern industrial society, which is based on economic, impersonal and artificial relationships; norms of economic value, labor, and consumption; and the bonds of social class and economic contract exchange. Such a typology closely parallels Comte's three stages, Spencer's militaristic-industrial dichotomy, and Durkheim's two forms of solidarity. What is emphasized here, however, is society as a particular kind of internal mental state in contrast to the more external and mechanical paradigms of earlier thinkers. The details of Tönnies's model are summarized in Figure 6.9.

Summary and Conclusions Tönnies perceived society as an expression of a particular kind of social will—the natural or rational. These wills operate at both individual and collective levels, representing an organic social system. Such an approach raises a number of issues, as follows:

1   The independent reality of this social will at the societal level

2   The foundation of the two types of will

3   Problems inherent in such a simplistic dichotomy

4   The contribution of other factors to the social system

Despite the above issues, Tönnies's work complements and contributes to the social-psychological type of organic theory, and his typology became the basis of much work to follow both in sociology and anthropology. The details of his framework as a whole are summarized in Figure 6.10.

FIGURE 6.10
TONNIES' THEORETICAL FRAMEWORK SUMMARIZED

FERDINAND TONNIES
(1855–1936)

BACKGROUND:
1   Rural, farm family
2   Enlightenment tradition
3   Experienced economic unrest and industrial development

AIM:
To understand society as a function of human will

ASSUMPTIONS:
1   Society is a product of human will
2   Individual "acts of will" combine to form collective "acts"
3   Interaction represents "acts of will" in interchange
4   There are two types of will: natural will and rational will
5   Society is an organic whole

METHODOLOGY:
1   "Pure," "applied," and "empirical" sociology
2   Use of historical induction

TYPOLOGY:
Gemeinschaft and Gesellschaft

ISSUES:
1   Independent existence of "social will"
2   Foundations of "social will"
3   Simplistic typology of wills
4   Relevance of other societal factors

The Systemic Type of Organic Theory Summarized

Any comparison of Durkheim and Tönnies reveals a number of distinct similarities:

1 They were both concerned with understanding normative or social phenomena.

2 Both assumed the independent existence of such phenomena.

3 Both delineated the foundation of social phenomena as a society's type of economic system.

4 Both outlined two major types of these phenomena, namely, the mechanical-organic and gemeinschaft-gesellschaft distinctions.

5 Both advocated and used comparative historical methods.

6 The typologies of both are almost identical.

What we have, then, in the case of Durkheim and Tönnies is organic theory at a more advanced and social-psychological stage but nevertheless representing Enlightenment reaction to the perceived political, economic, and social developments of the day. It can be seen how that theory is dynamic and progresses rather than remains static as a basic paradigm is further elaborated. The major elements of this branch of organic theory are summarized in Figure 6.11.

THE ORGANIC APPROACH SUMMARIZED

In this chapter we have attempted to show how organic theory in sociology represents the reaction of upper-class intellectuals, educated in the tradition of Enlightenment philosophy (namely, naturalism, rationalism, social evolutionism, social reform, and the positivist method) to a societal context experiencing high levels of political revolution, social breakdown, and industrial development. This reaction consisted of the conceptualization of society as an organic system defined by natural laws. The foundation of this system was its division of labor or role structure, upon which the normative system was based. This system was seen as evolving from the traditional toward the modern and industrial, with distinct modifications of its normative structure in the process.

FIGURE 6.11
THE STRUCTURE OF SYSTEMIC ORGANIC THEORY

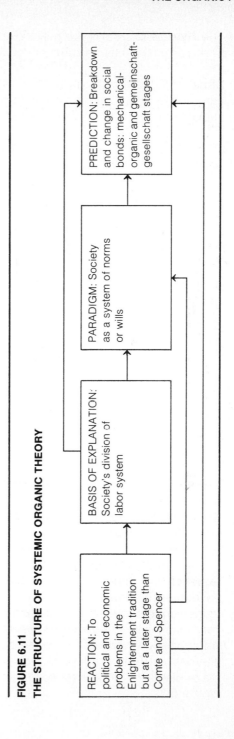

REACTION: To political and economic problems in the Enlightenment tradition but at a later stage than Comte and Spencer

BASIS OF EXPLANATION: Society's division of labor system

PARADIGM: Society as a system of norms or wills

PREDICTION: Breakdown and change in social bonds: mechanical-organic and gemeinschaft-gesellschaft stages

For clarity's sake, the major elements of the organic framework as a whole may be summarized as follows:

Aims   This framework grew out of the attempt to understand the natural laws of societal evolution in order to bring about greater social harmony and societal integration.

Assumptions

1   Society is an organic, interrelated system.

2   The social system evolves in reference to its underlying needs.

3   Society evolves from the traditional and nonindustrial toward the modern and industrial.

4   The social structure consists of society's normative structure, based on its underlying division of labor system.

5   The social system may be divided generally into social structure (social statics) and social process (social dynamics).

Methodology

1   Empirical observation (positivism)
2   Comparative and experimental methods
3   Utilization of historical induction

Typologies   Society is divided into typological stages of social evolution (i.e., Comte's three stages, Spencer's militarist-industrial types, Durkheim's mechanical-organic types, and Tönnies's gemeinschaft-gesellschaft types of social will).

From the above it can be seen that the organic approach represents a naturalistic, evolutionary way of looking at society developed in the tradition of Enlightenment philosophy. Such a framework provided the foundation for sociological theory and is very much part of sociology's general, underlying paradigm, as we shall see when we turn to the conflict and social-behaviorist alternatives. Before doing so, however, we shall summarize the major elements of the organic form of sociological explanation in Figure 6.12.

FIGURE 6.12
THE STRUCTURE OF ORGANIC SOCIOLOGICAL THEORY

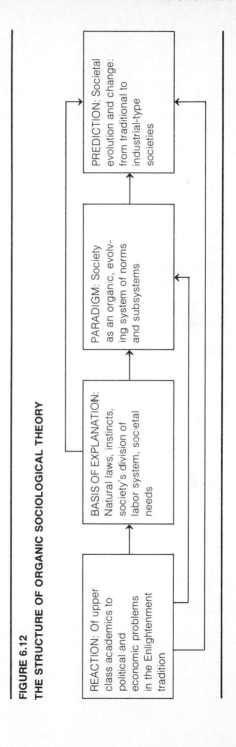

EXERCISES

1 Consider the following social trends:

a The general decline in the overall American birthrate

b The movement from the extended to the nuclear family

c The general increase in bureaucratization

d The general increase in deviant forms of behavior

e The general increase in protest-oriented social movements.

Account for each trend, using the general explanations provided by Comte, Spencer, Durkheim, and Tönnies. Compare in detail the different types of explanations you develop, using each theorist. To what extent are they similar? Can you develop an overall organic explanation of each trend?

READINGS

General Works

Aron, R.: *Main Currents in Sociological Thought*, vols. 1 and 2, Doubleday, Garden City, N.Y., 1970, for chaps. on Comte and Durkheim.

Coser, L. A.: *Masters of Sociological Thought, Ideas in Historical and Social Context*, Harcourt, Brace, Jovanovich, New York, 1971, for chaps. on Comte, Spencer, and Durkheim.

Martindale, D.: *The Nature and Types of Sociological Theory*, Houghton Mifflin, Boston, 1960, chaps. 3, 4, and 5.

Nisbet, R. A.: *The Sociological Tradition*, Basic Books, New York, 1966, chaps. 3 and 4.

Truzzi, M. (ed.): *Sociology, The Classic Statements*, Random House, New York, 1971, selections 4, 5, 7, 14.

Specific Works by Theorists

Comte

Simpson, G. (ed.): *Auguste Comte: Sire of Sociology*, Crowell, New York, 1969.

Comte, A.: *The Positive Philosophy*, H. Martineau (trans.), C. Blanchard, New York, 1959.

————: *System of Positive Polity*, B. Franklin, New York, 1966.

Spencer

Andreski, S. (ed.): *Herbert Spencer: Structure, Function and Evolution*, M. Joseph, London, 1971.
Carneiro, R. L. (ed.): *The Evolution of Society*, University of Chicago Press, Chicago, 1967.
Spencer, H.: *The Principles of Sociology*, Appleton, New York, 1923.

Durkheim

Simpson, G. (ed.): *Emile Durkheim*, Crowell, New York, 1963.
Wolff, K. H. (ed.): *Emile Durkheim, 1858–1917*, Ohio State University Press, Columbus, 1960.
Durkheim, E.: *Division of Labor in Society*, Free Press, Glencoe, Ill., 1947
———: *The Rules of Sociological Method*, Free Press, Glencoe, Ill., 1950.
———: *Suicide*, Free Press, Glencoe, Ill., 1951.

Tönnies

Tönnies, F.: *Community and Society*, Harper Torchbooks, New York, 1957.
———: *On Sociology: Pure, Applied, and Empirical*, University of Chicago Press, Chicago, 1971.

THE CONFLICT PARADIGM

In contrast to the organic approach, conflict theory views society as a system of competing groups representing the struggle to obtain resources for basic material needs. Primary factors behind this struggle include the problems of social organization itself (e.g., changing population and division of labor systems) or human nature (e.g., instincts or traits).

Such a paradigm, as we shall see, is as naturalistic, evolutionary, and systemic as organic theory, developed, to a large extent, within the tradition of Enlightenment philosophy also. However, conflict theory was developed by a group of thinkers whose background and social experience were strikingly different from that of the organic theorists and who were committed to human needs and societal change rather than systemic problems and the attempt to reassert social order. While the *structure* of the conflict paradigm is markedly similar, then, its ideological foundation is not, underlining once again the view of sociological theory as the reaction of a particular group of thinkers to the perceived problems of their day. It is to these contextual characteristics that we turn first, before moving to analyze the ideas of Karl Marx, Robert Park, Vilfredo Pareto, and Thorstein Veblen.

INTRODUCTION

The conflict theorists we shall be concerned with span a long period of time (1818–1944) and consist of thinkers who are far from homogeneous. Nevertheless, these theorists tend to possess certain general similarities: their social origins tend to be lower- rather than middle- or upper-class; they received an Enlightenment-type education in subjects such as classics, philosophy, history, law, and economics; they were involved in politics and activism; they experienced political repression, conflict, and polarization in their own societies; and they were socialized in the Enlightenment ideals of naturalism, idealism, evolution, rationality, pragmatism, and socialism. This theorizing process is summarized in Figure 7.1.

On the other hand, conflict theory should *not* be viewed as uniformly radical in ideology; conservative forms of the paradigm exist as well. Thus conflict theory tends to vary in ideology according to the underlying type of explanation used: the "societal problem" approach of Marx and Park is more radical in implication, while the "naturalistic" view, particularly as developed by Pareto, is more conservative in tone and purpose. Nevertheless,

100

both types emphasize conflict and change in their conceptualizations of society.

The above differences may be further elaborated as follows: according to the societal problem approach, struggle over need fulfillment results in conflict and change; the naturalistic approach, on the other hand, argues that there are certain characteristics inherent in human nature (e.g., traits or residues) which account for these same processes. Second, Marx and Park viewed economic and ecological conditions as accounting for conflict-oriented behavior, while Pareto and Veblen saw ideas and values—i.e., a normative approach—as more explanatory of these same processes. However, both types of conflict theory are systemic, evolutionary, and naturalistic, founded on a view of society which sees it as based on some type of equilibrium, no matter how temporary or unstable.

Conflict theory, then, represents a systemic paradigm of society and is similar to the organic approach in the structure of its explanation; however, it differs in its view of society as based on

FIGURE 7.1
MAJOR FACTORS BEHIND CONFLICT THEORY

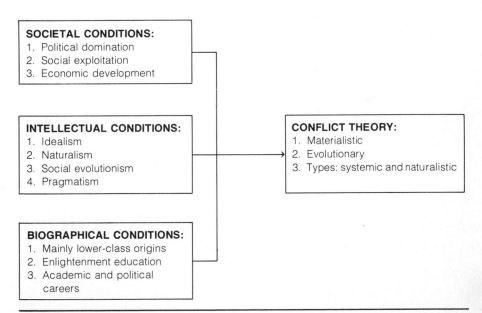

competition, domination, and conflict rather than consensus and integration. Furthermore, conflict theories differ in their emphasis upon macroscopic-societal or microscopic-naturalistic factors as the underlying foundation of these processes. Finally, they differ markedly from the organic theories in their general emphasis upon humanity's needs rather than societal or systemic priorities. While the *structure* of these theories may be similar, their *ideological content* is clearly different.

Having completed our introduction to this type of sociological theory, we turn to a discussion of its major subtypes, beginning with a consideration of the systemic approach.

THE SYSTEMIC APPROACH TO CONFLICT THEORY

According to this view, economic and ecological factors account for the development of social conflict. We shall discuss two major proponents of this type of theory—Marx and Park—examining their backgrounds and thoughts.

Karl Marx (1818–1884)

Background   Marx was born in Germany, the son of a Jewish lawyer. Educated in history, philosophy, and law, he participated in journalism and political radicalism, including the International Association of Workers and the Congress of the Communist League. He reacted to the political and economic repression present in Germany within the intellectual context of German idealism, French socialism, and British economic theory. His major publications include his *Critique of Political Economy* (1867, 1885, 1894), and *The Communist Manifesto* (1848). Reacting to the social, political, and economic problems of his day from the perspective of philosophical idealism, he developed a conflict-oriented theory of society which has had profound effects through to contemporary sociological thought.

Aims   Marx's major aim was to analyze the relationship between life conditions (society's economic substructure) and "ideas" (society's normative superstructure) on an ongoing and changing basis through society's historical development. Such an interactive relationship was basic to Marx's thought as he analyzed the corruption of "natural man" to "alienated man" through industriali-

102

zation and capitalistic exploitation. The ideological aim behind his theorizing, then, was the retransformation of society into a state in which "natural" rather than "alienated man" would be resynthesized with his natural and social environments. He planned a detailed historical study of political economics within the context of dialectic materialism to this pragmatic end. Marx, then, was an applied theorist using the German Hegelian tradition. In reacting to the political and economic oppression of his day, he developed a dialectic, change-oriented theory of society with particular emphasis on its economic substructure.

Assumptions

1 Marx's most basic assumption is that "existence determines consciousness," that is, that the material conditions of life define one's type of social or normative consciousness.

2 In this manner, the material determines the ideological, with materialistic change (material or economic contradictions) resulting in social change (changes in norms or social consciousness).

3 Accordingly, society too is "rooted in the material conditions of life," in which the economic substructure, developed in people's attempts to satisfy their primary needs (i.e., the human) struggle with nature) defines that society's legal and political superstructures. Society thus represents an evolutionary balance in which relationships and social consciousness are defined by its primary mode of material production, i.e., its economic system.

4 The dialectical interaction (the interchange and eventual synthesis of opposing elements) between economic substructure and normative superstructure leads society through a number of evolutionary stages: increasing population and economic needs result in an increase in the system's division of labor or role structure. This development, in turn, leads to the amassing of private property, which, under the influence of industrialization, results in the capitalistic system, with economic domination and alienation of the proletariat from nature and the means of production. Finally, contradictions and problems within the capitalistic economic system result in changes in consciousness and eventually revolution, moving the society toward a state of socialism in which, according to Marx, "natural man" will be restored. In such an

103

evolutionary model, as Marx applied the dialectic notion to society's historical development, the interactive relationship between substructure and superstructure is clear. Thus, the state and class conflict are the result of economic development and, in turn, lead to the marked change of that economic structure with a revolutionary change in humanity's social consciousness. Such an approach is clearly both evolutionary and dynamic.

To summarize, in applying the Hegelian dialectic to a materialistic view of social history, Marx saw the material determining the social in the trend toward capitalism as a result of an increase in society's division of labor and surplus in private property. The dialectic within capitalism, in turn, is seen as the beginning of a movement toward socialism in which there will be a return to "natural man" as he is reunited with his natural and social environments.

Social conflict, then, is a function of the ongoing dialectic between substructure and superstructure as humanity attempts to meet its primary needs on an ongoing and changing basis. Sociology, according to this view, represents the historical study of society's changing economic structure as the basis of social conflict. Finally, "society" is but a temporary equilibrium of this dialectic at particular stages of its economic development.

Methodology Marx is well known for his *dialectical materialism* approach to social history. The dialectic, rooted in German philosophy—particularly the work of Friedrich Hegel—sees in phenomena the forces of their own change in the trend from *thesis* (original state) to *antithesis* (opposite state) through a *synthesis* (combination of first two states) to a new *thesis* (new state). Such a dialectical development focuses on the dynamics of evolution and change in phenomena.

Marx took this philosophical device and applied it to the materialistic view of society just discussed. Accordingly, he believed that the materialistic structure of societies accounts for their changing evolution and development. Applying this to history, Marx delineated a particular societal dialectic sequence as follows: primitive communism ⟶ slavery ⟶ feudalism ⟶ capitalism ⟶ socialism. In this manner, dialectic materialism becomes a sociological tool in the historical analysis of societal development as materialistic forces and contradictions produce counterforces, leading to changes in the economic

and social structure of society.

Applying this device, Marx attempted a historical sociology, concentrating on the changing relationship between a society's mode of production and its social structure. He developed a history of social institutions, attempting thereby to abstract the pure events of social processes with the ideological aim of providing a scientific basis for socialism. Social analysis was thus aimed at societal change.

The Typology Applying his method of dialectical materialism, Marx outlined a number of societal stages of development representing predominant modes of production at each particular stage.[1] This evolutionary typology begins with *tribalism*, in which hunting, fishing, and agriculture predominate, the society is essentially patriarchal, and the division of labor represents an extension of the family system. Private property and the division of labor are thereby at a minimum.

As tribes amalgamate, we move to the stage of *communalism*, consisting of slavery, the beginning of private property, and a division of labor system. With a decline in agriculture, this changes to *feudalism*, a paternalistic, land-based economy in which the nobility controls the enserfed peasantry. Such a structure, however, becomes inefficient and breaks down in the face of urbanization, the development of a town bourgeoisie, increased needs for a manufacturing economy, and the general effects of world travel and colonization.

The major result of these developments is the evolution of *capitalism*, a system in which resources are monopolized in the form of capital by the owners of the means of production, labor is the major commodity of the worker, the predominant ideology is utilitarian and money-oriented, and society becomes stratified into the classes of owners, supervisors, and laborers. As with previous states, however, capitalism does not remain static: through the problems of overproduction and increasing alienation of the workers, the proletariat, according to Marx, becomes organized and revolts against the capitalistic bourgeoisie.

Capitalism begins the process of its own dissolution, moving society toward its ultimate end, the state of utopian *socialism*. Within this system, under the "revolutionary dictatorship of the proletariat," private property is abolished, there are no classes, and the individual is completely "socialized," while society and

[1]For details, see T. B. Bottomore (ed.), *Karl Marx, Selected Writings in Sociology and Social Philosophy*, McGraw-Hill, New York, 1964.

nature are reunited since private property and the division of labor have all but disappeared completely. In a sense, then, socialism implies a return to society's initial state of tribalism, where individuals are closely related to their physical and social environments. This evolutionary typology of societal stages is summarized in Figure 7.2.

Summary and Conclusions Marx assumed a materialistic and dialectical view of society. Attempting to analyze the dynamic relationship between society's economic foundation and its normative superstructure in order to resynthesize the individual and nature, he assumed that the material determines the nonmaterial, resulting in an increase in the division of labor system and private property and moving the social system through a sequence of specific stages: tribalism, communalism, feudalism, capitalism, and eventually socialism, reuniting humanity with nature. This materialistic-evolutionary framework is summarized as a whole in Figure 7.3.

Marx's paradigm highlights a number of distinct issues as follows:

1 His naturalistic, systemic, evolutionary model is similar in form although not in ideological and conceptual content to that of earlier organic theorists such as Comte and Spencer.

2 His view of society as an evolutionary balance is similar in form to their work also, thereby creating a link between organic and conflict theory.

3 Marx's materialistic determinism is similar to the approach of Comte and Spencer, along with that of other thinkers such as Sumner and Veblen, as we shall see.

4 Further, Marx's delineation of the major source of social change as systemic and societal is similar to the work of earlier theorists as well, while his emphasis upon knowledge as societally determined closely parallels the earlier work of Comte.

5 An important issue is the extent to which a society's division of labor defines its kind of consciousness or vice versa. While Marx and Durkheim opt for the former, Weber, as we shall see, tends to accept the latter interpretation.

6 Finally, Marx's projected socialism may be viewed as romantic philosophizing rather than sociological analysis. He has been

FIGURE 7.2
MARX'S TYPOLOGY

TRIBALISM ⟶ COMMUNALISM ⟶ FEUDALISM ⟶ FEUDAL DECLINE ⟶ CAPITALISM ⟶ REVOLT ⟶ SOCIALISM

TRIBALISM	COMMUNALISM	FEUDALISM	FEUDAL DECLINE	CAPITALISM	REVOLT	SOCIALISM
1. Hunting, fishing, agriculture 2. Division of labor = extension of family 3. Patriarchal structure	1. Begin private property 2. Begin division of labor 3. Use of slavery	1. Country base 2. Land base 3. Nobility power	1. Inefficiency 2. Development of bourgeoisie 3. Urbanization 4. Development of capitalism 5. Manufacturing needs	1. Labor as chief commodity 2. Structure: owners, laborers 3. Utilitarian ideology 4. Unnatural materialism 5. Alienation and servitude 6. Development of overproduction	1. Caused by alienation and degradation 2. Organization of proletariat	1. Classless 2. No private property 3. Totally "socialized individual" 4. Reunion: individual and nature

SOCIAL DYNAMISM: Struggle over Resources: Lack of Fit—Structure and Superstructure

FIGURE 7.3
MARX'S THEORETICAL FRAMEWORK SUMMARIZED

KARL MARX
(1818–1883)

BACKGROUND:
1 Jewish family
2 Educated in law, philosophy, history
3 Involved in journalism and activism
4 Enlightenment education
5 German political oppression

AIM:
Analysis of the relationship between ideas and life conditions

ASSUMPTIONS:
1 Existence determines consciousness
2 Material determines the nonmaterial
3 Society is rooted in material conditions of life
4 Dialectic: substructure and superstructure = evolutionary development

METHODOLOGY:
1 Historical sociology
2 Application of dialectical materialism method

TYPOLOGY:
Stages of societal development

ISSUES:
1 Similarities to organic theory
2 Evolutionary balance notion
3 Materialistic determinism
4 Sociology of knowledge
5 Material determines nonmaterial issue
6 Utopian socialism projection

repeatedly called to task by more contemporary thinkers for this inaccuracy and failure to take into account the complex rather than simplistic effects of industrialization on the capitalist social system.

Despite the above similarities and problems, however, Marx's thought represents the foundation of conflict theory, and his critical influence continues today in the form of contemporary conflict theory and radical sociology. We turn now to Robert Park, another systemic conflict theorist.

108

Robert Park (1864–1944)

Background Park was born in Pennsylvania, the son of a businessman. Educated in the universities of Harvard, Minnesota,
and Berlin, he was trained in philosophy and psychology. He
was also influenced by George Simmel's teachings in Berlin. His
career included journalism and activist participation in the Congo
Reform Association, and he also took a leading role in the sociology department at the University of Chicago. Steeped in the
traditions of American progressivism and idealism as well as the
works of John Dewey, William James, Simmel, and Tönnies, Park
took an ecological, process-oriented approach to society, focusing on competition and conflict as central to social change. His
major publications include *The Immigrant Press and Its Control*
(1922), *Introduction to the Science of Sociology* (1921), and *Race
and Culture* (1950).

Aims Park saw sociology as seeking to "arrive at natural laws
and generalizations in regard to human nature and society, irre-
spective of time and place" with a natural law being a "statement
which describes the behavior of a class of objects. . . ."[2] Viewing
society as similar to other systems in nature, he focused on its
ecological foundation, particularly the spatial distribution of individuals and groups. His viewpoint's relevance to conflict theory
lies in his focus on humanity's ecological struggle for existence,
resulting in dynamic processes such as conflict and accommodation which are temporary states in society's ongoing development. Park thus presented us with an ecological conflict theory
which is similar to Marx's in its emphasis on the central role of
societal problems.

Assumptions Park's ecological orientation to society consists
of a number of major assumptions, as follows:

1 The foundation of social stability lies in the process of evolution. Like Marx, however, Park saw social equilibrium as based on
societal development.

2 He assumed that human beings are continually engaged in a

[2]See R. E. Park and E. W. Burgess, *Introduction to the Science of Sociology*, University of Chicago Press, Chicago, 1921.

struggle for existence, with competition as a fundamental process.

3 Out of such struggle, a natural order emerges, discernible in the territorial distribution of individuals and groups as well as in their interdependence.

4 Within this "biotic" order, competition results in the ecological processes of dominance and succession.

5 The major social processes within this order consist of competition, conflict, accommodation, and assimilation. The first is based in the evolutionary process, resulting in the subsequent sequence of *social* processes leading eventually to cultural assimilation. Social processes, therefore, are based on underlying natural forces, particularly competition for resources, leading to a particular sequence of these processes. Conflict, then, is a biotic and evolutionary universal, resulting in particular societal consequences. Such an approach is not markedly different from Marx's delineation of the struggle for resources leading to particular forms of domination and resulting ultimately in socialism, a form of assimilation.

6 The social system, according to Park, consists of its ecological foundation, on which its economic, political, and moral orders are based. These are influenced by the underlying forces discussed above. Central to this system is the social control function—the central fact and problem of society. The parallel here with Marx, once again, is clear.

7 In this dynamic approach to society, Park's theory assumes that social change proceeds through a particular sequence: first dissatisfaction and unrest; then social movements resulting eventually in institutional modifications and restructuring.

8 Finally, Park saw an individual's self-concept as a function of his or her position in society's status hierarchy. Macroscopic social organization thus operates on the individual and social-psychological level as well.

To summarize, Park saw society as based on an underlying ecological order and the natural process of competition and evolution. Accordingly, the social system—consisting of ecological, economic, political, and moral orders—reflects these processes and functions primarily to control the individual and the process of competition. As it evolves, this system proceeds through the sequential stages of competition, conflict, accommodation, and assimilation, operating at the microscopic level as well through the individual's self-concept.

Such an ecological-conflict theory is similar to Marx's in its emphasis upon conflict as natural and universal, the control function of society, evolutionary stages of societal development, and the societal basis of normative phenomena. Such "societal problem" approaches to societal dynamics are basic to the conflict framework.

Methodology   In the ecological tradition, Park utilized the natural history technique—a composite of the case-study and life-history approaches. Such a methodology was used to trace sequential stages of development at all levels of the social system. Once again, the parallels with Marx's method of historical induction are evident.

The Typology   Park's typology consists of his "conceptual pyramid of levels of organization"—an ecological model of the social system. The foundation of the system is its *ecological order* (i.e., civilization, community), consisting of the spatial distribution of individuals and groups in their struggle for *usable space*—the focus of the ecological process. Next is the *economic order*, concerned with the production and consumption of goods and services. Following this is the *political order*, focusing on the resolution of conflict through the interpretation of social sanctions. Finally, the *moral order* (i.e., culture, society), at the highest level, regulates the order below it through the operation of mores and the society's social heritage in general.

This general system of social organization is influenced by the ecological forces of dominance and succession as well as the sequential stages of contact, competition, conflict, accommodation, and cultural assimilation. The typology as a whole is summarized in Figure 7.4.

Summary and Conclusions   We have seen how Park, viewing society as a natural system, developed an ecological-conflict approach, applying basic ecological processes to the social order. Perceiving competition and evolution as universal, he applied these, using the natural history technique, to the development of the social system (consisting of ecological, economic,

FIGURE 7.4
PARK'S TYPOLOGY

LEVELS OF SOCIAL ORGANIZATION

	I. Ecological order (civilization community)	II. Economic order	III. Political order
Function:	1. The spatial distribution of individuals and groups	1. The production and consumption of goods and services	1. The resolution of conflict through interpretation of social sanctions
Type of group:	2. Primary	2. Primary-secondary	2. Primary-secondary
Concern or emphasis:	3. Struggle for usable space, emphasis on techniques of trade and commerce	3. Values that can be treated as commodities	3. Determination of whether an act falls under one or another accepted social sanctions

	IV. *Moral order* (culture, society)
Function:	1. The regulation of the orders below it
Type of group:	2. Primary-secondary
Concern or emphasis:	3. Mores, social heritage

← Ecological processes: contact, competition, conflict, accommodation, assimilation →

political, and moral orders) through a number of sequential ecological stages (namely, contact, competition, conflict, accommodation, and assimilation) in reaction to the underlying forces of dominance and succession. This ecological conflict framework is summarized as a whole in Figure 7.5.

This paradigm raises a number of issues, as follows:

1 It is similar to Marx's in its description of conflict and evolution as natural and universal, social stability as based on evolution, society as a control system, stages of societal conflict, and normative phenomena as based on the status hierarchy.

2 The issue of the extent to which direct application of natural and ecological processes to society may be made remains a central question.

3 Park's sequential stages are so broad and general as to make their theoretical and applied use almost impossible, since it is extremely difficult to differentiate empirically between each stage.
4 Park's assimilation stage has also been criticized as vague and possibly ethnocentric in its emphasis upon the assimilation of minorities into elite culture.

FIGURE 7.5
PARK'S THEORETICAL FRAMEWORK SUMMARIZED

ROBERT PARK
(1864–1944)

BACKGROUND:
1 Businessman's son
2 Educated in philosophy and psychology
3 Involved in journalism and sociology
4 Influenced by Dewey, James, and Simmel
5 American idealism

AIM:
Sociology: seeks to arrive at natural laws and generalizations in regard to human nature and
          society, irrespective of time and place

ASSUMPTIONS:
1 The foundation of social stability is in the processes of evolution
2 Individual is continually and fundamentally engaged in a struggle for existence
   and competition
3 The processes produce a natural order, which is discernible in the territorial distribution
   of individuals, groups, organizations, etc., and their interdependency
4 Domination and succession = major ecological processes
5 Social system consists of ecological, economic, political, and moral orders
6 Social change is a sequential process
7 Self-concept is a function of social status

METHOD:
Natural history technique: composite of case-study and life-history approaches

TYPOLOGY:
Levels of social organization

ISSUES:
1 Similarity to Marx
2 Application of ecological processes
3 Sequential stages: broad
4 "Assimilation" stage: broad
5 Description rather than theory

5 Finally, taking the above into account, the paradigm as a whole may be viewed as descriptive rather than explanatory.

Despite the above problems, however, we have seen the extent to which Park tends to complement and further elaborate Marx's pioneering work in the field of conflict theory. His theory remains an important example of the societal problem approach to conflict theory—an approach we shall summarize before considering the more naturalistic view.

THE SYSTEMIC APPROACH TO CONFLICT THEORY SUMMARIZED

A number of major similarities between Marx and Park may be seen as follows:

1 Both theories evolved within the context of evolution-oriented modes of thought.

2 Both view analysis of the relationships between society's natural or material foundation and its social structure as their central concerns.

3 Both see society as an evolutionary balance between competition and evolution, with its central function being that of social control.

4 The material is seen as defining the nonmaterial.

5 Competition is viewed as universal and the cause of conflict.

6 Society is seen as being in a constant state of evolutionary development.

7 Both theorists outlined a particular sequence of evolutionary stages.

8 The end state of evolution is seen as a resynthesis or assimilation of previously discordant elements.

9 The individual's social identity is seen as a function of his or her material condition or position in the social structure.

10 Both use historical induction as their major methodology.

11 Both develop typologies of stages of societal development.

12   Both develop models of the social system in which the material substructure determines the normative superstructure.

From the above it should be evident that the theories of Marx and Park, while different in certain respects, represent a materialistic, evolutionary, conflict approach to society—the foundation of conflict theory and contemporary radical sociology. The structure of their kind of explanation is outlined in Figure 7.6. Having considered this structure, we shall now go on to examine the second major type of conflict theory—the naturalistic approach.

THE NATURALISTIC TYPE OF CONFLICT THEORY

This type of conflict theory is more microscopic and inductive: both Pareto and Veblen saw psychic states or traits accounting for competition, conflict, and social change, in contrast to Marx and Park's focus on more macroscopic and societal factors as causal. Nevertheless, society is viewed, again, as a dynamic, evolving, and changing structure which reacts to certain underlying forces and pressures. While the causal factors in this process are somewhat different, the conceptual argument is similar. We turn, then, to a consideration of Pareto and Veblen.

Vilfredo Pareto (1848–1923)

Background   Pareto was born in 1848, the son of an Italian nobleman. Educated in classics, economics, and science, he was a professor of political economics at the University of Lausanne and an Italian senator. His career included academia, business, and politics. He experienced much political conflict in Italy: the struggles for liberty and unification as well as conflict between parties of the left and right. He was exposed to the ideas of Machiavelli, positivism, and Social Darwinism. His major publications include *Course in Political Economics* (1896–1897) and *The Socialist System* (1901).

Aims   Pareto's main aim was to "identify and interpret the real forces that determine a state of equilibrium in the social system (namely, the elements that act upon the system and in turn are reacted upon by it)." This implies not an emphasis upon static

115

FIGURE 7.6

THE STRUCTURE OF THE SYSTEMIC APPROACH TO CONFLICT THEORY

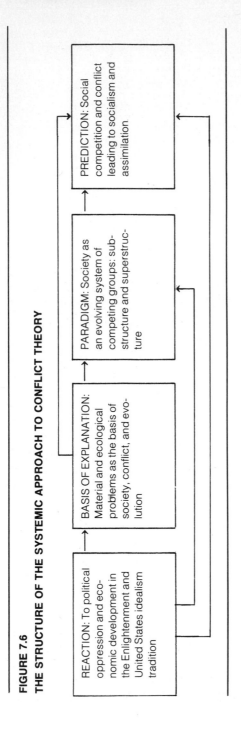

REACTION: To political oppression and economic development in the Enlightenment and United States idealism tradition

BASIS OF EXPLANATION: Material and ecological problems as the basis of society, conflict, and evolution

PARADIGM: Society as an evolving system of competing groups: substructure and superstructure

PREDICTION: Social competition and conflict leading to socialism and assimilation

social situations but a focus on the social dynamics of conflict and change. The prime elements behind these processes, according to Pareto, are microscopic, consisting of *psychic states* and social *rationales* which in turn define social action and societal processes. His theory is normative and inductive, with a naturalistic base in the notion of *residues*, based on nature, as prime elements in the understanding of society.

Assumptions

1 Pareto's main assumption is that social activity may be divided into two major types: *logical*, in which the objective end and subjective purpose are identical; and *nonlogical*, in which the objective end differs from the subjective purpose.

2 Further, he saw the bulk of social activity consisting of the latter (nonlogical action), founded on psychic states and based on nature, with an "instinct for combinations" (i.e., they combine to form residues or social forces).

3 Nonlogical ideas are viewed as the basis of a number of classes or types of forces or residues which define social equilibrium. They are class I: Instinct for Combinations (e.g., generic likeness assimilation); class II: Group Persistences (e.g., family relations); Class III: Need of Expressing Sentiments by External Acts (e.g., religious ecstasies); class IV: Residues Connected with Sociality (e.g., conformity, pity, cruelty, self-sacrifice); class V: Integrity of the Individual and His Appurtenances (e.g., equality, integrity); and class VI: The Sex Residue. These residues or social forces define social action and equilibrium.

4 The residues are socially reinforced by their "derivations" or societal rationalizations, based on humanity's need for logic. Pareto classifies these derivations as class I: Assertion; class II: Authority; class III: Accords with Sentiments or Principles; and class IV: Verbal Proofs. In this manner residues operate in social reality through their normative rationales or derivations.

5 The residues are differentially distributed in society through the class structure, making for social equilibrium and interdependence. As the distribution of these residues changes—particularly class I (Instinct for Combinations) and class II (Group-Persistence)—however, this equilibrium changes to a state of circulation between *governing* and *nongoverning* elites. Changes in the distribution of residues—with the higher strata absorbing more decadent elements, and the lower strata obtaining more elements of superior quality—cause revolutions, resulting in an oscillation between two kinds of dominant elite. These are the "lions," moved by class II residues, and the "foxes," defined by class I residues. This "lion-fox" circulation is constant and on-going, dependent on the changing distribution of class I and class II residues. Society, then, is a dynamic balance, dependent on the changing distribution of residues, which results in ongoing competition, conflict, and circulation.

6 Finally, Pareto saw society as a reciprocal system consisting of three major elements: (*a*) physical factors and conditions; (*b*) external elements (e.g., influences of other societies); and (*c*) internal elements (i.e., race, residues, and derivations). These three elements are interdependent, reciprocal, and dynamic in influence.

To summarize, Pareto viewed society as based primarily upon *nonlogical ideas* acting through classes of *residues* which, along with their accompanying *derivations* or rationalizations, are differentially distributed through the class structure, making for states of social equilibrium and circulation as the distribution of these residues changes between the "lions" and "foxes." Such an approach is naturalistic, systemic, dynamic, and conflict-oriented, similar to those of Marx and Park but naturalistic and inductive rather than sociological and deductive. A major difference, too, lies in the manner in which normative phenomena define the material rather than vice versa. Nevertheless, the overlap and structural similarities are evident.

Methodology In accordance with the above paradigm, Pareto saw the focus of sociology on the identification, classification, and distribution of residues in society as well as the tracing of their rhythm and change. Appropriate techniques included the use of scientific observation and experimentation as well as a focus on functional relationships, uniformities, regularities, and correlations. In general, sociology would involve the scientific study of residues in society.

The Typology Pareto's theoretical typology is implicit in his description of two major types of societal elite: the "lions" and the "foxes." The former are dominated by class II residues (Group-Persistence); are typified by military and religious elites; emphasize loyalty, solidarity, and patriotism as central values; and are prepared to use force when necessary. "Foxes," in contrast, typify class I residues (Instinct for Combinations), are often financiers, are manipulative and developmental in orientation, and are efficient in the fusion and further development of political empires. Society rests on the equilibrium of this constant elite circulation process, which is dependent on the distribution of the two classes of residues or sets of ideas. This model is summarized in Figure 7.7.

Summary and Conclusions Pareto, reacting to the political conflict of his day in the context of a Darwinistic and positivistic tradition, developed a naturalistic-inductive theory of social conflict: society is viewed as based on particular ideas and norms and as under the control of particular classes or elites who represent these orientations. Conflict and change are based upon the relative distribution of these residues, leading to a constant elite circulation process—itself the basis of societal equilibrium. Society represents a balanced system of normative forces and elites that are in a constant state of circulation according to the distribution of these forces. This framework as a whole is summarized in Figure 7.8.

Pareto's theory raises a number of distinct issues, as follows:

1 His notion of residues based on nature raises the danger of naturalistic reductionism; that is, every sociologically relevant norm becomes a function of a basic residue, in a similar manner to instinct theory.

2 Focusing on elites as the source of social change, Pareto created a very limited and essentially elitist theory of social change.

3 He tended to overlook the role of social structure as an *independent* as well as dependent variable.

4 His emphasis on derivations or normative explanations is important in its similarity to Marx and other theorists concerned with the sociology of knowledge.

5 Finally, his delineation of constant circulation as well as an

FIGURE 7.7
PARETO'S TYPOLOGY

DIMENSIONS	TYPE OF ELITE — CIRCULATION	
	"LIONS"	**"FOXES"**
1. Predominant residue 2. Group types 3. Orientations	Class II: Group persistence Military, religious a. Loyalty, solidarity, patriotism b. Use of force c. Conservative	Class I: Instinct for combinations Financiers a. Manipulative b. Economic manipulations c. Develop political empires

underlying equilibrium is important for its relevance to organic theory, as well as providing a link between organic and conflict theory.

Pareto, then, while limited in the structure of his theorizing, made an important contribution to conflict theory which was further elaborated by Veblen. We shall turn to him next.

FIGURE 7.8
PARETO'S THEORETICAL FRAMEWORK SUMMARIZED

VILFREDO PARETO
(1848–1923)

BACKGROUND:
1 Noble family
2 Educated in classics, science, and economics
3 Involved in politics, business, and academia
4 Enlightenment education
5 Italian political conflict

AIM:
To identify and interpret the real forces that determine a state of equilibrium in the social system (namely, the "elements" that act upon the system and in turn are reacted upon by it)

ASSUMPTIONS:
1 Social activity: logical and nonlogical
2 The bulk of social activity is based on nonlogical action
3 Classes of residues
4 Classes of derivations
5 Differential distribution of residues
6 Circulation of elites

METHODOLOGY:
1 Identify and classify residues, their distribution and "rhythm"
2 Use of scientific method

TYPOLOGY:
Types of elites

ISSUES:
1 Naturalistic, reductionism
2 Elitist theory of conflict
3 Role of social structure
4 Importance of normative phenomena
5 Underlying equilibrium

Thorstein Veblen (1857–1929)

Background Veblen was born in Washington, the son of Norwegian immigrants. Educated at Carleton College in classics, philosophy, and economics, he pursued varied academic and civil service careers. With his lower-class origins and experiences of America's industrial expansion, unrest, and political polarization, Veblen focused on the interaction between economic and societal development in the philosophical traditions of William Sumner, Marx, evolutionary theory, and pragmatism. His major publications include *The Theory of the Leisure Class* (1899), *The Theory of the Business Enterprise* (1904), and *The Instinct of Workmanship* (1914).

Aims Veblen's major aim was to "study human evolution using sociological reasoning rather than classical economics." Accordingly, he developed a theory of technological evolutionism, tracing the influence of the individual's economic instinct on the social processes of competition and societal change. Like Pareto, he developed a naturalistic, inductive theory of social conflict, but Veblen concentrated more on the effect of economic factors.

Assumptions

1 Veblen's major assumption was that human nature consists of three major traits: (*a*) a parental bent; (*b*) the instinct of workmanship or practical efficiency; and (*c*) idle curiosity. These traits he saw as representing the foundations of society's institutions.

2 Furthermore, it is idle curiosity, according to this theory, which leads to technological change—the prime mover in a societal evolution and social change.

3 The process of social evolution begins with a change in human values, resulting in the development of technology. Technology, in turn, leads to a change in values or ideas, and the "cumulative process of adaptation of means to ends" continues in Veblen's theory of the "process of economic life."

4 Basic to this theory is the notion of the human "economic interest" which accounts for the "process of cultural growth" and "a cumulative sequence of economic institutions." To this extent, Veblen is an economic determinist.

5 Within this growth process, evolution is organic and interdependent, each stage representing a technological balance in which "the interplay of parts has such a character of mutual support and dependence that any substantial addition or subtraction at any one point will involve more or less derangement all along the line." His approach here is one of technological functionalism.

6 Evolution is also viewed as cumulative and operates in reaction to changing material problems, representing selective and competitive adaptation to the environment.

7 Furthermore, this evolutionary process proceeds through a number of distinct stages in a manner similar to that posited by Marx: society begins with the state of the peaceable savage (low division of labor, high solidarity) and continues through the lower barbaric stage (the beginnings of ownership and the division of labor) and the higher barbaric stage (high ownership, development of a leisure class) to arrive at the fourth or pecuniary stage (a technocracy, high vicarious consumption and materialism)—the stage at which humanity's natural traits are most distorted. In this manner, the individual's "idle curiosity" leads to technological changes producing competition, conflict, and an exploitive economic system and class structure (i.e., capitalism). The parallels here with Marx's evolutionary model are obvious.

8 Finally, Veblen was concerned with the intersocietal process of acculturation and cultural borrowing—the crossbreeding of ideas. In this regard, he viewed some societies as more capable than others of adapting outside ideas to their own purposes, thereby accelerating their technological evolution.

To summarize, Veblen saw the basic traits of human nature as leading to technological change—the prime mover in societal evolution. This process is adaptive and equilibrium-oriented. It moves through a number of stages and leads to the emergence of a division of labor system and ownership of property. It eventually results in a state of bureaucratized capitalism, at which point the traits have become most distorted and exploited. Furthermore, at the macroscopic level, societies vary in their rates of evolution according to their borrowing and adapting capacity. Such a theory is naturalistic, evolutionary, and conflict-oriented, with strong parallels to the Marxian approach. Veblen's naturalistic foundation and failure to predict an ultimate utopian end-state, however, are distinctly different.

Methodology   Veblen's major focus was to study the sociological effects of technology, using a scientific approach from a "skeptical" point of view. Major forms of data would be historical, economic, and archeological as the researcher traced the process of technological evolutionism through its major stages in a number of different societies. Such an approach is also similar to Marx's in its use of historical induction as a major methodological tool.

The Typology   Veblen's typology consists of society's evolutionary stages, described earlier in our discussion, as the system experiences the effects of technology and "disintegrating animism."

The peaceable savage stage represents the initial and most natural period of humanity's existence. At this stage people are closely related to nature, there is little division of labor, the instinct of workmanship is free to operate in its purest form, religion is central to the society, and there is a high level of community and social solidarity.

With economic development, however, comes the lower barbaric stage. At this point the division of labor has begun and invidious distinctions are emerging, along with the ownership of private property.

The higher barbaric stage is even more negative: there is increased wealth and private property, a leisure class has evolved, and there are other monopolistic elites. The societal foundations of capitalism have thus been laid.

At the fourth and most negative level—society at the pecuniary stage—the natural instincts have become most distorted: leisure and consumption have become "conspicuous" and "vicarious," the basis of the economic system is advertising and war, relationships are instrumental and impersonal, values are highly materialistic, and motivations at the individual and institutional level are basically those of individual gain, leading to the domination of society by a business elite. Capitalism and bureaucratization have thus reached their zenith—the most unnatural state.

Central processes in this evolutionary development consist of technological development, cultural borrowing, and the crossbreeding of class. The typology as a whole is summarized in Figure 7.9.

124

FIGURE 7.9
VEBLEN'S TYPOLOGY

STAGES OF DEVELOPMENT

I. Peaceable ⟶	II. Lower Barbaric ⟶	III. Higher Barbaric ⟶	IV. Pecuniary
Savage			(distorted)
1. Little division of labor	1. Division of labor	1. Leisure class	1. Vicarious leisure
2. Feminism	2. Invidious distinctions	2. Increasing wealth	2. Vicarious consumption
3. Pure instinct of workmanship		3. Industrial work is relegated	3. Conspicuous consumption
4. Solidarity		4. Ownership of property	4. Pecuniary emulation
5. Importance of religion		5. Material selection	5. Advertising and war economy
6. Individual in close relation with environment			6. Motivation: individual gain

Idle curiosity   Technical change   Evolution
⟶

Declining animism
⟶

Cultural borrowing and crossbreeding of ideas
⟶

Summary and Conclusions   Veblen's theory represents a pragmatic reaction to the startling effects of industrialization during his lifetime. He accordingly developed a naturalistic, evolutionary, and economically deterministic theory of societal conflict and development, similar to Pareto's in its naturalistic base. In attempting to understand human evolution sociologically, he saw this process as based on human economic nature and resulting in social conflict and change through a number of distinct stages. Such a conceptual framework is summarized, for convenience, in Figure 7.10.

Veblen's approach raises a number of issues, as follows:

1   The use of naturalistic traits tends to be deterministic and reductionistic.

2   Veblen's technological determinism is similar, in its economic base, to Marx's and Durkheim's.

125

3 His typology of evolutionary stages is also similar to the work of Tönnies, Durkheim, Marx, and Weber.

4 His prediction of the negative effects of increased bureaucratization parallels the work of Weber.

FIGURE 7.10
VEBLEN'S THEORETICAL FRAMEWORK SUMMARIZED

THORSTEIN VEBLEN
(1857–1929)

BACKGROUND:
1 Son of Norwegian farmers
2 Classical education
3 Varied academic and government career
4 Education in moral philosophy
5 American industrial expansion

AIM:
The study of human evolution, using sociological reasoning rather than classical economics

ASSUMPTIONS
1 Nature of human being consists of three traits: parental bent, workmanship, idle curiosity
2 Idle curiosity leads to technological change—the "prime mover"
3 Values and technology in ongoing interaction
4 "Economic interest" results in "cultural growth"
5 Evolution—organic and interdependent
6 Change—cumulative and in reaction to dealing with material problems
        —selective adaptation to environment
        —no goal
        —competitive
7 Evolution proceeds through distinct stages

METHODOLOGY:
Study effects of technology, using historical, economic, and anthropological data

TYPOLOGY:
Stages of societal development

ISSUES:
1 Reductionistic argument
2 Technological determinism
3 Similarities to Tönnies, Durkheim, Marx, and Weber
4 Similarities to Weber and organic theory
5 Incomplete predictions

5 His notion of technological balance is also similar to the views of organic and structure-functional theories.

6 Finally, Veblen's evolutionary model, unlike Marx's, is incomplete: what is the ultimate end of social evolution? Apart from continuing distortion, this is unclear.

Despite the above problems, however, Veblen's is a major economic theory of societal conflict and evolution, further complementing and elaborating the earlier work of Marx.

The Naturalistic Approach to Conflict Theory Summarized

A number of major similarities between Pareto and Veblen may be seen, as follows:

1 Both theories evolved within the context of evolutionary and scientific norms, with the theorists exposed to high levels of political and economic conflict.

2 The aim of both is an understanding of major factors behind societal equilibrium, conflict, and evolution.

3 Both see society as based on instincts or traits.

4 Both see society as in equilibrium, if only on a temporary basis.

5 For both, norms or ideas are based on human instincts or traits.

6 These norms or ideas, in turn, are behind social development and conflict.

7 Societal evolution occurs in specific stages or cycles.

8 The direction of evolution is toward new problems and conflict.

9 The methods of both theorists concentrate on the effects of human instincts or traits, using historical induction.

10 Their typologies depict types of elites or stages of societal development.

From this it is evident that the views of Pareto and Veblen represent a naturalistic, evolutionary type of conflict theory which complements and further elaborates the earlier work of Marx. The commonalities in their approaches are summarized in Figure 7.11.

THE CONFLICT PARADIGM SUMMARIZED

In this chapter we have attempted to demonstrate how conflict theory represents an application of Enlightenment ideals concerning human nature to a historical analysis of social conflict. The general features of this approach as a whole may be summarized as follows:

Aims An attempt to understand the material and naturalistic factors behind societal equilibrium, conflict, and evolution.

Assumptions

1 Society is a system of competing elements based on its division of labor system and traits or instincts.

2 Society represents a temporary state of equilibrium.

3 The material and naturalistic determine the nonmaterial or normative.

4 Nonmaterial and normative, in turn, influence societal evolution.

5 Evolution follows a number of distinctive stages.

6 Evolution moves society toward increasing conflict, capitalistic development, and elitist exploitation.

Methods The major methodological tool used by conflict theorists is historical induction.

Typologies Evolutionary development is divided into specific stages or types of societal elites.

From this it can be seen that conflict theory represents a materialistic, naturalistic, evolutionary approach to society, developed in the tradition of Enlightenment philosophy and American pragmatism by a group of intellectuals who experienced high levels of political and economic turmoil. In direct contrast to organic theory, such an approach is more radical and oriented

FIGURE 7.11
THE STRUCTURE OF NATURALISTIC CONFLICT THEORY

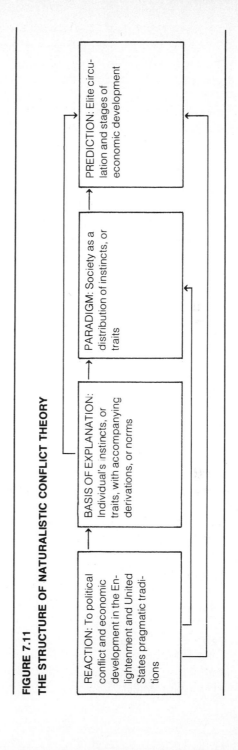

REACTION: To political conflict and economic development in the Enlightenment and United States pragmatic traditions

BASIS OF EXPLANATION: Individual's instincts, or traits, with accompanying derivations, or norms

PARADIGM: Society as a distribution of instincts, or traits

PREDICTION: Elite circulation and stages of economic development

toward human rather than societal needs, and it is more concerned with social change than with control. Nevertheless, parallels between the two types of theory exist in the *form* of their arguments: both are naturalistic, evolutionary, and macroscopic. Conflict theory is summarized in Figure 7.12. Social behaviorism, the approach we turn to next, differs markedly from conflict theory in its focus and level of analysis.

EXERCISES

1   Consider the following social trends:
   a   The increase in racial conflict in the United States during the 1960s

   b   The occurrence of student protest groups on United States campuses during the 1960s

   c   The recent women's liberation movement

   d   The general increase in bureaucratization throughout United States society

   e   The general increase in the United States divorce rate

Account for each trend, using the general explanations provided by Marx, Park, Pareto, and Veblen. Compare in detail the different types of explanation you develop, using each theorist. To what extent are they similar? Can you develop an overall conflict explanation of each trend?

READINGS

General Works

Aron, R.: *Main Currents in Sociological Thought*, vols. 1 and 2, Doubleday, Garden City, N.Y., 1970, for chaps. on Marx and Pareto.
Coser, L. A.: *Masters of Sociological Thought, Ideas in Historical and Social Context*, Harcourt, Brace, Jovanovich, New York, 1971, for chaps. on Marx, Park, Veblen, and Pareto.
Martindale, D.: *The Nature and Types of Sociological Theory*, Houghton Mifflin, Boston, 1960, chaps. 6, 7, and 8.

FIGURE 7.12
THE STRUCTURE OF CONFLICT THEORY

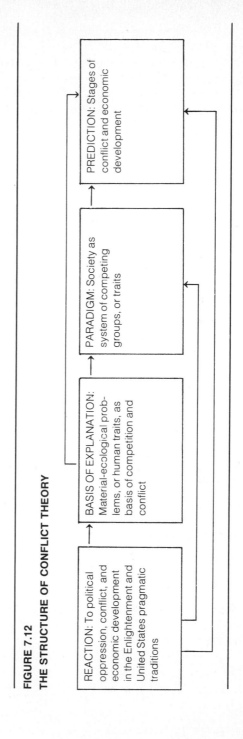

REACTION: To political oppression, conflict, and economic development in the Enlightenment and United States pragmatic traditions

BASIS OF EXPLANATION: Material-ecological problems, or human traits, as basis of competition and conflict

PARADIGM: Society as system of competing groups, or traits

PREDICTION: Stages of conflict and economic development

Nisbet, R. A.: *The Sociological Tradition*, Basic Books, New York, 1966, chaps. 5 and 7.

Truzzi, M. (ed.): *Sociology, The Classic Statements*, Random House, New York, 1971, selections 12, 19, 21, 29, and 34.

Zeitlin, I. M.: *Ideology and the Development of Sociological Theory*, Prentice-Hall, Englewood Cliffs, N.J., 1968, chaps. 10 and 12.

Specific Works by Theorists

Marx

Bottomore, T. B. (ed. and trans.): *Karl Marx, Selected Writings in Sociology and Social Philosophy*, McGraw-Hill, New York, 1964.

Marx, K., and F. Engles: *The German Ideology*, International Publishers, New York, 1930.

———— and ————: *Manifesto of the Communist Party*, Kerr, Chicago, 1888.

Park

Park, R. E.: *Human Communities*, Free Press, New York, 1952.

————: *Race and Culture*, Free Press, New York, 1950.

————: *Society*, Free Press, New York, 1955.

————: and E. W. Burgess: *Introduction to the Science of Sociology*, University of Chicago Press, Chicago, 1921.

Pareto

Finer, S. E. (ed.): *Vilfredo Pareto, Sociological Writings*, Praeger, New York, 1966.

Lopreato, J.: *Vilfredo Pareto, Selectons from His Treatise*, Crowell, New York, 1965.

Veblen

Veblen, T.: *Absentee Ownership*, Viking, New York, 1938.

————: *The Higher Learning in America*, Huebsch, New York, 1918.

————: *The Place of Science in Modern Civilization*, Huebsch, New York, 1919.

————: *The Theory of the Leisure Class*, Modern Library, New York, 1934.

Rosenberg, B.: *Thorstein Veblen, Selections from His Work*, Crowell, New York, 1963.

8

SOCIAL
BEHAVIORISM

MAJOR TOPICS:

The systemic type of social
behaviorism: Weber and Mead

The naturalistic type of social
behaviorism: Simmel and Sumner

Social behaviorism summarized

As human circumstances changed, so did modes of sociological thought: with industrialization, sociological paradigms became more microscopic, individualistic, and inductive in contrast to earlier macroscopic, societal, and deductive forms of thought. With social behaviorism—a study of the individualistic factors defining social behavior—we are presented with a rather different view of sociological reality: society is seen more from the individual's perspective as a set of values and interacting persons. Normative and cultural phenomena at the microscopic level become the central focus as these thinkers attempt to understand society on the individual level and as humanity's subjective and societal consciousness increases in the wake of the general effects of industrialization. As urbanization and general economic development proceed, sociology attempts to understand this changing social structure at the individual level in the light of traditional Enlightenment values of idealism as well as the more recent emphasis on the individualistic values of the Protestant ethic and subsequent pragmatism.

Despite the above differences, it will be evident that social behaviorism has certain features in common with earlier paradigms: as a model of social reality, it is systemic, evolutionary, idealistic, and equilibrium-oriented. To a certain extent, this paradigm represents a microscopic version of the earlier organic approach, which was developed and applied under different social circumstances. Once again, sociological theory represents a systemic paradigm of social reality—developed within a particular social context, whose characteristics we turn to next.

INTRODUCTION

The social behaviorists we discuss span a period of ninety years (1840–1931) and vary in background and thought. However, they may be viewed as a set of thinkers reacting to particular problems within a common tradition of thought for the following reasons: except for Simmel, they tend to have Protestant backgrounds; they received broad educations in history, philosophy, and theology; their careers were primarily academic; they experienced the dynamic effects of industrialization and urbanization; and most were socialized in Enlightenment idealism, Darwinian evolutionism, and modern pragmatism.

Social behaviorism may thus be viewed as the reaction of a group of predominantly Protestant thinkers, in the tradition of Enlightenment idealism and contemporary pragmatism, to the modern problems of social change. A new form of microscopic organicism thus emerged in response to systemic needs at the microscopic level. Such a theorizing process is summarized in Figure 8.1, in which its parallels with the organic approach are readily apparent.

Like other paradigms, social behaviorism is far from uniform, possessing a number of subtypes: the social interaction model and naturalistic argument, i.e., systemic and naturalistic types. The former, evident in the work of Weber and Mead, sees the individual as a social product and concentrates on underlying sociological processes; the latter, in contrast, views human instincts or needs as the foundation of microscopic social processes, which it sees as basic to society. Once again, we are presented with sociological and naturalistic subvariants of the same paradigm. The former tend to represent later and more pragmatic views of reality, while Simmel and Sumner emerged from the evolutionary traditions of Darwin and Spencer. Nevertheless, both

FIGURE 8.1
MAJOR FACTORS BEHIND SOCIAL BEHAVIORISM

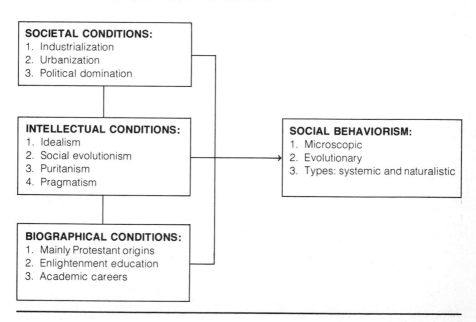

SOCIETAL CONDITIONS:
1. Industrialization
2. Urbanization
3. Political domination

INTELLECTUAL CONDITIONS:
1. Idealism
2. Social evolutionism
3. Puritanism
4. Pragmatism

BIOGRAPHICAL CONDITIONS:
1. Mainly Protestant origins
2. Enlightenment education
3. Academic careers

SOCIAL BEHAVIORISM:
1. Microscopic
2. Evolutionary
3. Types: systemic and naturalistic

types represent a microscopic, evolutionary, inductive, and systemic approach to social reality. While they differ in foundation, their societal paradigms are similar.

We begin our discussion with the social interaction model, exemplified in the work of Weber and Mead.

THE SYSTEMIC MODEL

According to this approach, the individual is rational and represents the product of a particular set of social relations. Society is viewed as a set of relations and values, along with socialization and interaction processes. Accordingly, the individual is society writ large, reflecting predominant value orientations which have emerged within specific societal contexts. Such a normative and systemic view of social reality is clearly exemplified in the writings of Weber and Mead.

Max Weber (1864–1920)

Background   Born in Germany, the son of a right-wing liberal Protestant, Weber received a broad education in economics, history, law, philosophy, and theology. Schooled in the tradition of German idealism, Weber was concerned with the human spirit, especially values, viewing the individual as an actor rather than the passive puppet of history. He was actively involved in German politics on the one hand while attempting to develop an objective or value-free sociology on the other. His major publications reflect Weber's concern with the development of mankind's value system and include *The Protestant Ethic and The Spirit of Capitalism* (1905), *Economics and Society* (1913), and *Sociology of Religion* (1920).

Aims   Weber defined sociology as a "science which attempts the interpretive understanding of *social action* in order thereby to arrive at a *causal explanation* of its cause and effects."[1] Implicit in this definition are a number of key elements: the attempt to interpret or understand; a focus on social action—behavior to which

---

[1]For this definition and many of the concepts that follow, see M. Weber, *Basic Concepts in Sociology*, Peter Owen, London, 1962.

subjective meaning is attached[2] (i.e., an emphasis on social values as primary elements); and the attempt to develop causal explanations of these phenomena. Weber was thus preoccupied with the *scientific understanding of social behavior* as sociology's central concern. Accordingly, he focused on the objective understanding of social values in historical context and attempted to assess their sociological impact on society.

His major works include studies of the Protestant ethic, the spirit of capitalism, charismatic authority, bureaucracy, and rationality as well as the Puritan ethic, mysticism, and the spirit of asceticism. For Weber, sociology was the study of crucial values defining social behavior at particular points in society's historical development. It can be seen that such an approach differs markedly in focus from the macroscopic and structural emphases of the theorists who developed the organic and conflict paradigms.

Assumptions

1 According to Weber, social action is meaningful to the actor when it assumes subjective meaning as well as taking "account of the behavior of others and is thereby oriented."[3]

2 There are a number of distinct types of meaning: "actually intended meaning for concrete individual action" (subjective meaning); the "average of actually intended meaning" (the group or normative level); and "meaning appropriate to a scientifically formulated pure type" (an abstract, theoretical model). All three types are relevant to a multilevel type of causal explanation.

3 Social action is viewed as varying in its level of *rationality*. Weber delineates four types of social action, varying from least to most rational, as follows: (*a*) *traditionally oriented social action* (habitual behavior, defined by tradition); (*b*) *affectually oriented social action* (emotional behavior); (*c*) *rational orientation toward an absolute value* (social action defined by a particular set of ethics or values); and (*d*) *rational orientation toward a system of individual ends* ("when the end, means, and secondary results are all rationally taken into account and weighed)."[4] Such a typology, according to Weber, is neither exclusive nor exhaus-

[2]Ibid.
[3]Ibid.
[4]Ibid.

tive; rather, it represents a continuum of types of social orientations ranging from cultures with low individualism and high traditional control to those with high individualism and low traditionalism.

4 He further elaborates this typology by delineating the kinds of legitimacy, relationships, associations, corporate groups, and control inherent within each orientation from the *traditional,* the *affectual*, through the *rational orientation* (defined by absolute values) to the *rational orientation* (defined by individual ends) as follows: within the traditional, legitimacy is based on religious attitudes, solidary relationships are communal, association is compulsory, corporate groups are political, and control is based on discipline. The affectual, on the other hand, is founded on affectual loyalty and is communal; in it, association is voluntary, corporate groups are revolutionary, and control is based on power. The rational orientation defined by absolute values is legitimized in terms of these values; in it, relationships are associative, association is compulsory, corporate groups are hierocratic, and control is based on discipline. Finally, the rational orientation based on individual ends is founded on self-interest, associative relationships, compulsory association, and political corporate groups; it is controlled on the basis of power. Thus different types of society or social actions are based on differing types of values or levels of rationality, i.e., the extent to which behavior is defined by individual or group interests.

5 The evolution of more rational forms of social action, according to Weber, stems from the process of competition, which results in the "selection of those of superior personal qualities."[5] Such competition alternates between peaceful and violent types as well as between traditional and charismatic values; it is influenced by the kind of opportunity structure that is inherent in the society concerned.

6 Finally, Weber viewed rationality as resulting in a particular kind of bureaucratic type or structure in which social action is closely defined by an elaborate system of roles, norms, and sanctions. At this point in its evolution, society is highly controlled, organized, and impersonal (bureaucratic) in response to the need for economic efficiency with industrialization.

140   [5]Ibid.

To summarize, Weber was primarily concerned with understanding the meaning of social action; he attempted to delineate the relationship between types of social action and the kinds of social structures that are based on them as society in general moves from the traditional to the modern or rational in the wake of industrialization and the influence of the Protestant ethic. Society, reacting to the process of social selection through competition, was viewed as becoming more rational or bureaucratic as higher levels of industrialization increased the need for efficiency. In general, Weber was concerned with the relationship between *individual values* and the *social structure*.

Methodology   As discussed earlier, Weber defined a number of types of social meaning and was concerned with the development of a multilevel approach. This involves two major methodological techniques: *interpretive understanding* and the *imaginary experiment*. The former implies an attempt to interpret the *meaning* of behavior at individual and group levels as well as the abstraction of formal models or ideal types of social meaning. The latter approach complements the former by involving the conjecture of possible kinds of social meaning—"thinking out possible chains of motivation."[6] In both cases, emphasis is placed on the attempt to reveal the particular kind of *motivation* behind the *social action* involved. In his own work, Weber used these methods to link the Protestant ethic with capitalism,[7] the Puritan ethic with asceticism,[8] and religious asceticism with bureaucratization.[9] It is evident, then, that his major concern was the link between motives and the social action, values and social behavior.

The Typology   Two major typologies are inherent within Weber's work: types of social action and his bureaucratic model, the latter representing major characteristics associated with the most rational type of the former. We shall discuss both in turn.

Weber's typology of social action is summarized in Figure

[6]Ibid.
[7]See M. Weber, *The Protestant Ethic and the Spirit of Capitalism*, G. Allen, London, 1930.
[8]See M. Weber, "The Social Psychology of the World Religions," in H. H. Gerth and C. W. Mills (eds. and trans.), *From Max Weber: Essays in Sociology*, Routledge, London, 1948, pp. 267–301.
[9]See M. Weber, "The Protestant Sects and the Spirit of Capitalism," ibid., pp. 302–358.

8.2, which contains the major characteristics discussed above. In addition, major elements defining the extent to which behavior is meaningful—the extent to which it is meaningful to the individual (i.e., the individuality of his decision making), takes account of the behavior of others, and takes account of it in a meaningful fashion—are presented as a part ot the typology. The major char-

FIGURE 8.2
WEBER'S TYPOLOGY OF SOCIAL ACTION

TYPES OF SOCIAL ACTION

DIMENSIONS	RATIONAL ORIENTATION (Ind. Ends)	RATIONAL ORIENTATION (absolute value)	AFFECTUAL ORIENTATION	TRADITION
1. Social Action				
a. Meaningful	Yes	Yes	Yes	No
b. Take account	Yes	Yes	No	No
c. Meaningfully take account	Yes	No	No	No
2. Legitimacy		Belief in absolute value	Affectual loyalty	Religious attitudes
a. Basis	Self-Interest			Change
b. Development	Increasing rationalization ←	← Charisma ←		through prophets
	Law ←	Convention ←	Slow develop- ← ment	Order
3. Solidary relationships	Associative	Associative	Communal	Communal
4. Openness	Most open and closed	Less open	Closed	Most closed
5. Conflict	Increasing rationalization	Selection process Increasing institutionalization	Alternation: peaceful vs. violent conflict	
6. Association	Corporate and compulsory	Compulsory	Voluntary	Compulsory
7. Corporate groups	Political and state	Hierocratic and church	Revolutionary movements	Political
8. Type of control	Power: individual and group	Imperative and discipline	Power	Discipline

FIGURE 8.3
WEBER'S BUREAUCRATIC MODEL

PRECONDITIONS ⟶ Inevitable ⟶ RESULT ⟶ Inevitable ⟶ CONSEQUENCES

1. Money economy	BUREAUCRATIZATION	1. Leveling of
2. Taxation	1. Fixed areas of	economic and
3. Demand for	competence	social differences
specialized knowledge	2. Office hierarchy	2. Increased class
4. Demand for management	3. Documents	differences
5. Warfare	4. Training	3. Bureaucracy-
6. Welfare needs	5. Full capacity of	democracy conflict
7. Consumption needs	officeholder	4. Increased
8. Modern communications	6. Management rules	capitalism
9. Religious asceticism	7. Office vocations	5. Rationalization
10. Absence of strong,		of educational
moral values		and religious
		institutions
		6. Rationalization
		of value
		system

acteristics of each type of social action are clear here, ranging from the traditional and least rational to the individualistic and thereby most rational. The interaction between traditional and charismatic values leading to increased rationalization, as well as the competitive selection process, is also present. We are thus presented with a major typology of values, social processes, and consequent social systems developed and fully elaborated by Weber in his historical research. Such a contribution is major in its description of types of societies, their major elements, and their evolution; it is unsurpassed in scope and depth in traditional as well as in modern sociology.

Weber saw societal evolution as tending toward increasing bureaucratization or rationalization. This brings us to his second major typology, the bureaucratic model. Figure 8.3 delineates three major elements in this model: (1) major preconditions of this process, (2) characteristics of bureaucratization itself, and (3) its societal consequences. Such a model has been developed from a number of his major works.[10] It can be seen that major preconditions consist of the development of a money economy, taxation, certain economic needs and demands, the contribution of certain

[10]For these major elements, see Weber's major works on "Power," "Religion," and "Social Structures," in Gerth and Mills, ibid., 159–442.

religious values, and the absence of strong, moral, traditional values.

Bureaucratization itself consists of a hierarchical role structure, impersonal and well-defined norms, a filing system, role training, and the full capacity of role players. Major consequences of this process include the leveling of social differences, increased class differences, conflict between bureaucracy and democracy, and the increased rationalization of society's major institutions—educational, religious, and political. Thus, while on the one hand bureaucratization makes for organizational efficiency, it also results in higher levels of control and in impersonal relationships.

Summary and Conclusions   Weber, whose work is a major example of social behaviorism, was concerned with understanding the *meaning* of social action on the individual and group level as the basis of society. Placing this meaning on a continuum of *rationality*, he proceeded to examine its societal context and evolution, moving from the traditional through the affectual and ideological to the individualistic and most rational. He also delineated the preconditions, characteristics, and consequences of society's most rational level—the bureaucratic—in historical depth and detail. Such macroscopic *and* microscopic analysis has left sociology with an important and multilevel framework which has yet to be fully appreciated or surpassed. The major elements of that analysis are summarized in Figure 8.4.

Before we turn to Mead, it is important to consider the issues Weber's work raises, as follows:

1   The extent to which Weber's typology of social action is either adequate or useful is immediately raised; i.e., it may be viewed as too simplistic and abstract for practical purposes.

2   His application of the principle of natural selection, while popular among other theorists such as Spencer, raises problems of suitability and the question of whether superior qualities are in fact produced as a result.

3   The extent to which rationalization comes to dominate society's institutional structure as a whole is also open to question.

4   Finally, Weber perceived values defining social structure, in contrast to the reverse relationship posited by Marx. This raises the question of adequately defining the interactive relationship

144

FIGURE 8.4
WEBER'S THEORETICAL FRAMEWORK SUMMARIZED

MAX WEBER
(1864–1920)

BACKGROUND:
1   Protestant family
2   Educated in economics, history, law, philosophy, theology
3   Involved in academic and political activities
4   Educated in German idealism
5   Bismarck politics

AIM:
". . . the interpretive understanding of *social action.*"

ASSUMPTIONS:
1   Subjective meaning of action
2   Types of meaning
3   Social behavior varies in rationality
4   Four types of social behavior
5   Natural selection leads to rationalization
6   Rationalization results in bureaucratization

METHODOLOGY:
1 Interpretive understanding of: a. Actually intended meaning
                                      b. Average or group meaning
                                      c. Meaning appropriate to ideal type
2   Use of the imaginary experiment

TYPOLOGY:
Types of social action and bureaucratic model

ISSUES:
1   Adequacy of typological differences
2   Application of "natural selection" to society
3   General rationalization
4   Values define social structure (cf. Marx)

between these two sets of phenomena—a relationship which is not altogether clear in Weber's work.

Despite the above issues, Weber remains one of social theory's giants, whose contributions remain overwhelming. We turn now to George Mead, a second social behaviorist whose views complement Weber's paradigm.

145

George Mead (1863–1931)

Background   Mead was born in Massachusetts, the son of a Puritan clergyman. Educated at Oberlin College, Harvard, Leipzig, and Berlin in the tradition of German idealism and American pragmatism, this thinker represents a synthesis of the thought of Simmel and Dewey. Working with the latter at the University of Chicago, Mead focused on understanding interaction and the "social self" within the context of a society experiencing high levels of industrialization, urbanization, reformism, pragmatism, and idealism. Humanity's consciousness of itself was increasing accordingly, and Mead was in the forefront. His major works include *Mind, Self, and Society* (1934) and *The Philosophy of the Act* (1938).

Aims   Mead's primary aim was to "study the activity or behavior of the individual as it lies within the social process."[11] His focus, as he attempted to understand such phenomena as a function of their sociological or societal context, was upon microscopic social *behavior* (in contrast to *meaning*). Accordingly, he concentrated on the sociological significance of social interaction, mind, language, and self-consciousness. He may thus be thought of as one of the earliest social psychologists.

Assumptions

1   In a similar fashion to Weber, Mead saw the individual as rational and the "product of social relations."

2   He perceived reality as *both* individual *and* social. Such a multilevel approach is in important contrast to previous paradigms, which were primarily macroscopic and systemic.

3   Mead viewed society as dynamic and evolutionary, constantly providing new and changing socialization patterns for individuals. Such a dynamic and normative approach to society has parallels with Weber's focus on meaning and rationality.

4   Mead described the social self as evolving through a particular chain: social interaction precedes nonverbal communication and

[11]See G. H. Mead, *Mind, Self, and Society*, University of Chicago Press, Chicago, 1934.

language; through language, attitudes and emotions are learned, thereby creating the mind and the self; the social self evolves through a number of stages proceeding from primary (initial) to secondary (formal) socialization, responding first to the significant other (personal and subjective self) and eventually to the generalized other (group self). A number of experiences are crucial to such development: initial role playing, which is relevant to the the process of primary socialization, and group games, which are crucial to assumption of the generalized other.

5 The end-product of these processes is formulation of the social self, which consists of two main elements: the "I," the individual's response to others' attitudes; and the "me," the social attitudes learned and assumed through socialization. Mead thus delineated the evolutionary process through which the individual's social personality is formed.

6 Finally, it is important to note that he did not take a deterministic approach to the social self—rather, he assumed that despite socialization, the self possesses a creative and spontaneous aspect which contributes to social change and new patterns of socialization. Human individuality thus contributes to constant societal dynamism and change.

To summarize, Mead viewed society as representing a dynamic system of socialization within which the social self is formulated through interaction, language, and socialization, proceeding through a number of distinct stages. In this way his paradigm is both systemic and microscopic, defined by an evolutionary perspective. Consequently, social reality is being constantly recreated, in response to the individual's creativity and spontaneity, in the evolution of new forms of socialization and social selves.

Methodology   As with Weber, Mead's methods were *interpretive* and *introspective*; that is, he advocated studying behavior as the best index of society by attempting to "get inside the individual." Understanding of general social processes would result. Such an inductive, interpretive methodology is typical of social behaviorists in general.

The Typology   Mead's typology is implicit in his description of the process whereby the social self evolves. This may be summarized in the following statements, already discussed above: **147**

1 Social interaction precedes mind, language, and self-consciousness.

2 Through language, the individual learns attitudes and emotions.

3 As the individual responds to the significant and then the generalized other through verbal and nonverbal communication, the social self is formed, consisting of the "I" (reaction to others) and the "me" (assumed attitudes).

4 This social self also possesses a creative and spontaneous aspect which contributes to new patterns of socialization and, consequently general social change. This typology is summarized in Figure 8.5, demonstrating Mead's inductive-microscopic view of society.

Summary and Conclusions As a social behaviorist, Mead viewed society as a dynamic and evolving system of socialization

FIGURE 8.5
MEAD'S TYPOLOGY

MODEL OF THE SOCIAL SELF

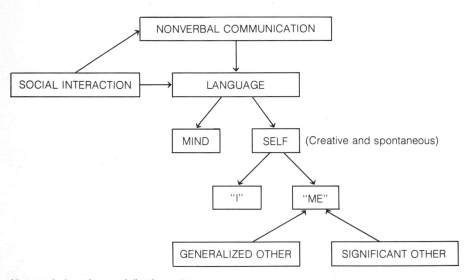

New and changing socialization patterns

representing the individual's underlying creativity and spontane-ity. Within this system the social self—the social personality—evolved through interaction and communication, contributing to ongoing social change through the introduction of new elements into the socialization process. Such a paradigm is significant in its inductive, evolutionary, and microscopic-macroscopic elements, representing an attempt to examine society in terms of human characteristics, in contrast to the reverse emphasis implicit in ear-lier approaches. The major elements of Mead's approach are sum-marized in Figure 8.6.

Mead's theory of society raises a number of distinct issues, as follows:

1   The analytical synthesis between the individual and society is unclear; i.e., the systemic characteristics of both are defined in general terms only and the reader is left wondering what the characteristics of society, apart from its normative aspects, really are.

2   Society's evolutionary qualities are also very general and un-clear.

3   The creative and spontaneous aspects of the social self are only defined in general terms.

4   The methodological problems of an interpretive-introspective approach continue to plague any researcher attempting to certify their validity.

Despite the above questions, Mead's analysis of the human being's social self remains one of the most valuable and inge-nious and provided the foundation for much of contemporary so-cial psychology, particularly the approach of symbolic interac-tionism.

THE SYSTEMIC APPROACH TO SOCIAL
BEHAVIORISM SUMMARIZED

A number of major similarities between Weber and Mead may be outlined as follows:

1   Both theorists were Protestants viewing society from the per-spective of German idealism within the context of high levels of economic and industrial change.

2 Both were concerned with the interpretive understanding of social behavior.

3 Both saw society as an evolutionary system based on particular patterns of values or socialization processes.

4 Both were concerned with the relationship between values and behavior.

FIGURE 8.6
MEAD'S THEORETICAL FRAMEWORK SUMMARIZED

GEORGE MEAD
(1863–1931)

BACKGROUND:
1 Puritan family
2 Educated in philosophy
3 Taught at University of Chicago
4 Educated in pragmatism and idealism
5 American industrialization and urbanization

AIM:
Study the activity or behavior of the individual as it lies within the social process

ASSUMPTIONS:
1 Individual is rational and the product of social relations
2 Society is dynamic and evolutionary, providing new and changing socialization of individuals
3 Reality is individual *and* social
4 Social interaction precedes mind, language, self-consciousness
5 Social interaction leads to nonverbal communication
6 Language creates minds and selves
7 Attitudes and emotions are learned through language
8 As individual matures he or she responds to significant other, then to generalized other
9 Social self possesses a creative and spontaneous aspect

METHODOLOGY:
1 Study behavior as the best index
2 Get inside the individual
3 Atomistic approach is futile

TYPOLOGY:
Model of the social self

ISSUES:
1 Individual-society relationships
2 Society's evolutionary qualities
3 Creative and spontaneous qualities of the social self
4 Problems of introspective methods

5 Both were concerned with changing systems of values and socialization processes.

6 Both used and advocated interpretive-introspective methods for studying these phenomena.

7 Both used a microscopic-inductive method in their analysis.

8 Both developed typologies of systems of values at the microscopic level, moving to the macroscopic.

9 The theories of both raise problems concerning the link between the individual and societal levels of analysis and present difficulties of methodology.

From the above it can be seen that Weber and Mead take a microscopic, inductive, evolutionary, systemic, and normative approach to society—the foundation of modern social psychology. Before we turn to the naturalistic approach, the structure of this type of explanation is delineated in Figure 8.7.

THE NATURALISTIC TYPE OF SOCIAL BEHAVIORISM
This type of social behaviorism is as microscopic, inductive, and normative as the systemic approach; however, it is based on assumed characteristics concerning human nature and humanity's instinct for the negation of others (in Simmel's case) and its inborn motives (in Sumner's). We turn, then, to consider each in turn.

Georg Simmel (1858–1918)

Background Simmel was born in Berlin, the son of a Jewish businessman. Having received a broad gymnasium education in history and philosophy, he was influenced strongly by the work of Kant, Darwin, and Spencer. He was a lecturer at the University of Berlin and cofounder of the German Society for Sociology. His major works include *On Social Differentiation* (1890), *The Philosophy of Money* (1900), and *Sociology: Investigations on the Forms of Sociation* (1908).

Aims In the formalistic spirit of Kant, Simmel was concerned with the *patterns* and *forms* of interaction and association in society, i.e., with abstracting the major forms of social behavior in

151

FIGURE 8.7
THE STRUCTURE OF THE SYSTEMIC APPROACH TO SOCIAL BEHAVIORISM

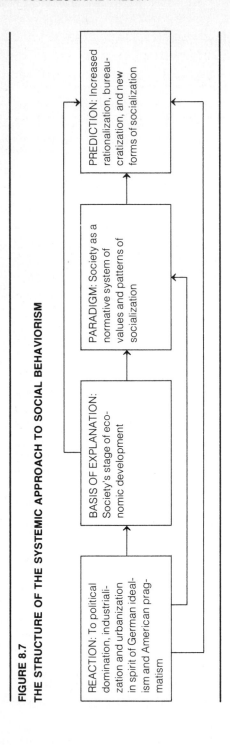

society. Such an approach was microscopic but, more significantly, it involved a rejection of earlier organismic views of social reality. Thus, for Simmel, society did *not* exist as a separate system; rather, it was inherent in the forms of reciprocal social relations, representing no more or less than the interacting individuals concerned. It was the forms of these relationships that Simmel wished to study.

Assumptions

1 As mentioned above, Simmel viewed society not as an organism but as a "name for interacting individuals." Accordingly, sociology becomes the study of patterns of interaction and forms of association, since it is assumed that only these phenomena exist in reality and they exist as *process*.

2 Society exists as a function of socialization rather than as an independent reality.

3 Accordingly, the individual is a product of society; but, as for Mead, he is assumed to be unique nevertheless. Thus *both* the individual and society are important subject matter for sociology.

4 Simmel saw certain group characteristics structuring interaction and association—in particular, *group size*. Accordingly, he assumed that group size defines the form of association or that *size determines form*. Thus the single individual or monad represents high freedom; there is dependence in the dyad; authority prevails in the triad; mores govern small groups; and laws rule large groups (of five or more persons). In understanding each type of group, special attention is paid to the leader-follower relationship.

5 At work within any group, according to Simmel, is the human instinct for the "negation of others," i.e., competition. This construct represents a central element in his theory.

6 Such an instinct results in ongoing conflict—"the essence of social life"—and social evolution. Consequently, the relationship between the individual and society is *dialectical*, while industrialization results in greater individual freedom but increased alienation as well. His view of the effects of progress is thus one of ambivalence; that is, conflict results in societal evolution but increases problems of individual meaning.

153

To summarize, Simmel saw society consisting of individuals in association and interaction and as defined by the "instinct for negation," conflict, group size, and societal evolution in the wake of industrialization, with increased individual freedom and simultaneous alienation. Such a paradigm is similar to Mead's with the exception, perhaps, of its instinctual base.

Methodology   Simmel was concerned with the development of a *formal sociology*, i.e., with the study of the perennial and limited *forms* of *interaction*. In other words, specific types of interaction represent the basis of specific types of social structures in Simmel's view. Consequently, he advocated and used an abstract, analytical, historical, and comparative approach to these phenomena as he attempted to apply the principles of his theory historically. He also encouraged the study of social types— "typical attributes of the social structure." Consequently, he analyzed types such as the "stranger," "mediator," "poor person," "man in the middle," and "renegade" in great detail. These types represent what is typical of particular patterns of association.

The Typology   Simmel developed a model of typical characteristics of groups of a certain size. This typology is summarized in Figure 8.8. Of central interest here is the relationship between form (i.e., group size) and type of association or relationship (e.g., level of freedom and type of authority). As mentioned above, certain specific correlations are evident: monads represent high levels of freedom, dyads offer high dependence and absorption, triads involve an authority structure, small groups result in the evolution of mores, while large groups involve the evolution of formal laws. Running through this model is the assumption that as society becomes larger, more industrialized, and more efficient, the problem of individual meaning and alienation increases markedly, thereby posing new dilemmas.

Summary and Conclusions   For Simmel society represented groups of individuals in interaction and it was defined by humanity's competitive instinct, conflict, group size, and societal evolution. Second, as the basis of the economy became material products contributed by an impersonal labor force, industrialization had the effect of increasing not only freedom but also the levels of individual alienation. This approach is summarized in Figure 8.9.

FIGURE 8.8
SIMMEL'S TYPOLOGY

TYPES OF GROUPS

MONAD	DYADIC	TRIADIC	SMALL GROUP	LARGE GROUP
Single individual	Two persons	Three persons	Four persons	Five or more persons
High freedom	Dependence relationship	Authority structure	Development of mores	More formal
	Intense absorption of individuals	Unity and synthesis		Development of laws

Problem of individual meaning in modern culture

Money results in freedom and alienation

Such a paradigm raises a number of questions:

1 To what extent, for example, was Simmel totally rejecting the organic approach in his notion of a formal sociology? That is, would a group of individuals in interaction and association not represent a kind of system with certain conscious and unconscious normative effects?

2 To what extent does size really determine form? That is, what

---

FIGURE 8.9
SIMMEL'S THEORETICAL FRAMEWORK SUMMARIZED

GEORGE SIMMEL
(1858–1918)

BACKGROUND:
1 Jewish family background
2 Educated in history and philosophy
3 Lecturer at University of Berlin
4 Educated in Spencer and Darwin
5 Marked political, economic, and industrial development

AIM:
The study of societies—the patterns and forms of interaction and association

ASSUMPTIONS:
1 Rejection of the organicist approach
2 Society: name for number of individuals, connected by interaction
3 Size determines form
4 Individual's instinct for negation of others
5 Relationship between individual and society is dialectical

METHODOLOGY:
1 Study perennial and limited forms of *interaction*—formal sociology
2 Use of abstraction, analytical, historical, comparative approach
3 Study of social types

TYPOLOGY:
Types of social groups

ISSUES:
1 Total rejection of organic approach
2 Size—form relationship
3 Individual's instincts issue
4 Methodological problems of studying interaction

---

are the underlying and intervening conditions which greatly complicate such a relationship?

3 What is the actual basis of the individual's "instinct for negation," and to what extent is such an assumption nonscientific?

4 Finally, what other methodological techniques are necessary to study the *dynamics* of interaction and association, in contrast to Simmel's historical and rather static approach?

Despite the above issues, Simmel made an important contribution to the social-behaviorist understanding of society and in many ways complemented and expanded the insights provided by Mead. We turn next to the work of another relevant theorist, William Sumner.

William Sumner (1840–1910)

Background Sumner, the son of a British motor mechanic, was educated at Yale and Oxford in French, Hebrew, and theology. Despite his church training and early religious career, Sumner was heavily influenced by Spencer and Darwin and had strong interests in anthropology and archeology. Heavily involved in the political, social, and economic issues of his time, Sumner was committed to the improvement of his social environment. His major works are *Folkways* (1906) and *The Science of Society* (1927). Our major interest in him within the context of this chapter relates to his work on society's normative structure (i.e., folkways) and its instinctual base. Thus, while he may also be viewed as a macroscopic conflict theorist, our interest in him here concerns the social behaviorist elements in his general theory, which tend to represent its foundation.

Aims Applying the views of Spencer and Darwin to society, Sumner saw sociology as the study, on both macroscopic and interpersonal levels, of society's evolutionary laws. He felt, then—like Comte—that the sociologist's central task was to trace these evolutionary laws in sociological phenomena in order to maximize orderly societal development. At the social-behaviorist level, this involved analysis of the relationship between individual motives and the evolution and development of his or her normative systems (i.e., folkways and mores).

Assumptions

1 In applying the theories of Spencer and Darwin to society, Sumner made the basic assumption that evolution is a basic force and law.[12] Society evolves to higher levels of organization through the processes of competition, cooperation, and survival of the fittest. Inherent in this development is the "law of population" (which says that "Population tends to increase up to the limit of the supporting power of the environment. . . .") and the "law of diminishing returns" (i.e., "More labor gets more from the land, but not proportionately more."). Population, combined with the law of diminishing returns, then, represents the "great underlying condition of society," leading Sumner to describe societies as underpopulated or overpopulated. The former are characterized by economic surplus, democracy, high self-reliance, and low social caste; the latter maximize the use of resources, are controlled by power elites, and are differentiated by high levels of social caste.

In this way, Sumner attempted to delineate the typical effects of population growth on natural resources. Within this framework, he also assumed in a deterministic fashion that poverty is a result of ignorance (i.e., ignorance of evolutionary laws), while nature deals with deviance (such as alcoholism) by eventually removing "things which have survived their usefulness." At the macroscopic level, Sumner's work represents the rather simplistic and direct application of evolutionary principles to society. Of more concern, though, is his analysis of social behavior at the microscopic level.

2 At the interpersonal level, Sumner assumed that behavior is patterned by folkways and mores—the habits and customs of social life. In this way, he took a normative approach to microscopic phenomena.

3 Further, underlying the operation of folkways and mores are human interests or motives: hunger, love, vanity, and fear. Underlying these interests, in turn, is humanity's major motivation—advantage and expediency.

4 Out of these interests and motives, folkways develop in an unconscious, spontaneous, and uncoordinated fashion. Then so-

[12]See M. R. Davie (ed.), *William Graham Sumner*, Crowell, New York, 1963, for this and other references.

cietal forces are influenced by change, trial and error, and the pleasure-pain principle. They also indicate a "strain toward consistency," are defined as "right and true," and are reinforced by taboos and sanctions. They are further reinforced by in-group–out-group ethnocentrism and patriotism.

5 Through constant ritual, folkways are eventually established as mores—norms regarding societal or group welfare. These are likewise sanctioned by taboos; they experience strain toward consistency and represent the basis of social control, the class structure, subcultural differentiation, and the institutional system. Folkways thus become institutionalized as the moral basis of the social structure.

6 This structure, however, is far from static; mores may become degenerate, inert, or too rigid; are subject to modification in the process of intergenerational transmission; may be subject to opposition; and may become inappropriate as society experiences a change in its "life condition." Accordingly, these normative phenomena are subject to constant change and development in response to changing societal conditions.

To summarize, while at the macroscopic level Sumner applied naturalistic evolution to societal development in a simplistic fashion, at the microscopic level he conceptualized social phenomena in normative terms, viewing social reality as a set of developing and changing folkways and mores that were evolving and responding to humanity's natural motives and interests. Evolution at this level, then, was defined in normative terms.

Methodology Sociological methods, for Sumner, included the use of techniques such as classification, comparison, sequence making, cross-cultural analysis, and historical induction. These techniques were applied to folkways and mores in an attempt to verify their foundation, evolution, and relationship to life conditions; that is, Sumner attempted to apply the scientific method to normative phenomena.

The Typology Major elements in Sumner's model of folkways and mores, their foundation and evolution, have already been discussed above. However, these elements and their interrelationships are summarized in Figure 8.10. A number of aspects are highlighted here: the naturalistic foundation of folkways, their

159

**FIGURE 8.10
SUMNER'S TYPOLOGY**

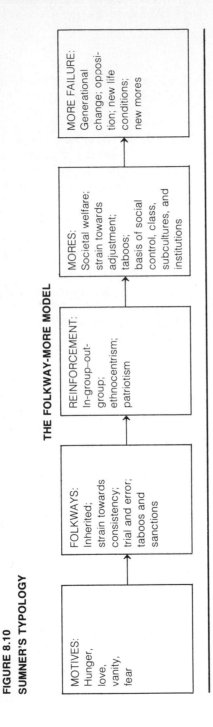

THE FOLKWAY-MORE MODEL

MOTIVES:
Hunger, love, vanity, fear

FOLKWAYS:
Inherited; strain towards consistency; trial and error; taboos and sanctions

REINFORCEMENT:
In-group–out-group; ethnocentrism; patriotism

MORES:
Societal welfare; strain towards adjustment; taboos; basis of social control, class, subcultures, and institutions

MORE FAILURE:
Generational change; opposition; new life conditions; new mores

expedient evolution and strain toward consistency, their normative reinforcement and further development as mores, their institutionalization as the social structure, and dynamic qualities in the face of opposition and change. Sumner thus developed a dynamic, evolutionary, and normative theory of society, a theory based on naturalistic assumptions concerning humanity's motives and interests.

Summary and Conclusions On the basis of naturalistic assumptions, Sumner developed an inductive, evolutionary, and normative theory of society which is both microscopic and societal in scope, structural and dynamic. While his notions concerning societal evolution are somewhat simplistic, his analysis of society at the microscopic level is both dynamic and far-reaching, containing a number of parallels with Durkheim's earlier work. His approach as a whole is summarized in Figure 8.11.

Sumner's theory raises a number of rather obvious issues:

1 His simplistic application of natural evolution principles to society raises problems of relevance and suitability.

2 The relationship between population and societal characteristics is likewise simplistic, failing to specify intervening contingencies which would obviously complicate matters.

3 His delineation of human motives and needs raises the obvious problem of naturalistic determinism.

4 Problems of the group dimension in society and the dysfunctional effects of power elites tend to be overlooked or deemphasized.

Sumner thus tended to develop a naturalistic, deterministic, functionalist, and reductionistic type of theory. Nevertheless, his conceptualization of society as a dynamic and elaborate set of normative phenomena made an important contribution to early sociology and is still referred to in the attempt to understand why and how norms develop.

NATURALISTIC SOCIAL BEHAVIORISM SUMMARIZED
Simmel and Sumner reveal a number of important similarities:

1 Both reacted to the problems of industrialization and urbanization in the tradition of Darwin and Spencer.

2 Both were concerned with normative phenomena at the microscopic level.

3 Both viewed behavior as naturalistically based on human motives.

4 Both highlighted the effects of group or population size on society.

5 Both saw a dialectical relationship between the individual and society.

FIGURE 8.11
SUMNER'S THEORETICAL FRAMEWORK SUMMARIZED

WILLIAM SUMNER
(1840–1910)

BACKGROUND:
1 Son of British mechanic
2 Educated in theology
3 Tutor at Yale
4 Educated in Spencer and Darwin
5 Marked political, economic, and social development

AIM:
Study of society's evolutionary laws

ASSUMPTIONS:
1 Evolution is underlying societal force
2 Behavior is patterned by folkways and mores
3 Individual's interests are hunger, love, vanity, and fear
4 Folkways developed in reaction to individual's interests
5 Folkways became mores through ritual
6 Mores are dynamic and subject to change

METHODOLOGY:
Application of the scientific method to normative phenomena

TYPOLOGY:
Folkway-more model

ISSUES:
1 Application of natural evolution to society
2 Relationship: population and societal characteristics
3 Individual's instinctual motives
4 The group dimension in society

6 Both saw society as evolutionary.

7 Both advocated and used the technique of historical induction.

8 Both developed typologies of the effects of group size on society.

Their theories thus represent naturalistic, microscopic, evolutionary, organic, and inductive views of society, complementing and elaborating the earlier work of Comte and Spencer at the interpersonal level of analysis. Such a contribution remains important in contemporary sociology and is summarized in Figure 8.12.

SOCIAL BEHAVIORISM SUMMARIZED
In this chapter we have attempted to show how social behaviorism represented the reaction of a group of predominantly Protestant thinkers to the contemporary problems of social change in an industrialized society in the traditions of Enlightenment idealism and American pragmatism. What evolved may be viewed as the application of earlier organic paradigms to contemporary society at the *microscopic level*, i.e., conceptualization of society as a naturalistic, evolving, systemic phenomenon from either the sociological or naturalistic point of view.

The major elements of social behaviorism as a whole may be summarized as follows:

Aims   The interpretive understanding of normative phenomena at the microscopic level of analysis.

Assumptions

1 Society is an evolving system of normative phenomena.

2 Social behavior is a function of values or interests.

3 As normative phenomena change, social change occurs.

4 The link between the individual and society is dialectical, contributing thereby to societal evolution.

Methodology   The utilization of interpretive, historical induction.

Typologies   The delineation of systems of values as basic to types of societies.

FIGURE 8.12

THE STRUCTURE OF THE NATURALISTIC APPROACH TO SOCIAL BEHAVIORISM

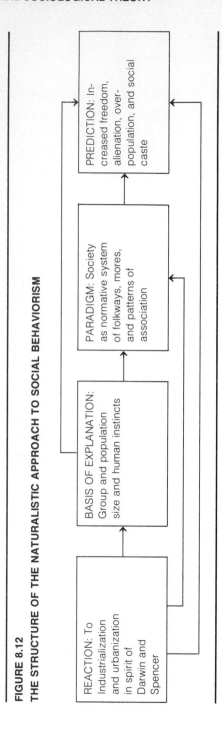

REACTION: To Industrialization and urbanization in spirit of Darwin and Spencer

BASIS OF EXPLANATION: Group and population size and human instincts

PARADIGM: Society as normative system of folkways, mores, and patterns of association

PREDICTION: Increased freedom, alienation, overpopulation, and social caste

From this it can be seen that social behaviorism represents a naturalistic, evolutionary, organic approach to society at the microscopic or interpersonal level of analysis, an approach developed within the context of Enlightenment idealism and American pragmatism. Such an elaboration of earlier organic views contributed to the development of modern social psychology and made an important contribution to sociology as a whole. Its major elements are summarized in Figure 8.13.

EXERCISES

1 Consider the following social trends:

   a Increased bureaucratization in American society from the 1950s through the 1970s

   b Increased middle-class alienation in the United States during the 1960s

   c Marked changes in social norms and laws in the United States from the 1950s through the 1970s

   d The increased trend toward a vocational orientation in American higher education during the 1970s

Account for each trend, using the general explanations provided by Weber, Mead, Simmel, and Sumner. Compare the different types of explanation you develop in each case. To what extent are they similar? Can you develop a general social-behaviorist explanation of each trend?

READINGS

General Works

Aron, R.: *Main Currents in Sociological Thought*, vols. 1 and 2, Doubleday, Garden City, N.Y., 1970, for chaps. on Weber.
Coser, L. A.: *Masters of Sociological Thought, Ideas in Historical and Social Context*, Harcourt, Brace, Jovanovich, New York, 1971, for chaps. on Weber, Mead, and Simmel.
Martindale, D: *The Nature and Types of Sociological Theory*, Houghton Mifflin, Boston, 1960, chaps. 12, 13, and 14.
Nisbet, R. A.: *The Sociological Tradition*, Basic Books, New York, 1966, chaps. 3, 4, and 5.

FIGURE 8.13
THE STRUCTURE OF SOCIAL BEHAVIORISM

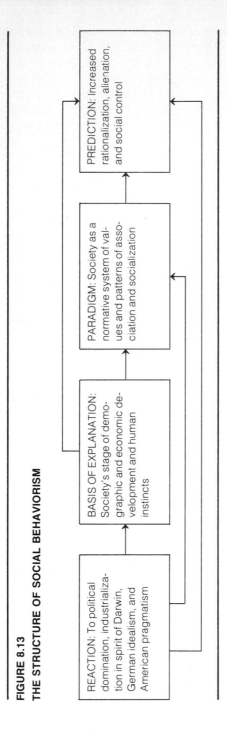

Truzzi, M. (ed.): *Sociology, The Classic Statements*, Random House, New York, 1971, selections 8, 16, 18, 23, 26, and 30.
Zeitlin, I. M.: *Ideology and the Development of Sociological Theory*, Prentice-Hall, Englewood Cliffs, N.J., 1968, chap. 11.

Specific Works by Theorists

Weber

Weber, M.: *Basic Concepts in Sociology*, Citadel, New York, 1964.
————: *The Theory of Social and Economic Organization*, Free Press, Glencoe, Ill., 1947.
Gerth, H. and C. W. Mills (eds.): *From Max Weber: Essays in Sociology*, Routledge, London, 1948.

Mead

Mead, G. H.: *Mind, Self, and Society*, University of Chicago Press, Chicago, 1934.
————: *Movements of Thought in the Nineteenth Century*, University of Chicago Press, Chicago, 1936.
————: *The Philosophy of the Act*, University of Chicago Press, Chicago, 1938.

Simmel

Wolff, K. H. (ed. and trans.): *The Sociology of Georg Simmel*, Free Press, New York, 1950.
———— and R. Bendix (trans.): *Conflict and the Web of Group Affiliations*, Free Press, Chicago, 1956.

Sumner

Sumner, W. G.: *Folkways*, Ginn, Boston, 1907.
————: *The Science of Society*, Yale University Press, New Haven, Conn., 1927.
Keller, A. G., and M. R. Davie (eds.): *Essays of William Graham Sumner*, Yale University Press, New Haven, Conn., 1934.

9

TOWARD A TYPOLOGY OF TRADITIONAL SOCIOLOGICAL THEORIZING:

SUMMARY OF SECTION TWO

So far in our analysis of theory in general and sociological theory in particular, we have made a number of major points.

1 We have defined *theorizing* as "the process by which the individual accounts for his or her physical and social environments within the context of a specific social setting, thereby defining both physical and social reality."

2 We described *formal theory* as "a set of accepted, abstract, and logical propositions which attempts to explain relationships between phenomena, using a paradigm, a set of concepts and their logical relationships, a set of operationalized variables and indexes, a methodology designed to test these predicted relationships, data analysis and interpretation, and, finally, general evaluation of the theory as a whole."

3 We defined *sociological theory* as "a set of paradigms concerning society and social phenomena in reference to their separate societal reality."

4 It was also evident that these paradigms represent a person's attempt to account for his or her physical and social environment within specific societal, intellectual, and biographical conditions. Theorizing thus represents a dynamic and changing reaction to these changing conditions; that is, as these conditions change, so does the theory defining them, making it increasingly secular, microscopic, scientific, and sociological.

5 Three major paradigms were defined as central to sociological theory: the organic-structure-functional, emerging from the secularization of earlier metaphysical, theological, and philosophical views of reality; the conflict-radical; and the social-behaviorist–social-psychological. The first of these views society as a system of functionally interrelated parts subject to the influence of natural laws, the society's division of labor system, and underlying system problems. The conflict-radical approach, in contrast, views society as a system of competing forces in reference to the struggle to meet primary needs and subject to naturalistic and systemic pressures as well. The third approach, social-behaviorist–social-psychological paradigm, conceptualizes society at the microscopic and interpersonal level, in an inductive fashion, focusing on the individual's relation to the social environment through socialization, roles, exchange, role playing, and individual definitions of reality. All three types of explanation, however, were seen as conceptualizing social order and change, utilizing naturalistic and systemic forms of explanation, and representing the response of particular groups to societal problems from particular philosphical perspectives.

6 In examining the organic paradigm in particular, it was shown how this type of theory represented the reaction of upper-class academics to political and economic problems of their day in the Enlightenment tradition. These individuals conceptualized society as an organic, evolving system of norms and subsystems that was reacting to natural laws, instincts, and society's division of labor system. Details of this paradigm as exemplified in the case of particular theorists are summarized in Figure 9.1. It can be readily seen that the naturalistic type tends to represent the

FIGURE 9.1
A SUMMARY OF THE ORGANIC PARADIGM

TYPE	NATURALISTIC		SYSTEMIC	
THEORIST	COMTE	SPENCER	DURKHEIM	TONNIES
BACKGROUND	Monarchist, trained in medicine and physiology	Nonconformist with classical education	Jewish with Enlightenment education	Enlightenment education
AIMS	Eliminate revolution	Trace societal evolution	Understand social phenomena	Understand social will
ASSUMPTIONS	Naturalistic evolution applies to society	Organic evolution	Social facts exist	Society represents social will
METHODS	Positivism	Positivism	Measure social facts	Historical induction
TYPOLOGY	Social statics and social dynamics	Social statics and social dynamics	Mechanical and organic solidarity	Gemeinschaft and gesselschaft
ISSUES	Naturalistic explanations	Organic arguments	Nominalism versus realism	Characteristics of social will

response of upper-class intellectuals to political and economic problems within the traditions of naturalism and positivism, resulting in a naturalistic, organic approach to society. Durkheim and Tönnies, on the other hand, react to these same societal problems from an idealistic perspective, resulting in a normative or moralistic view of society. The paradigm as a whole, however, represents an organic, evolutionary, and naturalistic conceptualization of society.

7 Further, the conflict paradigm was seen as the reaction of generally lower-class individuals to political oppression, conflict, and economic development in the traditions of Enlightenment philosophy and American pragmatism. This reaction resulted in a materialistic-ecological approach to society as a system of competing groups. The systemic approach, exemplified by Marx and Park, is summarized in Figure 9.2. It is evident that their theories may be viewed as reactions to social conflict in the tradition of Enlightenment idealism, resulting in a materialistic-ecological view of society in conflict terms. The naturalistic argument inherent in the work of Pareto and Veblen, on the other hand, represents the application of Enlightenment naturalism to political and economic conflict, resulting in an approach which may be labeled *naturalistic determinism*. Conflict theory in general, however, may be viewed as the application of materialistic, ecological, and naturalistic principles to society by individuals who have observed and/or experienced political and economic conflict, in particular members of the lower classes.

8 Social behaviorism may be viewed as the reaction of predominantly middle-class intellectuals—in the spirit of Darwin, German idealism and American pragmatism—to the problems of industrialization and urbanization. This reaction resulted in a microscopic conceptualization of society as a normative system of values, associations, and socialization, a system based on society's demographic development and humanity's instincts. Figure 9.3 reveals how the systemic type, exemplified by Weber and Mead, represents a reaction to the effects of industrialization in the tradition of idealism and pragmatism, resulting in a microscopic and normative model of society. Simmel and Sumner, on the other hand, take a more naturalistic and instinctual approach to society at the interpersonal level.

Social behaviorism as a whole, however, represents the application of idealistic and pragmatic principles to the problems of

FIGURE 9.2
A SUMMARY OF THE CONFLICT PARADIGM

TYPE	SYSTEMIC		NATURALISTIC	
THEORIST	MARX	PARK	PARETO	VEBLEN
BACKGROUND	Lower-class Jew with Enlighten-ment education	Businessman's son, educated in philosophy and psychology	Noble family with Enlightenment education	Farmer's son with classical education
AIMS	Understand life conditions and ideas	Develop natural laws of society	Understand social forces behind equilibrium	Understand human evolution
ASSUMPTIONS	Material defines nonmaterial	Natural order as foundation of society	Society is function of nonlogical action—residues	Individual's three major traits
METHODS	Dialectical materialism	Natural history	Scientific method	Historical induction
TYPOLOGY	Stages of societal development	Model of social organization	Circulation of elite	Stages of societal development
ISSUES	Materialistic determinism	Ecological determinism	Naturalistic determinism	Naturalistic determinism

modern industrialization, resulting in a microscopic, normative approach to society in distinct contrast to earlier paradigms and in reaction to society's changing characteristics. On the other hand, all three paradigms represent systemic and evolutionary conceptualizations of society as a separate reality at either the macroscopic or microscopic level. In this way, society is viewed as a "real" system with normative or naturalistic qualities.

CONCLUSIONS: TOWARD A MODEL OF TRADITIONAL SOCIOLOGICAL THEORIZING

We have seen how sociological theory represents the reaction of a *particular* group of intellectuals to *particular* societal problems

FIGURE 9.3
A SUMMARY OF SOCIAL BEHAVIORISM

TYPE	SYSTEMIC		NATURALISTIC	
THEORIST	WEBER	MEAD	SIMMEL	SUMNER
BACKGROUND	Protestant with German idealism	Puritan with American pragmatism	Educated in Spencer and Darwin	Mechanic's son educated in Spencer and Darwin
AIMS	Understand social action	Study social activity	Study forms of association	Study societal evolution
ASSUMPTIONS	Social action varies in rationality	Social inter-action precedes self	Size deter-mines form	Behavior is defined by folkways
METHODS	Interpretive understanding	Interpretive understanding	Study forms of association	Apply scientific method to norms
TYPOLOGY	Types of social action	Model of social self	Types of social groups	Folkway-more model
ISSUES	Values and social structure	Sociological determinism	Naturalistic determinism	Naturalistic determinism

from the perspective of *particular* philosophical traditions, resulting in systemic conceptualizations of society which vary in *level* (macroscopic or microscopic) and *type of explanation* (naturalistic or systemic). Such a model involves a number of distinct elements: the theorist's *background* (general socioeconomic status); his *philosophical viewpoint* (idealism, pragmatism, or naturalism); the predominant *societal problems* of the day (political-economic domination or the effects of industrialization); and the resultant *sociological paradigm* (organic, conflict, or social behaviorist). It would appear that, in *broad* and *general* terms the model operates as follows: socioeconomic background, along with philosophical viewpoint, influences the reaction to predominant societal problems to produce a systemic paradigm of society which differs in level and explanation.

The elements and operation of such a model are summarized in Figure 9.4, from which it can be seen that the organic approach is primarily a reaction of upper-class individuals to

174

FIGURE 9.4

A MODEL OF TRADITIONAL SOCIOLOGICAL THEORIZING

PARADIGM	GENERAL BACKGROUND	PHILOSOPHY	SOCIETAL PROBLEMS	EXPLANATION

ORGANIC	Upper class
	Upper class
		Naturalism
		Idealism
			Political and
			    economic
			Political and
			    economic
				Naturalistic
				Systemic

CONFLICT	Lower class
	Lower class
		Idealism
		Naturalism
			Political and
			    economic
			Political and
			    economic
				Systemic
				Naturalistic

SOCIAL BEHAVIORIST	Middle class Middle class	Idealism- pragmatism Naturalism	Industrialization Industrialization	Systemic Naturalistic

political and economic problems within the tradition of Enlightenment idealism and naturalism; conflict theory is the reaction of lower-class thinkers to political and economic oppression, also in the traditions of Enlightenment idealism and naturalism; while social behaviorism may be viewed as the reaction of middle-class thinkers to the effects of industrialization from the perspective of Enlightenment idealism and naturalism as well as American pragmatism. Furthermore, the links between Enlightenment naturalism and naturalistic sociological paradigms—as well as the correlation between Enlightenment idealism, American pragmatism, and more sociological types of explanation—are also shown.

While such a model is both *general* and *simplistic,* it appears to highlight the manner in which sociological theorizing represents the *systemic response of a particular group of intellectuals to the predominant societal problems and developments of the day.* It is to an examination of this process within contemporary sociology, particularly in American society, that we turn to in Section 3, in our analysis of structure-functional, modern conflict, and social-psychological paradigms.

CONTEMPORARY SOCIOLOGICAL THEORY

10

INTRODUCTION TO CONTEMPORARY SOCIOLOGICAL THEORY

MAJOR TOPICS:

The background of American
sociological theory

Stages in the development of
contemporary theory

The context of contemporary theory

So far in our analysis we have examined three major paradigms; in this third section we turn to these paradigms as they have developed largely within contemporary America. The high level of continuity with earlier theory will be evident; nevertheless, *American sociology* possesses its own unique character—*the application and development of European paradigms within the context of a materialistic, pragmatic, and utilitarian culture.* Consequently, theory is more empirically oriented than its earlier European origins. However, links between the two types of sociology are very strong and *contemporary sociological theory,* to a large extent, represents the further *elaboration and application of early European paradigms.* Accordingly, the organic, conflict, and social-behaviorist paradigms are revived in the form of structure functionalism, radical sociology or modern conflict theory, and social psychology. In this introductory chapter we shall examine three aspects of contemporary theory: the background of American sociological theory, stages in its development, and the contexts of its three major paradigms.

THE BACKGROUND OF AMERICAN SOCIOLOGICAL THEORY (1905–1918)

The foundation of American sociology reveals its close links with nineteenth-century European thinkers:[1] reference to the work of Comte, Spencer, and Darwin; belief in natural laws, progressive social change, social reformism, and an individualistic conception of society;[2] a high percentage of individuals with theological and rural backgrounds; and a heavy emphasis on America's social problems in the wake of the society's post-Civil War industrial and urban development. In general, then, early American sociology may be viewed as the *response of middle-class intellectuals to America's social problems in the tradition of nineteenth-century European sociology.*

Such an approach was heavily organic, evolutionary, and idealistic in content, as is evident in the work of thinkers such as Lester Ward, William Sumner, Franklin Giddings, and Albion

---

[1] In this discussion we are indebted to the following works: L. L. Bernard and J. Bernard, *Origins of American Sociology,* Crowell, New York, 1943; R. C. Hinkle, Jr., and G. J. Hinkle, *The Development of Modern Sociology,* Random House, New York, 1954; and H. W. Odum, *American Sociology,* Longmans, London, 1951.
[2] See Hinkle and Hinkle, ibid., pp. 7–17.

Small. Early American sociological theory, then, tended to represent the application of the organic paradigm to the concerns and problems of post-Civil War America as it was experiencing the beginnings of industrialization. Thus both the content and context of American sociology were similar to their European counterparts: however, distinct differences emerged in the ongoing development of the former within the context of a heavily materialistic culture, as we shall see.

STAGES IN THE DEVELOPMENT OF CONTEMPORARY THEORY

According to Roscoe Hinkle and Gisela Hinkle,[3] the founding period in American sociology lasted from 1905 to 1918. From this point on, a number of distinct stages emerged, as follows:

The Scientific Stage (1918–1935)[4]

During this era American sociology attempted to become scientific, empirically oriented, professionalized, and academically organized. Its subspecialities began to emerge, while an emphasis on the influence of the social environment rather than innate characteristics became predominant. Crucial within this period also were the effects of two major events: World War I and the Depression of the 1930s. These societal problems reinforced the movement toward empiricism within American sociology. The basis of the discipline thus moved toward empiricism within the context of a materialistic and economically oriented society. Such a change had important repercussions for the type of sociology which followed, namely, its scientific, empirical, and specialized character.

Theory, Research, and Application (1935–1954)

During this period the emphasis on utilitarianism and professionalism increased, as did subfield proliferation and organization. The influence of certain European thinkers such as Durkheim, Freud, and Weber also increased, contributing to the development of social behaviorism and neopositivism—the foundations of

[3]Ibid., chap. 1.
[4]For this and the next stage we rely on ibid., chap. 1.

the social-psychological paradigm. In general, this era saw American sociology becoming increasingly empirical, organized, and applied to social problems predominant within the society. The empiricist movement had thus become institutionalized.

The Emergence of Modern Conflict Theory (1960s)

The 1960s saw a resurgence of conflict theory within American sociology in response to increased levels of social and racial conflict within the society as a whole as well as to the increasing obviousness of the negative effects of industrialization and bureaucratization. Consequently, an attempt was made to make sociology more conflict-oriented in order to deal with these events, while radical sociology attempted to examine its traditional counterpart critically and to develop a new, applied type of discipline more relevant to societal problems and needs. Within the field of race relations, a "colonial" approach to analyzing racism was also developed, based on neo-Marxism. Once again, then, theory responded to events within the society as a whole.

Technology and Modern Systems Theory (1970s)

Sociology's modern environment—particularly in an era of apparent recession—may be viewed as one in which technological and economic needs are predominant. Systemic planning and control priorities have reemerged as paramount, resulting in an updating of structure functionalism in the form of cybernetics and systems theory as applied to modern sociology. Heavy emphasis is placed upon information and planning *systems* which will respond efficiently to bureaucratic needs in an era of scarce resources and a wide range of social problems. Consequently, earlier organic and structure-functional paradigms have reemerged in new dress, responding to an environment in which systemic needs are once again paramount.

Conclusions

We have outlined a number of stages in the development of contemporary theory as follows: the European foundation; the scientific stage; theory, research, and application; the emergence of radical sociology; and technology and modern systems theory. While these stages may be viewed as distinct entities, it is also evident that theorizing in American sociology is a relatively uniform process: it is *the application of European philosophical ideas to the changing problems of a materialistic, pragmatic, and utilitarian society in which idealism has given way to empiricism and utilitarianism*. Consequently, contemporary theory represents the earlier organic, conflict, and social-behaviorist paradigms in its systemic, evolutionary, and equilibrium-oriented characteristics at both microscopic and macroscopic levels of analysis; but to a large extent it lacks the idealistic belief in inevitable societal progress and evolution inherent in traditional sociological theory. In this manner idealism gave way to realism and empiricism within the context of a society which was experiencing high levels of industrialization and urbanization.

Having briefly defined some of the major stages in the development of contemporary theory, it is important to specify the contexts in which each paradigm developed before examining each in detail.

THE CONTEXT OF CONTEMPORARY THEORY

We turn now to major characteristics of the contexts in which the structure-functional, modern conflict, and social-psychological paradigms developed.

The Context of Structure Functionalism

Like organic theory, structure-functionalism flourished under conditions in which systemic needs were paramount:

1 The problems of social and economic development in post-Civil War American society.

2 The devastating social and economic effects of the 1930s Depression.

3 Postwar difficulties in the 1920s and 1940s.

4 Contemporary problems of technological and economic development in the 1970s.

5 Philosophical orientations toward the above problems represented application of nineteenth-century European sociological thought in the emphasis upon *natural laws, progressive social change, social reformism,* and the *organic analogy* as applied to

183

society, with a deemphasis on idealism and increased belief in empiricism.

6 Finally, as with organic theory, these orientations tended to reflect the views of an intellectual elite—views of society that were essentially systemic and conservative.

Structure functionalism may thus be summarized as the application of nineteenth-century European sociological thought, in particular the organic model, to the systemic problems of a developing America within the context of a pragmatic and nonidealistic value system. In this manner the continuity between foregoing systems of thought and this particular paradigm is evident.

The Context of Modern Conflict Theory

Like structure functionalism, modern conflict theory represents the application of earlier systems of thought to events within contemporary society:

1 The application of eighteenth-century idealism and progressivism to modern society

2 The elaboration of neo-Marxist ideas to deal with the complexity of modern social conflict

3 Reaction to high levels of social and racial conflict within modern America

4 Reaction to the repressive effects of bureaucratization on the individual as well as on modern sociology

5 Application of earlier reformist notions to contemporary social problems in the wake of industrialization and urbanization

In short, modern conflict theory represents the application of neo-Marxist theory to the problems of conflict and bureaucratization in modern society, revealing, once again, the continuity of earlier social philosophy and modern social theory.

The Context of Social Psychology

The social-psychological paradigm reveals continuities also:

1 The application of earlier individualistic conceptualizations of society to the analysis of modern society

2 Elaboration of individualism—implicit within the Protestant ethic —to an analysis of modern society

3 The influence of European thinkers such as Durkheim and Weber on the development of a microscopic, internally oriented, and introspective view of society

4 The application of the evolutionary optimism in earlier Darwinism to modern social life[5]

5 Awareness of the impact of bureaucratization on the individual with his or her consequent alienation and search for personal meaning

In sum, the social-psychological paradigm may be viewed as the application of earlier notions of individualism and social evolution to events within contemporary society. The continuity between earlier value systems and sociology's reaction to contemporary societal problems is evident once again, with an added emphasis on a microscopic and inductive paradigm of society in contrast to the former two types.

Summary
A number of common themes in the above paradigms are evident:

1 Belief in the Enlightenment values of natural laws, progressive social change, and the organic analogy

2 The influence of European thinkers such as Durkheim, Darwin, Marx, and Weber

3 Belief in application of the scientific method to the solution of contemporary social problems

4 Reaction to changing societal developments, i.e., systemic needs, social conflict, and the effects of bureaucratization on the individual

5 A heavy emphasis on human economic, political, and social needs within the context of a materialistic, utilitarian, and pragmatic culture

[5]For a discussion of this, see L. Shaskolsky, "The Development of Sociological Theory in America—A Sociology of Knowledge Interpretation," *Ohio Valley Sociologist*, **32**:11–35, 1967.

To this extent contemporary sociological theory may be viewed as the relatively homogeneous application of European paradigms to developments in modern society within the context of a materialistic, pragmatic, and utilitarian culture. However, when the three paradigms are examined in order, the following trends also appear:

1 A movement from macroscopic to microscopic paradigms of society

2 A change from societal to individual structure functionalism

3 A movement from organic to technological-cybernetic structure functionalism

4 A change from static, equilibrium-oriented theory to dynamic, evolutionary structure functionalism

5 A movement from the method of historical induction to emphasis upon the scientific and experimental method

6 A change from the use of informal to formal research and methods of theory construction

These trends suggest a general movement away from macroscopic, societal, organic, and static theory toward the more microscopic, technological, and dynamic type. Nevertheless, contemporary social theory continues to represent the application of earlier European paradigms to changing developments in modern society within the context of a materialistic, pragmatic, and utilitarian culture.

CONCLUSIONS

In this introductory chapter we have attempted to demonstrate the degree to which contemporary sociological theory represents the application of earlier European paradigms to changing societal problems within the particular cultural context of American society. Thus structure functionalism was defined as the application of nineteenth-century European thought, in particular the organic model, to the systemic problems of a developing America; modern conflict theory represents application of neo-Marxist theory to the contemporary problems of conflict and bureaucratization; while the social-psychological paradigm may be viewed as the application of earlier notions of individualism and social evolution to events within contemporary society. In this manner, contemporary sociological theory may be viewed as the changing and dynamic application of the earlier European paradigms to the social, political, and economic problems of evolving American society within the boundaries of its utilitarian value system. Sociology's historical continuity and ongoing dynamic evolution is thus clear. This process is summarized in Figure 10.1. We shall then proceed to examine each paradigm in detail.

EXERCISES

1 Compare and contrast the historical circumstances behind the evolution of sociology in Europe and the United States. Describe significant differences between the two.

2 Compare and contrast the historical circumstances behind

FIGURE 10.1
THE EVOLUTION OF CONTEMPORARY SOCIOLOGICAL PARADIGMS

PARADIGMS:

Structure functionalism ⟶ Modern conflict theory ⟶ Social psychology

CHARACTERISTICS:

| Organic sociological thought and reaction to systemic needs | ⟶ | Eighteenth-century idealism and progressivism and reaction to modern conflict and bureaucratization | ⟶ | Individualism and Protestant ethic and reaction to contemporary social problems |

From macroscopic, societal, organic, and static to microscopic, technological, and dynamic paradigms ⟶

Sociological theory as a function of earlier paradigms and changing societal environment ⟶

the development of the three contemporary sociological paradigms. Delineate significant differences among the three of them.

3 Compare the three contemporary paradigms with respect to their settings and major characteristics. What major differences do you find?

4 Outline the interactive relationship between societal factors and the type of predominant paradigm which emerges. What do you conclude about the evolution and development of sociological theory?

READINGS

Bernard, L. L., and J. Bernard: *Origins of American Sociology,* Crowell, New York, 1948.

Friedrichs, R. W.: *A Sociology of Sociology,* Free Press, New York, 1970.

Gouldner, A. W.: *The Coming Crisis of Western Sociology,* Avon, New York, 1970.

Hinkle, R. C., Jr., and G. J. Hinkle: *The Development of Modern Sociology,* Random House, New York, 1954.

Martindale, D.: *The Nature and Types of Sociological Theory,* Houghton Mifflin, Boston, 1960, chaps. 12–19.

Mullins, N. C.: *Theories and Theory Groups in Contemporary American Sociology,* Harper & Row, New York, 1973.

Odum, H. W.: *American Sociology,* Longmans, London, 1951, chaps. 1, 2, and 3.

Reynolds, L. T., and J. M. Reynolds (eds.): *The Sociology of Sociology,* McKay, New York, 1970.

Shaskolsky, L.: "The Development of Sociological Theory in America—A Sociology of Knowledge Interpretation," *Ohio Valley Sociologist,* **32**:11–35, 1967.

Smith, D. L.: "Sociology and the Rise of Corporate Capitalism," *Science and Society,* **29**:1–18, 1965.

11

STRUCTURE FUNCTIONALISM:

THE ORGANIC PARADIGM CONTINUED

We begin our analysis of contemporary theory by outlining the major characteristics of structure functionalism—the foundation of American sociology—and the elaboration of the earlier organic paradigm. As in Section 2, we shall summarize the societal, intellectual, and biographical conditions under which this type of theory developed and delineate its major assumptions. We shall then discuss two major variants: the naturalistic and systemic types as evident in the work of four major contemporary theorists: Talcott Parsons, Walter Buckley, Amitai Etzioni, and Edward Tiryakian. We shall conclude our discussion by examining structure-functionalism as a whole.

INTRODUCTION

Like organic theory, structure functionalism represents the systemic reaction of establishment-oriented intellectuals to the political, economic, and social needs of contemporary society. We described these needs as stemming specifically from post-war, post-Depression, and contemporary social, economic, and technological problems.[1] We also described the philosophical orientations of this intellectual elite as representing the application of nineteenth-century European thought in its emphasis upon natural laws, progressive social change, social reformism, and the organic analogy to society within the context of a pragmatic and nonidealistic value system. Structure functionalism, then, as the foundation of contemporary theory, represents the application of the organic paradigm to the systemic needs of contemporary society by a particular intellectual elite.

This approach views society as a *systemic, interrelated, interdependent, evolving, equilibrium-oriented whole, representing underlying system needs or functions*. In this manner, *structure*, or the social system, represents *function*, or particular underlying system needs. An attempt is thus made to develop a general theory of society based on the assumption that society exists and possesses an independent reality or existence as a *social system*, with characteristics similar to other systems in the universe (i.e., natural and physical systems). The major focus of sociology, accordingly, is to examine and discover the major characteristics of this social system and the mode of its evolution in order to maximize orderly social change. The parallels in form between this kind of theory

190   [1]See Chap. 10 for further details.

and the organic paradigm are obvious in its systemic, evolutionary, and naturalistic characteristics.

Not all structure functionalists, however, hold identical views of what constitutes society's underlying functions. While, on the one hand, there are those who view society as having characteristics in common with organic systems, in particular the principle of *homeostasis* or equilibrium, others take a more sociological view, seeing society as a normative system existing within rather than outside the individual. As with organic theory, then, we are presented with two major types: the *naturalistic* type of theory, on the one hand, and the normative or *systemic,* on the other. Both, however, view society as a macroscopic, evolving, homeostatic system based on certain underlying functions. The major difference here is found in what these functions are rather than in the type or form of theory involved.

To summarize, structure functionalism, the earliest type of American sociological theory, evolved in response to political, economic, and social needs within American society. It was developed by an establishment-oriented intellectual community applying earlier European sociological thought within the context of a nonidealistic, pragmatic culture. The major consequence of these factors is a type of theory which is naturalistic, systemic, and conservative, varying according to whether the particular theorist is more or less naturalistic or systemic. This theorizing process is summarized in Figure 11.1.

We turn first to examine the naturalistic type of structure functionalism as evident in the work of Parsons and Buckley.

THE NATURALISTIC TYPE OF STRUCTURE FUNCTIONALISM

Parsons and Buckley are useful examples of this type of theory, the former in his use of the organic analogy and the latter in his cybernetic or systems theory approach to society.

Talcott Parsons (1902)

Background   Parsons was born in Colorado in 1902. He majored in biology at Amherst College, came into contact with anthropological functionalism at the London School of Economics, and was influenced by Weberian thought at Heidelberg, where he received

FIGURE 11.1

MAJOR FACTORS BEHIND STRUCTURE FUNCTIONALISM

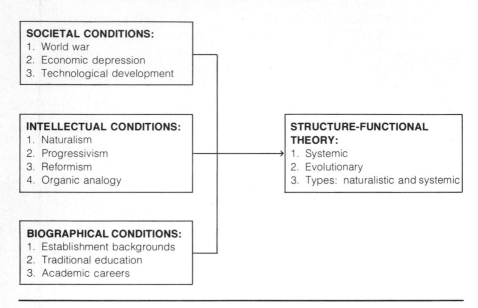

his D. Phil. in sociology and economics. His general theory of society represents a synthesis of biological, anthropological, and Weberian elements. His academic career since 1927 has consisted primarily of work at Harvard. He experienced both the Depression and the formative years of the society's high rate of industrialization.[2] His major works include *The Structure of Social Action* (1937), *The Social System* (1951), *Towards a General Theory of Action* (1951) and *The System of Modern Societies* (1971).

Aims   The major aim of Parsons' theorizing is the development of a *general theory of society*, i.e., a theory which applies to societies *in general* as part of all living systems. Such a functional theory of social organization is based on his view of the human being as a decision-making actor constrained by normative and situational factors. It is these latter factors which introduce system needs or

[2]For a useful discussion of the effects of these factors on Parsons, see A. W. Gouldner, *The Coming Crisis of Western Sociology*, Avon New York, 1970, chap. 5.

functions into the understanding of social behavior. Furthermore, since, according to his view, societies possess universal characteristics, it is possible to develop theories which apply to all societies, their evolution and development.[3]

Assumptions Parsons makes a number of major assumptions concerning society, as follows:

1 The social system is assumed to exist *sui generis;* i.e., society possesses an independent reality beyond the existence of the individual as a system of interaction.

2 Social structure or societal subsystems represent a number of underlying primary functions (structure represents function) or underlying system problems. These functions consist of *integration* (the social system based on norms which bind the individual to society through normative integration), *pattern maintenance* (the cultural system of values and value generalization), *goal attainment* (the personality system—the basis of differentiation), and *adaptation* (the behavioral organism—the basis of roles and the economic system).

3 The social system, in turn, consists of four subsystems: *societal community* (integrative norms), *pattern maintenance or fiduciary* (integrative values), *polity* (applying to goal attainment), and *economy* (applying to adaptation). In general, the major focus of the social system, according to Parsons, is internal, normative integration, while the basis of society is its "level of self-sufficiency relative to its environments. . . ."[4]

4 This view of society is "grounded in the essential nature of living systems at all levels of organization and evolutionary development. . . ." with the assumption that there is "strong continuity over the class of living systems. . . ."[5] The biological analogy is thus central to Parsons' paradigm of society.

---

[3]See in particular his recent work, *The System of Modern Societies,* Prentice-Hall, Englewood Cliffs, N.J., 1971, p. 1.
[4]Ibid., p. 8. For a discussion of Parsons' general model of the social system, see the same work, p. 11.
[5]T. Parsons, "Some Problems of General Theory in Sociology," in J. C. McKinney and E. A. Tiryakian (eds.), *Theoretical Sociology, Perspectives and Developments,* Appleton Century Crofts, New York, 1970, p. 35.

5 Furthermore, in line with this analogy (i.e., the view that society is similar to biological and natural systems), Parsons assumes that society's central focus or foundation is the tendency toward equilibrium or homeostasis. Central processes within this tendency are those which interrelate the four subsystems of action—their *interpenetration*, the *internalization* of social and cultural phenomena into the personality, and the *institutionalization* of normative components as constitutive structures.[6] The social system is thus viewed as highly integrated and equilibrium-oriented.

6 This system, however, is not viewed as static; rather, it possesses a capacity for *adaptive evolution* in a manner which results in increased goal attainment for society as a whole along with increased internal integration. Central processes of evolutionary change consist of *differentiation* (the further division or specialization of functional structures), *adaptive upgrading* (increased freedom of social units from resource restrictions), *inclusion* of new structures in the normative system, and *value generalization* (the evolution of value systems to higher levels of generality in order to maintain integration with evolution.[7])

7 Finally, Christian culture or the Western value of instrumental activism is viewed as a prime mover in the process of societal evolution and modernization, proceeding through a number of historical stages to present-day modern America.[8]

To summarize, Parsons views society as an independent system with characteristics in common with other living systems. Accordingly, its structure represents basic underlying functions, consists of distinct subsystems, is homeostatic, and evolves in an adaptive fashion. Such a paradigm is an important example of the organic approach updated and further elaborated to deal with Western society's more recent historical development. In many respects, however, it represents a mechanical application of the biological model to society.

Methodology Parsons assumes that his paradigm is *"at a certain level,* a deductive propositional system," based, as it is, on

[6]Parsons, *The System of Modern Societies*, p. 6.
[7]Ibid., pp. 26–27.
[8]Ibid., chaps. 3–8.

the "theory of living systems generally. . . ." and the "theory of cybernetic control. . . ."[9] Furthermore, in constructing such paradigms, he assumes that it is appropriate to "treat more complicated systems in terms of combinations of more elementary components on various different levels,"[10] thereby taking an *additive* approach to social reality. Third, the method Parsons employed to document the adaptive evolution of society consists of the *"match* between the theoretical scheme . . . and the statements of empirical fact that have been selected to validate theoretical interpretation."[11] Bringing these points together, it is possible to view the Parsonian method as the historical deduction of paradigms of societal relationships based on the biological analogy further elaborated and confirmed by *matching* the theoretical scheme with empirical facts. In this manner an elaborate structure-functional model of society is arrived at through historical and logical deduction based on acceptance of the biological definition of social reality.

The Typology   One of Parsons' major typologies is contained in his theory of modernization, which describes particular stages of societal evolution from early Christianity through the industrial revolution to modern America,[12] documenting the instrumental effects of Christian culture. Within each stage this orientation serves to move the society toward modernization (i.e., bureaucratization, rationalization, industrialization, and democratization) as follows:

1   *Early Christianity* (the functional specificity of the church's organizational structure)

2   *The medieval period* (the church's contribution to knowledge)

3   *Renaissance and Reformation* (the development of secular culture within the church, Reformation individualism)

4   *The Counterreformation* (the pluralization of values, the legitimation of secular society)

5   *Rise of the state* (the organization and institutionalization of secular society)

---

[9]Parsons, "Some Problems of General Theory in Sociology," ibid., p. 42.
[10]Ibid., p. 35.
[11]Parsons, *The System of Modern Societies*, p. 138.
[12]Ibid.

6 *The industrial and democratic revolutions* (industrialization and democratization)

7 *Modern America* (high secularization, industrialization, and democratization)

Thus Parsons attempts to demonstrate the manner in which the Christian church led to the disintegration of medieval unity, resulting in the functional evolution of modern society. In this macroscopic and historical fashion he attempts to validate his structure-functional paradigm of society. The details of his typology are summarized in Figure 11.2, in which the structure of societal evolution is clearly demonstrated.

Summary and Conclusions   Parsons, reacting to the systemic needs of his day in the tradition of biology, anthropological functionalism, and Weberian sociology, developed a particular para-

---

FIGURE 11.2
PARSONS' TYPOLOGY

STAGES IN MODERNIZATION

EARLY CHRISTIANITY:	⟶	MEDIEVAL PERIOD:	⟶	RENAISSANCE AND REFORMATION:	⟶	COUNTER-REFORMATION:
1. Functional specificity of church organization 2. Urban community		1. Guilds and equality 2. Church contribution to knowledge 3. Celibacy		1. Secular culture within church 2. Individualism		1. Value pluralization 2. Legitimacy of secular society

⟶ RISE OF STATE:	⟶ INDUSTRIAL AND DEMOCRATIC REVOLUTIONS:	⟶ MODERN AMERICA:
1. Landed aristocracies 2. Court centralization 3. Parliaments 4. Rationalism 5. Secular culture	1. Industrialization 2. Democratization	1. Republic 2. Educational revolution 3. Unions 4. High industrialization 5. Linguistic uniformity

Church disintegrates medieval unity	evolutionary change	modernization (i.e., industrial-democratic society)

⟶

digm of society and social evolution: a biologically based structure functionalism which is systemic, homeostatic, and evolutionary in content, utilizing the methods of historical and logical deduction, and applied to the evolution of modern Western society. His theory represents the nonidealistic elaboration of the earlier organic paradigm, is the foundation of American sociology, and raises a number of distinct issues, as follows:

1 The suitability of applying biological principles to society is open to severe questioning.

2 Viewing society as integrated and homeostatic deemphasizes problems of power and domination, leaving Parsons open to charges of elitism and conservatism.

3 Structure functionalism, while recently evolutionary, has tended to be static and nondevelopmental.

4 Parsons' notion of Western society as modern and other societies as less so raises the problem of ethnocentrism.

5 His method of historical matching may also be viewed as self-fulfilling, raising distinct problems of validity.

In general, then, Parsonian functionalism raises a broad range of problems relating to the biological analogy, homeostatic models, elitism, ethnocentrism, and methodological validity. Nevertheless, his paradigm represents the foundation of much of contemporary theory and is summarized as a whole in Figure 11.3.

We turn now to Buckley, a similar but more recent theorist.

Walter Buckley (1927)

Background   Buckley, born in 1927, was educated at Brown University (B.A., 1952) and the University of Wisconsin. He has pursued an academic career at various places, including the University of California at Santa Barbara. His primary intellectual interests focus on sociological theory, social stratification, and mobility. His publications include articles in the major journals as well as a book entitled *Sociology and Modern Systems Theory* (1967).

FIGURE 11.3
PARSONS' THEORETICAL FRAMEWORK SUMMARIZED

BACKGROUND:
1   Educated in biology, anthropological functionalism, and Weberian sociology
2   Experienced Depression, World Wars, industrialization
3   Academic career

AIMS:
Develop a general theory of society

ASSUMPTIONS:
1   The social system exists *sui generis*
2   Structure represents function
3   The social system consists of subsystems
4   Continuity with other living systems
5   Society is homeostatic
6   Society possesses the capacity for adaptive evolution
7   Christian culture is a prime mover in modernization

METHODOLOGY:
Historical deduction based on the biological analogy

TYPOLOGY:
Stages of modernization

ISSUES:
1   Application of the biological analogy
2   The homeostatic view of society
3   Static aspects of structure functionalism
4   View of Western society as modern
5   Problem of historical matching

Aims   One of Buckley's major aims has been to apply the perspective of modern systems theory to sociology in an attempt to develop a more dynamic conceptual framework of sociocultural reality. Viewing current theory as based too heavily on the mechanical and organic models of the past, Buckley attempted to utilize the *dynamics of information transmission*—the basis of the cybernetic approach—to develop a process-oriented view of social organization. As we shall see, this approach has certain features in common with general structure functionalism.

Assumptions

1   Buckley views the systems approach as focusing on the *"total emergent processes* as a function of possible positive and/or

198

negative *feedbacks* mediated by the *selective decisions,* or choices of the individuals and groups directly or indirectly involved."[13] According to this view, organization is a temporary state, dependent upon characteristics of information feedback and decision making at a particular point in time.

2 Applying this approach to sociology, Buckley divides society into two major parts: structure and process. The former consists of structure at two levels—the psychological and sociocultural.

3 The psychological system, according to Buckley, consists of four major components: (*a*) the biological individual, (*b*) environmental objects of interest to him or her, (*c*) another individual, and (*d*) communication and information exchanges, representing a complex adaptive system. These four elements as a system of interlinked components represent a dynamic, emergent communication system—the basis of social organization at the psychological level.

4 At the sociocultural level an attempt is made to reach an optimum level of stability and flexibility in order to adapt to the system's environment. There are five major elements in this adaptive process: (*a*) a source for the introduction of variety into the system; (*b*) maintenance of an optimum level of system tension and member satisfaction; (*c*) a two-way communication network with the environment for goal-attainment, comprising the system's major institutions (science, technology, magic, and religion); (*d*) a decision-making system; and (*e*) mechanisms for "propagating meanings, symbol systems, and information sets" (the internal socialization system). Within this structure, the higher the level, the greater the dependence on "communication" rather than "energy" linkage. Furthermore, social organization represents a temporary "constraint in the ensemble of possible interactions of social units," i.e., organization based on a particular set of decisions dependent upon particular information feedback at a particular point in time.

5 *Process* within the systems model consists of openness, information linkage, feedback loops, goal direction, and two main processes: (*a*) *morphostasis,* or form-preserving processes, and (*b*) *morphogenesis,* or "processes which tend toward elaboration

[13]W. Buckley, *Sociology and Modern Systems Theory,* Prentice-Hall, Englewood Cliffs, N.J., 1967, p. 80.

and/or system change." These processes are dependent upon elements in the adaptive process at the sociocultural level (i.e., variety, tension, institutions, etc.).

6 Finally, as examples of system dynamics, Buckley uses the processes of "negotiated order," the "resolution of role strain," and "role making."

To summarize, Buckley views social organization at the psychological and sociocultural level as based upon the process of information feedback and structured by the communication *systems* at these levels as well as the processes of morphostasis and morphogenesis. Like Parsons, he sees society as a system consisting of subsystems, structure and process, equilibrium and evolution; to Buckley, however, the underlying functions are cybernetic rather than biological.

Methodology   Buckley's method consists primarily of applying the principles of cybernetics and systems theory to an analysis of social organization—a process similar to Parsons' use of the biological analogy. Typical in structure functionalism, then, is the application of outside paradigms to the sociological analysis of social order.

The Typology   Buckley's typology is inherent in his systems model of society, discussed above, focusing on the information feedback loops between psychological and sociocultural systems and their environments that are influenced by the processes of morphostasis and morphogenesis. Accordingly, social organization at all levels of society represents a temporary set of decisions based upon information feedback at a particular point in time between subsystems and their environments. This typology is summarized in Figure 11.4.

Summary and Conclusions   Buckley represents a cybernetic type of structure functionalism. Applying systems theory to sociology, he views society as a set of psychological and sociocultural subsystems founded on the process of information feedback. These subsystems—representing dynamic, emergent communication systems—consist of structure and process, equilibrium and evolution, morphostasis and morphogenesis. They are adaptive and attempt to reach an optimum level of stability and flexibil-

FIGURE 11.4
BUCKLEY'S TYPOLOGY

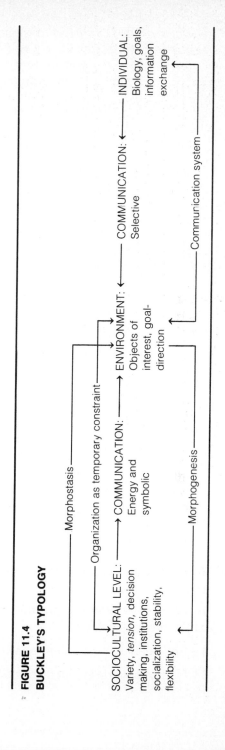

ity. Such a paradigm has obvious parallels with the work of Parsons: it emphasizes the biological individual, goal attainment, communication, adaptation, stability, institutions, socialization mechanisms, and system maintenance as well as evolution. The difference here, however, lies in the underlying functions being cybernetic rather than biological, while social organization is viewed as temporary and dynamic rather than static and stable.

Buckley's work also raises a number of issues:

1 The extent to which Buckley's theory is significantly different from Parsons' recent work is open to question.

2 The extent to which feedback loops make social theory significantly more dynamic is also problematic.

3 Macroscopic processes such as morphostasis and morphogenesis are somewhat unclear in definition and foundation.

4 Most of Buckley's examples of dynamics are microscopic in scope.

Despite such problems, systems theory is an important attempt to make contemporary theory more dynamic. Buckley's framework as a whole is summarized in Figure 11.5.

THE NATURALISTIC TYPE OF STRUCTURE FUNCTIONALISM SUMMARIZED

A number of basic similarities between the theories of Parsons and Buckley are evident:

1 Both attempt to develop a general theory of social organization.

2 Both view decision-making systems as central to such organization.

3 Both types of theory are systemic and divide the social system into subsystems.

4 Both view the individual as a biological organism.

5 Finally, both delineate a number of processes as central to the

FIGURE 11.5
BUCKLEY'S THEORETICAL FRAMEWORK SUMMARIZED

BACKGROUND:
1 Educated at Brown and Wisconsin
2 Academic career

AIMS:
Application of modern systems theory to sociology

ASSUMPTIONS:
1 Organization as temporary state dependent on information-feedback
2 Society as structure and process
3 The psychological system
4 The sociocultural system
5 Morphostasis and morphogenesis

METHODOLOGY:
Application of cybernetic principles to society

TYPOLOGY:
Systems model of society

ISSUES:
1 How different from Parsons
2 Dynamism of "feedback loops"
3 Unclear definitions
4 Microscopic illustrations

social system: goal attainment, adaptation, stability, institutions, socialization mechanisms, system maintenance, and evolution.

In general, this type of structure functionalism is macroscopic, systemic, and evolutionary, representing the attempt to develop a general theory of society in reference to underlying system needs. The main characteristics of this type of explanation are summarized in Figure 11.6. We shall then go on to consider the more systemic type of functionalism within contemporary theory.

THE SYSTEMIC TYPE OF STRUCTURE FUNCTIONALISM

This type of functionalism, while similar to the naturalistic in *form*—it is macroscopic, systemic, and evolutionary—differs in

203

FIGURE 11.6

THE STRUCTURE OF NATURALISTIC STRUCTURE FUNCTIONALISM

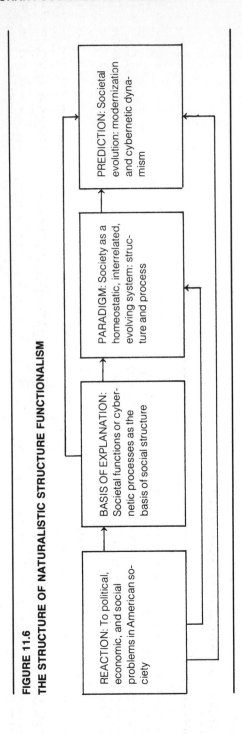

content in that the basis and types of functions in society are viewed as normative and internal to the individual rather than biological and external. In this section, we shall discuss two such theorists: Etzioni, who is concerned with a society's consensus-formation capacity, and Tiryakian, who takes a phenomenological view of social structure. Such approaches complement the more mechanistic paradigms of earlier functionalists.

Amitai Etzioni (1929)

Background Etzioni, born in 1929, was educated at Hebrew University and Berkeley, receiving his Ph.D. at the latter in 1958. His academic career has included chairmanship of the sociology department at Columbia University and membership of the Institute of War and Peace Studies there. His major publications include *A Comparative Analysis of Complex Organizations* (1961), *Political Unification* (1965), and *The Active Society* (1968). His intellectual interests center around social forecasting, futurism, sociological theory, and social change.

Aims The major aim of Etzioni's theory as applied to the "active society"[14] is the development of a *macrosociology*—study of the emergent properties of macroscopic (social) units which "account for a significant part of the variance of sociological data..."[15] in order to maximize "social goals." Here again, we have a macroscopic, systemic theory whose major aim is social control and social development.

Assumptions

1 Etzioni's initial assumption is that macroscopic units possess "emergent qualities" and "macroscopic consequences." Focus here is upon macroscopic phenomena as independent and explanatory.

2 These phenomena may be divided into units (e.g., roles), subunits (e.g., families), and supraunits (e.g., neighborhoods).

[14]A. Etzioni, *The Active Society,* Free Press, New York, 1968.
[15]A. Etzioni, "Toward a Macrosociology," in McKinney and Tiryakian, op. cit., p. 71.

The same structure may also be applied to societies, subsocieties, and suprasocieties.

3 *Relations* within the social system are of three kinds: *situations* (interunit relations), *systems* (unit interdependence), and *communities* (integrated units).

4 Of central importance in the system is the government, representing the "cybernatorial overlayer of society," providing the system with decision making communication, and feedback mechanisms. In viewing society in this fashion, Etzioni claims he is synthesizing voluntaristic theory—a central guidance system—and the cybernetic model in the form of a voluntaristic-cybernatorial theory of societal guidance.

5 Two major factors are central to this model of society: (*a*) *control*, the system's "cybernatorial capacities" (its knowledge input and decision-making structures) and "power" (assets and mobilization) and (*b*) its *consensus-formation capacity* (its internal consensus-formation structures).

6 Finally, using the two dimensions of control and consensus-formation, Etzioni produces a typology of societies in which the active type is high on both characteristics. Further macrosociological work will concentrate, according to the author, on outlining conditions which favor or block the rise of active societies.

To summarize, Etzioni attempts to develop a voluntaristic-cybernatorial theory of societal guidance by viewing government as society's "cybernatorial overlayer." This overlayer guides a system of units, subunits, and supraunits which are dependent upon its control and consensus-formation capacities. Such an approach is macroscopic, systemic, evolutionary, cybernetic, and structure-functional in its view of the social structure as having emergent qualities and being dependent upon external control and internal normative factors.

Methodology Etzioni essentially uses two major methods: (1) application of voluntaristic and cybernetic paradigms to societal development and (2) abstraction of a historical typology of societies based on these dimensions. The result is a dynamic, cybernetic theory of societal development that is dependent upon external and internal functions. Once again, structure-functional methods consist of the macroscopic application of other paradigms to societal evolution.

The Typology Etzioni develops a typology of societies on the basis of their positions on the two axes of control and consensus-formation capacity, as follows: (1) the "comparatively active" (high on both); (2) the "drifting society" (low on control but high on consensus); (3) the "overmanaged society" (high on control and low on consensus); and (4) the "passive society" (low on both). Such a model is summarized in Figure 11.7.

Summary and Conclusions In applying the assumptions of voluntarism and cybernetics to societal development, Etzioni develops a normatively based structure-functionalist theory of "societal guidance," relevant to the achievement of societal goals. Such an approach is similar to that of Parsons in its emphasis upon systems and subsystems, cybernetics, macroscopic emergency or evolution, external control, and internal normative integration. Etzioni's theory also raises similar issues as follows:

1 In its emphasis upon government and control as central, it runs the risk of being elitist-oriented.

2 Such an approach, accordingly, tends to underemphasize the problems of power and domination.

3 Application of the voluntaristic-cybernatorial approach is obscure and often highly generalized.

4 Finally, the development of abstract typologies and macroscopic theories of development raises the problems of relevance to public policy.

Despite such problems, Etzioni makes an important contribution to the development of a macrosociology. His framework as a whole is summarized in Figure 11.8. We shall then go on to the phenomenological type of functionalism developed by Tiryakian.

Edward Tiryakian (1929)

Background Tiryakian, educated at Princeton (B.A., 1952), and Harvard (1956), has pursued an academic career within sociology departments at Princeton, Harvard, and Duke universities. His intellectual interests have focused on the relationship between existentialism and sociology, the evolution and change of social systems, sociological theory, and ethnomethodology. Our

207

FIGURE 11.7
ETZIONI'S TYPOLOGY

CONSENSUS FORMATION

CONTROL

	High	Low
High	Comparatively active society	Drifting society
Low	Overmanaged society	Passive society

FIGURE 11.8

Etzioni's Theoretical Framework Summarized

BACKGROUND:
1 Educated at Hebrew and Berkeley
2 Academic career
3 Interests in social planning and change

AIMS:
The development of a macrosociology to maximize societal goals

ASSUMPTIONS:
1 Macroscopic units possess emergent qualities
2 Existence of units, subunits, and supraunits
3 Relations, situations, systems, and communities
4 Government as cybernatorial overlayer
5 Control and consensus-formation dimensions

METHODOLOGY:
Application of the voluntaristic-cybernatorial approach to societal development

TYPOLOGY:
Types of societies compared on control and consensus-formation functions

ISSUES:
1 Elitism problems
2 Underemphasis on power and domination problems
3 Obscurity of voluntaristic-cybernatorial approach
4 High level of abstraction

---

interest in him here relates to his development of a phenomenological type of structure functionalism.[16] His major publications include *Sociologism and Existentialism* (1962).

Aims Tiryakian attempts to develop a phenomenological theory
of social order in order to "uncover the fuller dimensions of the
cultural matrix of social reality . . ." and "make possible its relatively adequate control, so that progressive (that is, orderly) sociocultural change can be insured."[17] Once again, we are presented
with application of a nonsociological paradigm to societal evolution in order to maximize orderly social change.

[16]See especially E. A. Tiryakian, "Structural Sociology," in McKinney and Tiryakian, op. cit., pp. 11–135.
[17]Ibid., p. 135.

209

Assumptions

1   In contrast to the other functionalists, Tiryakian takes an internal, phenomenological view of social structures, treating them as "normative phenomena of intersubjective consciousness which frame social actions in social space."[18] Thus social structure is internal, existential, and normative, providing the basis for individual and group definitions of reality.

2   Social phenomena have a *"becoming* aspect . . ." and "are actualizations or manifestations from an existential ground of possibilities, and it is this ground which we refer to as social structure."[19] Social structure is thus dynamic and emergent rather than static.

3   Institutionalization or formalization represents the process by which social phenomena surface from the ground of possibilities, becoming visible and organized into social structure.

4   Furthermore, this ground of possibilities is divided into the realm of the *sacred* and the *secular,* which are ordered into an antithetical equilibrium—the basis of the social order.

5   Consequently, the social order emerges as "the regulation of the irrational, of the sacred"—the process of "social structuration."[20]

6   Finally, at the macroscopic level, culture represents a set of integrative symbols, dynamically influenced by the processes of structuration and destructuration as new elements surface from the ground of possibilities in society's movement from the sacred toward greater rationalization.

   To summarize, Tiryakian advocates a "structural sociology" —"a theoretical approach which is a macrodynamic analysis of societal systems, having as its starting point the analysis of the fundamental essences of a total society, located in its cultural framework, and which proceeds to consider the actualization of these possibilities."[21] Society is a cultural, symbolic, existential system within the individual, constantly shifting from the sacred to

[18]Ibid., p. 115.
[19]Ibid., p. 118.
[20]Ibid., p. 123.
[21]Ibid., p. 131.

the secular in antithetical equilibrium. It can be seen, once again, that such an approach is macroscopic, systemic, and evolutionary, while in this case the basis of society's underlying functions is phenomenological rather than biological or cybernetic. Tiryakian, in fact, states explicitly that "We see our approach as a renovation of structural-functional analysis."[22]

Methodology   As with other structure functionalists, Tiryakian's methodology consists of the application of a nonsociological paradigm, in this case phenomenology, to the problem of orderly social change, aided by historical induction. Consequently, he develops a theory which is macroscopic, systemic, equilibrium-oriented, and evolutionary.

The Typology   While Tiryakian does not develop a formal typology, one is implied in his differentiation between *sacred* and *secular* realms in society. The former are represented by religious beliefs and practices, while the latter consist of economic and political or goal-attainment activity. The former also contain "antithetical divine and demonic forces"[23] ordered into some kind of equilibrium within the social system. This system of forces, as we have stated, is subject to the influence of social structuration, moralization, and rationalization, all of which are contained within the boundaries of an integrative cultural system. Such a typological model of society is summarized in Figure 11.9.

Summary and Conclusions   Tiryakian conceptualizes society as a phenomenological system consisting of sacred and secular subsystems in antithetical equilibrium, integrated by culture and subject to the ongoing processes of structuration, destructuration, and rationalization. While his paradigm stands in contrast to those of other structure functionalists, it also raises a number of central issues:

1   Phenomenological concepts such as the *ground of possibilities, sacred, secular, structuration,* and *destructuration* are distinctly unclear in definition.

2   The societal contingencies underlying the operation of these phenomena are not clearly delineated.

[22]Ibid., p. 131.
[23]Ibid., p. 123.

211

FIGURE 11.9
TIRYAKIAN'S TYPOLOGY

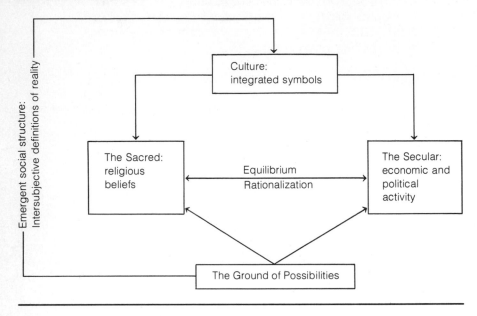

3 The characteristics of an antithetical equilibrium are also unclear.

4 Finally, the process of structuration and rationalization is likewise indistinct.

In short, while Tiryakian's paradigm is interesting, it requires further clarification. Nevertheless, it provides a useful contrast to the more formal and external types of traditional structure functionalism. The major characteristics of his framework are summarized in Figure 11.10.

THE SYSTEMIC TYPE OF STRUCTURE FUNCTIONALISM SUMMARIZED

This type of structure functionalism, as evident in the work of Etzioni and Tiryakian, consists of the following emphases:

1 The development of general theories of societal evolution in order to maximize orderly social change.

212

FIGURE 11.10
TIRYAKIAN'S THEORETICAL FRAMEWORK SUMMARIZED

BACKGROUND:
1   Educated at Princeton and Harvard
2   Academic career
3   Interests in social systems analysis

AIMS:
Develop a phenomenological theory of social order to ensure orderly sociocultural change

ASSUMPTIONS:
1   Phenomenal view of social structure
2   Social phenomena have "becoming" aspect
3   Institutionalization from ground of possibilities
4   Sacred and secular elements
5   Social order is regulation of the irrational
6   Culture is a set of integrative symbols

METHODOLOGY:
Application of phenomenology to the problem of orderly social change

TYPOLOGY:
Phenomenological model of social structure

ISSUES:
1   Clarity of concepts
2   Social contingencies are unclear
3   Antithetical equilibrium is unclear
4   Structuration processes are unclear

2   The application of nonsociological paradigms to societal evolution.

3   The division of society into system and subsystem.

4   A normative-phenomenological type of functionalism.

5   The assumption that the social system possesses emergent qualities.

6   The development of typologies of societal evolution.

This type of structure functionalism, then, is macroscopic, systemic, evolutionary, and normative. Its major characteristics are summarized in Figure 11.11. We shall then go on to outline the characteristics of structure-functional theory as a whole.   **213**

FIGURE 11.11

THE STRUCTURE OF SYSTEMIC STRUCTURE FUNCTIONALISM

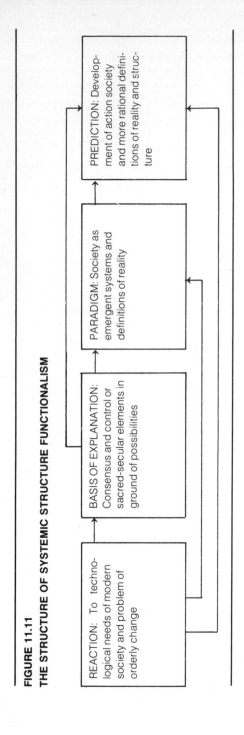

STRUCTURE-FUNCTIONAL THEORY SUMMARIZED

In this chapter we have attempted to show how structure functionalism represents a continuation of the earlier organic model in the form of the systemic reaction of establishment-oriented intellectuals to the political, economic, and social needs of contemporary society—in particular postwar, post-Depression, and contemporary social, economic, and technological problems. We also described the philosophical orientations of this intellectual elite as representing the application of nineteenth-century European thought in its emphasis upon natural laws, progressive social change, social reform, and the organic analogy to society within the context of a pragmatic, nonidealistic value system. The result is a view of society as a systemic, interrelated, evolving, equilibrium-oriented whole representing underlying system needs or functions.

Our examination of Parsons, Buckley, Etzioni, and Tiryakian has highlighted a number of similarities: except for Parsons, these theorists represent the early Depression–post-World War I generation; they received traditional educations in high-status institutions; they all pursued academic careers; and their intellectual interests have tended to focus on societal planning needs and large-scale social change. Their backgrounds, careers, and interests thus have much in common. Furthermore, their paradigms also have a number of similar elements, as follows:

Aims The attempt to develop a general theory of society in order to maximize societal goals and orderly social change.

Assumptions

1 Society possesses an independent existence.

2 Society or social structure is based on underlying system needs or functions.

3 Social structure consists of system and subsystem.

4 Society is equilibrium-oriented or homeostatic.

5 Society is adaptive toward its environment.

6 Society possesses emergent qualities.

7 Society is integrated through culture.

Methodology The application of nonsociological paradigms (e.g., the biological analogy, cybernetics, voluntarism, phenomenology) to the process of societal evolution.

Typologies Models of social structure and stages of societal evolution.

From the above it can be seen that structure functionalism represents a systemic, evolutionary, and homeostatic reaction to the needs of contemporary society developed by establishment-oriented intellectuals within the context of a pragmatic culture. The high level of correlation with the earlier organic model is clearly evident here, pointing to the continuity of sociological theory over time but modified by differing cultural contexts. Thus, while the kinds of functions in contemporary theory have come to vary, the form of the structure-functional argument remains substantially the same. The main elements of this approach are summarized in Figure 11.12. We shall then proceed to a discussion of modern conflict theory.

EXERCISES

Consider the following social trends:

a Increased bureaucratization in American society

b Increased voter participation in American society

c Increased plurality in American life-styles

d The women's liberation movement in American society

e The extent to which American society is more modern than many European societies

Account for each trend, using the general explanations provided by Parsons, Buckley, Etzioni, and Tiryakian. Compare in detail the different types of explanation you develop, using each theorist. To what extent are they similar? Can you develop an overall structure-functional explanation of each trend?

FIGURE 11.12
THE STRUCTURE OF STRUCTURE FUNCTIONALISM

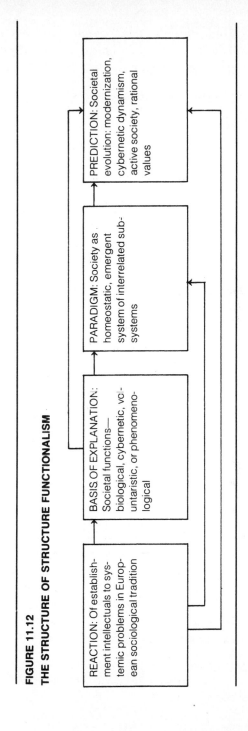

READINGS

General Works

Larson, C. J.: *Major Themes in Sociological Theory,* McKay, New York, 1973, chap. 5.
Martindale, D.: *The Nature and Types of Sociological Theory,* Houghton Mifflin, Boston, 1960, chaps. 17 and 18.
Timasheff, N. S.: *Sociological Theory, Its Nature and Growth,* 3d ed., Random House, New York, 1967, chaps. 17 and 18.
Turner, J. H.: *The Structure of Sociological Theory,* Dorsey, Homewood, Ill., 1974, chaps. 2 and 3.

Specific Works by Theorists

Parsons

Parsons, T.: *Societies: Evolutionary and Comparative Perspectives,* Prentice-Hall, Englewood Cliffs, N.J., 1966.
————: *The Social System,* Free Press, Glencoe, Ill., 1951.
————: *The Structure of Social Action,* McGraw-Hill, New York, 1937.
————: *The System of Modern Societies,* Prentice-Hall, Englewood Cliffs, N.J., 1971.

Buckley

Buckley, W.: *Sociology and Modern Systems Theory,* Prentice-Hall, Englewood Cliffs, N.J., 1967.

Etzioni

Etzioni, A.: *The Active Society,* Free Press, New York, 1968.
————: "Toward a Macrosociology," in J. C. McKinney and E. A. Tiryakian (eds.), *Theoretical Sociology, Perspectives and Developments,* Appleton Century Crofts, New York, 1970, pp. 69–98.

Tiryakian

Tiryakian, E. A.: "Existential Phenomenology and the Sociological Tradition," *American Sociological Review,* **30**:674–688, 1965.

————: "Structural Sociology," in J. C. McKinney and E. A. Tiryakian (eds.), *Theoretical Sociology, Perspectives and Developments,* Appleton Century Crofts, New York, 1970, pp. 111–135.

12

MODERN CONFLICT THEORY:

THE CONFLICT PARADIGM CONTINUED

While the foundation of contemporary theory in sociology is predominantly structure-functional in form, earlier European conflict theory—which is part of the establishment of American sociology too—has continued in reaction to contemporary class conflict and the negative effects of industrialization and bureaucratization within modern society. In this chapter, then, we shall deal with modern conflict theory[1] in the work of Ralf Dahrendorf, C. Wright Mills, Lewis Coser, and David Riesman. The former two represent the systemic type of conflict theory, the latter the more naturalistic type. Once again we shall describe the societal, intellectual, and biographical conditions under which this type of theory developed.

INTRODUCTION

Like earlier conflict theory, its contemporary counterpart represents the reaction of a particular group of intellectuals—in this case theorists familiar with European sociological thought—to a number of specific conditions. These conditions include high levels of social and racial conflict in the United States, the repressive effects of bureaucratization and industrialization, and the application of reformist orientations to the modern problems of industrialization and urbanization. The philosophical context of modern conflict theory, furthermore, represents the application of eighteenth-century idealism and progressivism to the problems of modern society, the elaboration of neo-Marxist ideas to deal with the complexity of modern social conflict, and the direct influence of European thought on modern class theory in the case of Dahrendorf. Consequently, modern conflict theory represents the application of the traditional conflict paradigm to the problems of contemporary society by an intellectual elite conversant with European thought.

This approach views society as *a systemic, evolving system of groups competing for resources and controlled by a dominant elite.* Various social and demographic conditions define the intensity, duration, and form of social conflict, while the social structure represents the type of domination present in the society at a particular stage of its evolution. Society represents underlying competition for resources, resulting in a particular form of coercion or domination. In other words, as in Marxian theory, superstructure or social structure represents substructure or a particular

---

[1]For purposes of this discussion, we are using the terms *modern conflict theory* and *radical sociology* as synonyms.

form of economic dominance (*structure* represents *domination*). Modern conflict theory applies this paradigm to modern society by delineating the social conditions that define conflict, the institutional structure of dominance, the effects of conflict, and its operation at the social-psychological level. To a large extent, it is neo-Marxist in foundation and systemic in form. Hence, it is similar to structure functionalism in form but strikingly different in ideological content.

Modern conflict theory may be divided into two major types: (1) the systemic, emphasizing social factors that define the operation of conflict, and (2) the naturalistic, describing the nonsocial and demographic context of conflict. In this regard, Dahrendorf and C. W. Mills represent the former, while Coser, in his dependence upon Simmel and the organic analogy,[2] and Riesman, in his emphasis upon demographic factors, illustrate the latter type. It should be emphasized, however, that such a classification is a matter of *degree* only, particularly in contemporary conflict theory in which purely naturalistic types of explanations are virtually absent. Differences here relate to the kinds of factors emphasized as primary in the understanding of social conflict.

To summarize, modern conflict theory represents the systemic reaction of intellectuals conversant with European conflict theory—from the perspective of eighteenth-century idealism and progressivism—to the problems of conflict and domination in contemporary industrialized society. The major consequence of these factors is a type of theory which is systemic, evolutionary, and conflict-oriented. This type of theorizing is summarized in Figure 12.1.

We turn first to examine the sociological type of modern conflict theory as evident in the works of Dahrendorf and Mills.

THE SYSTEMIC TYPE OF MODERN CONFLICT THEORY

Dahrendorf and Mills outline the social causes and structure of conflict within modern industrial society. The former is particularly concerned with the specific conditions under which class conflict emerges, while Mills is well known for his portrait of America's power elite and the white-collar classes. Both are useful examples of modern conflict theorists.

---

[2]See, for example, J. H. Turner, *The Structure of Sociological Theory*, Dorsey, Homewood, Ill., 1974, p. 108.

FIGURE 12.1

MAJOR FACTORS BEHIND MODERN CONFLICT THEORY

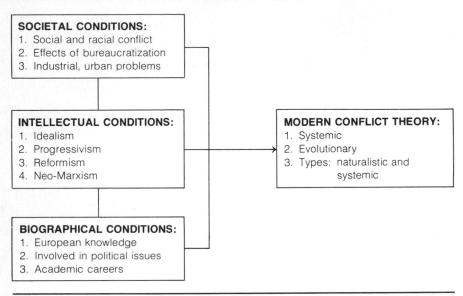

SOCIETAL CONDITIONS:
1. Social and racial conflict
2. Effects of bureaucratization
3. Industrial, urban problems

INTELLECTUAL CONDITIONS:
1. Idealism
2. Progressivism
3. Reformism
4. Neo-Marxism

BIOGRAPHICAL CONDITIONS:
1. European knowledge
2. Involved in political issues
3. Academic careers

MODERN CONFLICT THEORY:
1. Systemic
2. Evolutionary
3. Types: naturalistic and systemic

Ralf Dahrendorf (1929)

Background   Dahrendorf was educated at the University of Hamburg (D.Phil., 1952) and London University (Ph.D., 1956). During his distinguished academic career he has held sociology chairs at a number of German universities and has worked at the London School of Economics (1952–1954) and Stanford University (1957–1958). His major publication in English is *Class and Class Conflict in Industrial Society* (1959), which reflects his contact with David Lockwood, Reinhard Bendix, and Seymour Lipset.

Aims   In his major work, *Class and Class Conflict in Industrial Society,*[3] Dahrendorf is concerned with "the puzzling fact that social structures . . . are capable of producing within themselves the elements of their supersession and change."[4] Accordingly, he attempts to show how the groups and processes involved in this

[3]R. Dahrendorf, *Class and Class Conflict in Industrial Society,* Stanford University Press, Stanford, Calif., 1959.
[4]Ibid., p. viii.

phenomenon "can be identified theoretically and analyzed empirically."[5] This theorist attempts to state a general theory of class conflict and social change, using coercion theory.

Assumptions

1 Dahrendorf bases his approach on the coercion theory of society, which assumes ubiquitous (i.e., general) social change, social conflict, coercion, and the contribution of each element in society to "its disintegration and change."[6] Such assumptions are basic to the conflict paradigm of society.

2 Accepting this model of societal reality, he proceeds to the assumption that associations are imperatively coordinated (i.e., their members are subject to authority relations) and are structured by two aggregates of positions—domination and subjection.[7]

3 Further, each aggregate possesses common latent interests (i.e., unconscious orientations inherent in particular social positions) which represent the basis of quasi-groups—unorganized groups whose members share common latent interests.[8]

4 These latent interests may become articulated into manifest interests (i.e., conscious orientations which oppose the interests of other associations), and these quasi-groups may then become social classes (associations sharing manifest or latent interests related to the "authority structure of imperatively coordinated associations").[9]

5 Such articulation is dependent upon the presence of a number of particular factors or "conditions of organization": technical conditions (personnel, charter), political conditions (freedom of coalition), social conditions (communication, patterned recruitment), and psychological conditions (internalization of role interests).[10]

6 Should these conditions be present, the intensity of consequent class conflict depends on the extent to which these conditions

[5]Ibid., p. viii.
[6]Ibid., p. 162.
[7]Ibid., pp. 237–238.
[8]Ibid., pp. 237–238.
[9]Ibid., pp. 238–239.
[10]Ibid., p. 239.

exist, the extent to which group and class conflicts are superimposed, the distribution of authority and rewards, and the openness of the class system.[11]

7 Finally, the violence of class conflict depends on the extent to which the above conditions are present, the extent to which absolute deprivation gives way to relative deprivation, and the extent to which the conflict is effectively regulated.[12]

To summarize, Dahrendorf, accepting the coercion view of society, views its subgroups as imperatively coordinate and structured by underlying latent interests. Under certain social conditions, these become articulated into "manifest interests" and class conflict ensues. Both the intensity and violence of this conflict are dependent upon certain situational conditions. Society is viewed as a set of competing, imperatively coordinated associations, and as structured by underlying interests and surrounding social conditions. Thus society is provided with a source of continuous dynamism and social change. Such an approach is an important synthesis of Marx and Weber in the attempt to deal with conflict and social change in modern industrial society.

Methodology Dahrendorf proceeds by examining Marx's theory of class; he critiques it and attempts to deal with its problems by examining industrial and political conflict within modern industrial society. In developing his own theory of class conflict, he also uses Weber's concepts of *authority* and *imperatively coordinated associations*. Dahrendorf's methods may thus be viewed as an application and elaboration of Marx and Weber to class conflict within modern industrial society. The application of earlier paradigms to the analysis of a specific situation is typical of this kind of theory.

The Typology Dahrendorf's typology is inherent within his theory of social class and class conflict. Such a model, as discussed above, delineates a number of major elements within the coercion perspective, the class structure, underlying interests, and the conditions defining the articulation of class conflict as well as its level of intensity and violence. This is summarized in Figure 12.2, which outlines Dahrendorf's conflict paradigm of society and social change.

---

[11]Ibid., p. 239.
[12]Ibid.

FIGURE 12.2
DAHRENDORF'S TYPOLOGY

Summary and Conclusions Dahrendorf, reacting within the tradition of coercion theory to the problem of conflict in modern industrial society, applied an important synthesis of Marx and Weber to account for the emergence and evolution of class conflict. Viewing society as a set of competing associations which are imperatively coordinated and structured by underlying and opposing latent interests, he explains the articulation of these interests into class conflict in terms of certain conditions of organization, the intensity and violence of which are dependent upon the situational context. Such an approach is systemic and dynamic, viewing the basis and evolution of class conflict from the perspective of coercion theory. As a major conflict theory of society and class conflict, Dahrendorf's approach raises a number of issues, as follows:

1 His definition of major concepts relating to class and class conflict is unusually clear.

2 His synthesis of Marx and Weber is an important link between conflict and social-behaviorist theory, while it also deals with the issue of the extent to which these two theorists are in fact opposite types.

3 His theory attempts to account for the nonemergence as well

227

as the emergence of class conflict—an important elaboration of Marx that attempts to deal with the complexity of conflict in industrial society.

4 Finally, by his own admission, Dahrendorf's theory is temporary and incomplete, requiring further application and elaboration.

In general, Dahrendorf is one of the most important of contemporary conflict theorists, contributing one of the most sophisticated theories to date. His framework as a whole is summarized in Figure 12.3. We now turn to C. Wright Mills, an American conflict theorist.

C. Wright Mills (1916–1962)

Background   Mills obtained his Ph.D. at the University of Wisconsin in 1941, working with Hans Gerth—a German sociologist—and Howard Becker. He translated some of Weber's basic works with Gerth (*From Max Weber*, 1946), and from 1946 onward was a professor of sociology at Columbia University. His knowledge of European sociology was great and his interests and perspectives were in the conflict and radical tradition. He is well known for his critical analysis of capitalistic American society. His major works include *White Collar* (1951), *The Power Elite* (1956) and *The Sociological Imagination* (1959).

Aims   Mills was centrally concerned with the development of what he termed "the sociological imagination"—understanding of "the larger historical scene in terms of its meaning for the inner life and the external career of a variety of individuals."[13] The consequences of this type of understanding include involvement with public issues, greater awareness of the relationship between history and biography, awareness of the idea of social structure, and an orderly understanding of men and societies.[14] Furthermore, it asks three kinds of questions: (1): "What is the structure of this particular society as a whole?"; (2) "Where does this society stand in human society?"; and (3) "What varieties of men and women now prevail in this society and in this period?"[15] Finally, a major focus of this approach is on the "comparative understanding of social

[13]C. W. Mills, *The Sociological Imagination,* Grove Press, New York, 1961, p. 5.
[14]Ibid., chaps. 1, 7.
[15]Ibid., pp. 6–7.

FIGURE 12.3

DAHRENDORF'S THEORETICAL FRAMEWORK SUMMARIZED

BACKGROUND:
1 Educated at Hamburg and London
2 International academic career
3 Interests in class analysis

AIMS:
Develop a general theory of class conflict and social change

ASSUMPTIONS:
1 Coercion theory of society
2 Associations are imperatively coordinated
3 Each aggregate possesses common latent interests
4 Latent interests may be articulated into manifest interests under certain conditions
5 Articulation depends on conditions of organization
6 Intensity and violence of resulting class conflict depends on social conditions

METHODOLOGY:
Application of Marx and Weber to class conflict in industrial society

TYPOLOGY:
Model of class and class conflict

ISSUES:
1 Clarity of concepts
2 Synthesis of Marx and Weber
3 Theory of nonemergence and emergence
4 Temporary and incomplete

structures that have appeared and do now exist in world history."[16]
In his own work Mills attempted to use this perspective in the socio-
logical understanding of power and stratification in contemporary
American society in order to "grasp what is going on in the world."[17]
His focus, then, was practical as well as theoretical.

Assumptions   Mills made a number of major assumptions concerning the nature of social reality and the sociological effects of
industrial capitalism:

1   Social reality in Mills's view represents a combination of biography, history, and their "intersections within social structures."[18]

[16]Ibid., p. 134.
[17]Ibid., p. 7.
[18]Ibid., p. 143.

229

Such reality is both macroscopic *and* microscopic, for it is "In the welter of the individual's daily experience (that) the framework of modern society must be sought . . . ."[19]

2 Mills accepted the Weberian notion that industrialization results in increased societal rationality; however, the effects of this rationality are more negative than positive, as we shall see.

3 A major effect of rationalization is an increase in centralization and consequent elitism. In his work *The Power Elite,*[20] Mills describes this elite as consisting of the top executive layer of big business, the political order, and the military establishment. Members of this elite possess certain similar characteristics: similar social origins, interchangeable roles, and the ability to operate in secret. They also possess high prestige and self-confidence, deny their power, and destroy and create "lesser" institutions between which they develop increasing interdependence. Furthermore, society, under their control, has assumed a particular form: (a) the elite, (b) middle levels of power—a semiorganized stalemate, and (c) a mass society at the bottom levels, representing a well-controlled media market.[21] The consequences of increased rationality consist of high levels of institutional centralization and elitist control, i.e., institutionalized domination.

4 Rationalization also affects the occupational structure: individual entrepreneurs decline sharply, while the percentage of dependent employees increases markedly.[22] This, in turn, has made for the "decline of the independent individual and the rise of the little man in the American mind."[23] In this manner, increased control applies to all levels of the social structure.

5 The consequences of these processes at the individual level consist of a decline in freedom and an increase in alienation in which the middle class is particularly subject to uneasiness, alienation from work and self, is deprived of individual rationality, and is politically apathetic as a result.[24] Rationalization thus results in psychological as well as institutional control, the result of which is the decline of freedom on all levels of society.

[19]C. W. Mills, *White Collar, The American Middle Classes,* Oxford University Press, New York, 1956, p. xx.
[20]C. W. Mills, *The Power Elite,* Oxford University Press, New York, 1956.
[21]Ibid., chap. 1.
[22]Mills, *White Collar*, p. xii.
[23]Ibid.
[24]Ibid., p. xviii.

To summarize, Mills viewed industrial capitalism as leading to increased societal rationalization. The major effects of this on society are as follows: at the institutional level, there is increased elitism and centralization; at the occupational level, a decline in entrepreneurs and an increase in dependent employees; and on the individual level, there is a decline in freedom and a corollary increase in alienation. Consequently capitalistic domination affects all parts of the social system.

Methodology   Mills advocated the methods of the "classic craftsman" as central to the "sociological imagination." This involves a high level of historical awareness, flexibility, clarity of conception, simultaneous deduction-induction, a synthesis of theory and research, attempted comparative understanding of social structures, and a focus on individual experiences as a reflection of societal characteristics. In short, this method consists of a sensitive, flexible, and creative attempt to "grasp history and biography and the relations between the two in society."[25] It is unbound by time, empirical constraints, or levels of analysis. Mills's works are case studies in the use of this method as he employs a wide variety of historical and empirical data in the sociological portrayal of the power elite and the middle class in America.[26]

The Typology   Mills's delineation of types of social structure is implicit in the discussion above: capitalistic structures are high on rationality, centralization, elitism, a dependent-employee occupational structure, and alienation, and they are low on freedom and entrepreneurship. Noncapitalistic, nonindustrial societies, on the other hand, tend to lack these characteristics. Such a typology is reminiscent of the views of earlier theorists such as Marx, Weber, Spencer, Tönnies, and Durkheim. An important sociological model of the effects of modern capitalism, it is summarized in Figure 12.4.

Summary and Conclusions   Using earlier ideas generated by Marx and Weber, Mills developed a coercion-oriented analysis of modern capitalistic America in which the effects of increased rationality—the major product of industrialization—involve a con-

---

[25]Mills, *The Sociological Imagination*, p. 6.
[26]For further details of Mills's methods, see his essay "On Intellectual Craftsmanship," in *The Sociological Imagination*, pp. 195–226.

FIGURE 12.4
MILLS'S TYPOLOGY

TYPE OF SOCIETY	NONCAPITALISTIC	CAPITALISTIC
DIMENSIONS:		
Economy	Nonindustrial	Industrial
Organization	Low rationalization	High rationalization
Centralization	Low	High
Elitism	Low	High
Occupational structure	Entrepreneurial	Dependent employee
Freedom	High	Low
Alienation	Low	High

sequent increase in centralization, elitism, employee roles, control, and individual alienation. We are presented with a major conflict-oriented portrait of American society, representing a valuable extension of the earlier work of Marx and Weber. Such a theory, nevertheless, raises a number of issues:

1 To what extent, for example, are his data impressive, nonsystematic, and descriptive, resulting in simplistic conclusions?
2 To some, his approach may be viewed primarily as projections of his personal ideology rather than objective sociology.
3 He emphasized the overwhelmingly negative consequences of rationalization to the exclusion of any positive functions.
4 Finally, his methods may be viewed as too informal to be considered scientific.

Despite such criticisms, Mills remains a major conflict theorist in contemporary sociology, providing the stimulus for a certain type of sociology.[27] Figure 12.5 sums up his contribution.

THE SYSTEMIC TYPE OF MODERN CONFLICT THEORY SUMMARIZED

It is clear from the above that a number of common characteristics can be seen in Dahrendorf and Mills:

1 Both were influenced by European sociology, particularly the work of Marx and Weber.

[27]See, for example, I. L. Horowitz (ed.), *The New Sociology*, Oxford University Press, New York, 1964.

FIGURE 12.5
MILLS'S THEORETICAL FRAMEWORK SUMMARIZED

BACKGROUND:
1 Educated at Wisconsin
2 Familiar with Weber
3 Academic and radical career

AIMS:
Application of the sociological imagination to an understanding of social structure

ASSUMPTIONS:
1 Social reality is a combination of biography and history
2 Industrialization results in increased rationality
3 Rationalization increases centralization and elitism
4 Rationalization increases the percentage of dependent employees
5 Rationalization reduces freedom and increases alienation

METHODOLOGY:
Application of classic craftsmanship

TYPOLOGY:
Types of social structure

ISSUES:
1 Simplistic conclusions
2 Problem of subjectivity
3 General negativism
4 Informal methods

---

2 Both were concerned with understanding conflict and domination within modern industrial society.

3 Both adhered to the coercion theory of society.

4 Both viewed power and domination as central to the social structure.

5 Both used the method of historical induction.

6 Both applied a synthesis of Marx and Weber to the analysis of conflict and domination.

7 Both outlined types of social structures.

This kind of modern conflict theory is concerned with the social conditions under which such conflict emerges and the sociological characteristics of domination at its various stages of development. Such an approach represents a major attempt to develop a dynamic analysis of contemporary conflict and domination in the earlier European tradition. Its major features as a type of explanation are summarized in Figure 12.6. We shall then turn to the more naturalistic variant of this theory.

THE NATURALISTIC TYPE OF MODERN CONFLICT THEORY

We turn now to consider the type of conflict theory developed by Coser and Riesman. The former is concerned with the functions of conflict that lead to greater societal adaptation; he bases his work on earlier propositions developed by Simmel. In these respects, his approach may be viewed as naturalistic to the extent that it is based on the organic analogy and Simmel. Riesman may also be classified as naturalistic insofar as he views social conflict, domination, and change as functions of changing demographic factors, in particular population trends. In both cases, however, the naturalistic argument is utilized to a lesser extent than in traditional theory. We turn to examine these views as important examples of modern conflict theory in the naturalistic vein.

Lewis Coser (1913)

Background Coser, born in Germany, received his doctorate from Columbia University in 1954 and has pursued a distinguished academic career. At present he is professor of sociology at the State University of New York, Stony Brook. A former student of Robert Merton, his intellectual interests have focused on sociological theory, knowledge, and science. His major publications include *The Functions of Social Conflict* (1956), *Continuities in the Study of Social Conflict* (1967), and *Masters of Sociological Thought* (1971). In our discussion here we are specifically concerned with his theoretical work on conflict.

Aims In his work on conflict, Coser aims to "clarify and to consolidate conceptual schemes which are pertinent to data of social conflict," focusing on the "functions, rather than the dysfunctions, of social conflict . . . with those consequences of social conflict

234

FIGURE 12.6

THE STRUCTURE OF SYSTEMIC MODERN CONFLICT THEORY

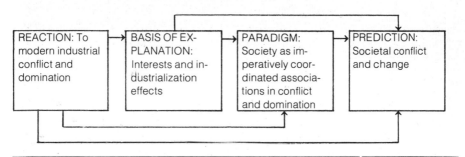

| REACTION: To modern industrial conflict and domination | → | BASIS OF EX-PLANATION: Interests and in-dustrialization effects | → | PARADIGM: Society as im-peratively coor-dinated associa-tions in conflict and domination | → | PREDICTION: Societal conflict and change |

which make for an increase rather than a decrease in the adaptation or adjustment of particular social relationships or groups."[28] Conflict for Coser is "a struggle over values and claims to scarce status, power and resources in which the aims of the opponents are to neutralize, injure or eliminate their rivals."[29]

Assumptions

1 Coser's initial assumption is that conflict may increase rather than decrease social adjustment, adaptation, and the maintenance of group boundaries; i.e., conflict is functional as well as dysfunctional.[30] He then proceeds to delineate the source, situational contingencies, and possible functions of conflict.

2 Conflict arises, according to Coser, when "there exists an excess of claimants over opportunities for adequate reward. . . ."[31] Its consequences are then defined by the type of social structure within which it occurs and the types of issues concerned, all of which influence the functions of this process within the general society.

3 Social structures vary in patterns of social mobility,[32] the existence of safety-valve institutions, the institutionalization and tolerance of conflict, the degree to which groups are close-linked, the

[28]L. A. Coser, *The Functions of Social Conflict*, Free Press, Chicago, 1956, pp. 7–8.
[29]Ibid., p. 8.
[30]Ibid., p. 8.
[31]L. A. Coser, *Continuities in the Study of Social Conflict*, Free Press, New York, 1967, p. 27.
[32]Ibid., p. 26.

level of group participation, and the length of conflict.[33] Thus *the more closed the stratification system, the fewer the safety-valve institutions, the lower the institutionalization and tolerance of conflict, the more close-knit the groups, the higher the group participation, and the longer the group struggle, the more intense and disruptive will be social conflict within the society*.

4   The types of issues over which conflict takes place are also a major factor in its effects: issues which concern societal legitimacy and involve disagreement over basic assumptions tend to result in high levels of conflict. Furthermore, issues may be *realistic* (i.e., the frustration of *specific* demands) or *nonrealistic* (issues involving a need for general "tension release.").[34] The latter type result in more intense conflict.

5   Finally, a positive combination of the above factors may result in conflict being functional for the social system as follows: it may stabilize relationships, revitalize existing norms, contribute to the emergence of new norms, provide a mechanism for the continual readjustment of the balance of power, develop new associations and coalitions, decrease social isolation, and contribute to the maintenance of group boundary lines.[35] In general, then, under particular conditions, conflict may result in a more stable, flexible, and integrated social system.

To summarize, conflict over realistic issues within an open social structure may contribute to the structure's greater adaptation, flexibility, and integration, while nonrealistic conflict in a closed and inflexible environment will lead to violence and disintegration. Whatever the case the functions of social conflict within society are the central focus of this type of theory.

Methodology   Coser's method consists of distilling basic propositions from social conflict theories, in particular Simmel's, and extending them by relating them to "other findings of a theoretical or empirical nature."[36] As is somewhat typical of conflict theorists, Coser extends and applies the perspectives of earlier theorists to the study of contemporary social conflict.

[33]Coser, *The Functions of Social Conflict*, chap. IX.
[34]Ibid.
[35]Ibid.
[36]Ibid., p. 8.

FIGURE 12.7
COSER'S TYPOLOGY

TYPE OF SOCIETY	"CLOSED"	"OPEN"
DIMENSIONS:		
Stratification system	Closed	Open
Safety-value institutions	No	Yes
Institutionalization of conflict	No	Yes
Tolerance of conflict	No	Yes
Group types	Close-knit	Loosely structured
Group participation	High	Low
Functions of conflict	Disintegrative	Integrative

The Typology A particular typology is evident in our discussion of Coser's work: that of an open, flexible social structure, on the one hand, in which realistic conflict leads to greater flexibility and integration, and a closed, rigid society, on the other, in which nonrealistic conflict results in violence and disintegration. This typology of the situational conditions and effects of social conflict is summarized in Figure 12.7. Such an approach is an important example of modern conflict theory in which the work of earlier thinkers is elaborated to deal with the complexity of conflict in modern society. Coser's organismic analogy also provides an important conceptual link with structure functionalism.

Summary and Conclusions In assuming that social conflict may have functional consequences, Coser proceeds to describe the sociological conditions under which particular effects of conflict may emerge—the open, realistic, situation on the one hand and the closed, rigid, and unrealistic one on the other. Such an attempt to develop a theory which specifies the conditions and effects of this dynamic process in contemporary society is a major contribution to modern sociological theory. Nevertheless, his work raises certain issues, as follows:

1 While he attempts to compensate for the one-sidedness of structure functionalism, Coser may be accused of falling into the same trap by viewing conflict as "adaptive" and "integrative."[37]

[37]For further discussion of this, see Turner, *The Structure of Sociological Theory*, pp. 108–109.

2 His delineation of the source of social conflict may be viewed as too simplistic.

3 His propositions may be viewed as too general and macroscopic to be relevant to the understanding of specific situations.

4 Finally, his theory may be viewed ultimately as closer to structure functionalism than to conflict theory, thereby contributing little to the latter.

Despite the above criticisms, Coser's work may be considered an important contribution to modern conflict theory, complementing the approach of Dahrendorf and Mills; his approach as a whole is summarized in Figure 12.8.

David Riesman (1909)

Background   Riesman was educated at Harvard, where he completed his A.B., in 1931. His academic career has included a professorship in law at the University of Buffalo from 1937 to 1942; he then served as professor of social sciences at the University of Chicago and has held the same position at Harvard since 1958. His intellectual interests include the sociology of education and the study of social character. His major publications include *The Lonely Crowd* (1950) and *Individualism Reconsidered* (1954). Our interest in him relates to his description of social character, social conflict, and changing patterns of social conformity as dependent upon demographic change; these are discussed in *The Lonely Crowd*.[38] Of particular relevance here is his delineation of demographic change as the foundation of social conflict, thereby making a contribution to the naturalistic version of modern conflict theory.

Aims   Riesman is primarily concerned with "the way in which one kind of social character which dominated America in the nineteenth century, is gradually being replaced by a social character of quite a different sort."[39] Social change in the society's predominant type of social character is thus his central concern.

---

[38]We have used the following edition: D. Riesman, *The Lonely Crowd,* Yale University Press, New Haven, Conn., 1961.
[39]Ibid., p. 3.

FIGURE 12.8
COSER'S THEORETICAL FARMEWORK SUMMARIZED

BACKGROUND:
1 Educated at Columbia
2 Familiar with Simmel
3 Academic career

AIMS:
Analyze functions of social conflict

ASSUMPTIONS:
1 Conflict may increase social adjustment
2 Conflict originates in claimants/rewards ratio
3 Social structures may be open or closed
4 The types of issues concerned influence conflict
5 Conflict may be functional for the social system

METHODOLOGY:
Application and elaboration of Simmel in analysis of conflict

TYPOLOGY:
Types of social structures

ISSUES:
1 Relationship to structure functionalism
2 Simplistic source of conflict
3 General and macroscopic propositions
4 Low contribution to conflict theory

Assumptions

1 To begin with, Riesman defines *social character* as "that part of 'character' which is shared among significant social groups and . . . is the product of the experience of these groups."[40]

2 The link between this character and society "is to be found in the way in which society ensures some degree of conformity from the individuals who make it up."[41] Thus social character represents normative conformity.

3 These modes of conformity, in turn, are dependent upon particular demographic factors or "certain population shifts in Western society since the Middle Ages."[42] These shifts, according to

[40]Ibid., p. 4.
[41]Ibid., p. 5.
[42]Ibid., p. 7.

Riesman, have taken the form of the S-shape.[43] The bottom horizontal line of this S represents traditional societies in which births and deaths are almost equal—societies in the phase of high growth potential. When this potential actualizes, transitional growth occurs—represented by the vertical bar of the S—during which the birthrate is higher than the death rate. This growth rate slows down, however, in the third state of incipient population decline—represented by the top horizontal bar of the S—in which births and deaths are low.

4 Having delineated this S-shaped growth curve, Riesman states his major thesis: "that each of these three different phases on the population curve appears to be occupied by a society that enforces conformity and molds social character in a definably different way."[44] The author describes the relationship between character and societal type as follows: *tradition-directed* people are typical of the society of high growth potential, *inner-directed* types are part of transitional growth, while *other-directed* people predominate in the society of incipient population decline. The first type is characterized by traditional inherited behavior defined by kinship; the second is guided by internalized goals but not necessarily the means; while other-directed individuals are unsure of basic values and are oriented toward peer-group standards. The first type predominated in primitive societies and the European Middle Ages, the second during the Victorian era, and the third predominates in contemporary metropolitan America.

5 The causal nexus of this model of social change is located within the interactive relationship between population and social structure; i.e., as shifts in the former occur, in particular the birth-death ratio, society evolves new forms of conformity to ensure continuation of need satisfaction. Accordingly, social conflict and changing forms of conformity and domination are a function of changing population factors. Societies of transitional growth, for example, are likely to be "violent, disrupting the stabilized paths of existence in societies in which tradition-direction has been the principal mode of insuring conformity. The imbalance of births and deaths puts pressure on the society's customary ways. A new slate of character structures is called for . . . ."[45] Thus social conflict and domination are dependent upon the society's birth-death ratio,

[43]Ibid.
[44]Ibid., p. 8.
[45]Ibid., p. 14.

representing particular demographic pressures which result in particular forms of social structure and types of domination or conformity.

To summarize, Riesman perceives social structure, represented in the notion of *social character*, as dependent upon a society's birth-death ratio beginning with the society of high growth potential and *tradition-directed* types, moving through transitional-growth societies with *inner-directed* types, and finally leading to societies of incipient population decline, in which the other-directed type predominates. In this manner, social conflict and types of conformity or domination are defined by a society's underlying demographic structure.

Methods   Riesman's technique involves the application of demographic and economic theories of growth to social change and types of social structure or conformity,[46] using historical induction. Here again, methodology involves the application of other frameworks to the problem of social conflict and change.

The Typology   Riesman's model of "groups of social conformity" is overt: the tradition-directed individual is typical of high-growth-potential, kinship-based, nonprogressive, homogeneous, traditional societies; inner-directed types predominate in transitional-growth, expanding, fluid, dynamic societies; while other-directed individuals are typical of societies characterized by population decline, urbanization, bureaucratization, increased group contact, and the "new" middle classes. This model is summarized in Figure 12.9.

Summary and Conclusions   In accounting for social conflict and change inherent in varying social character types, Riesman perceives these phenomena as dependent upon a society's birth-death ratio, moving from the society of high-growth potential and tradition-directed types, through transitional-growth societies with inner-directed types, to contemporary societies of incipient population decline in which the other-directed personality represents the predominant conformity mode. Thus social conflict and types of domination are defined by a society's underlying demographic structure and consequent type of social structure. Such an approach clearly raises a number of issues:

[46]Ibid., pp. 7 and 9.

FIGURE 12.9
RIESMAN'S TYPOLOGY

TYPES OF SOCIAL CONFORMITY	TRADITION-DIRECTED	INNER-DIRECTED	OTHER-DIRECTED
FACTORS:			
Demographic	High growth potential	Traditional growth	Incipient population decline
Economic	Stable person-land ratio	Colonial expansion	Industrialization and urbanization
Socialization	Imitation in fixed social order	Inner implanted by elders	Peer group standards
Sanctions	Anxiety felt in deviants	Guilt if cannot conform	Shame-fear of isolation
Examples	Primitive societies, European Middle Ages	Victorian era	Metropolitan middle classes in United States, Australia, New Zealand

FIGURE 12.10
RIESMAN'S THEORETICAL FRAMEWORK SUMMARIZED

BACKGROUND:
1 Educated at Harvard
2 Law and academic careers
3 Interests in education and social character

AIMS:
Analyze changes in social character in the United States

ASSUMPTIONS:
1 Social character is shared among significant social groups
2 Social character represents modes of social conformity
3 Social character is dependent upon the society's birth-death ratio—the "S" curve
4 The tradition-directed, inner-directed, and other-directed types are based on the "S" curve
5 Social change is a function of demographic change

METHODOLOGY:
Application of demographic and economic theories of growth to social conflict and change

TYPOLOGY:
Types of social conformity

ISSUES:
1 Unclear demographic-societal relationship
2 Broad types of social character
3 Lack of data base
4 Link with structure functionalism

1   The interactive relationship between demographic and societal factors is general and unclear.

2   Riesman's types of social character are macroscopic and very broad, making it difficult to apply them to specific situations.

3   Controversy exists concerning both the accuracy and actual existence of his types, in particular the other-directed personality.[47]

4   Finally, Riesman's approach, like Coser's, bears a strong resemblance to structure functionalism in its implicit emphasis upon adaptive societal evolution. Its utility as a conflict theory is thus limited.

Despite the above problems, Riesman's theory remains a major analysis of social conflict, evolution, and contemporary culture; it is summarized as a whole in Figure 12.10.

THE NATURALISTIC TYPE OF
MODERN CONFLICT THEORY SUMMARIZED

In taking a more organismic or naturalistic approach to the analysis of social conflict and change, Coser and Reisman reveal a number of similarities; they both:

1.   Analyze the relationship between societal structure and the types of conflict and domination within it

2   View conflict as functional to the processes of social evolution and change

3   View conflict as a function of the societal-environmental relationship

4   Delineate types of social structure

5   Apply other frameworks to the analysis of social conflict.

This type of modern conflict theory, then, is macroscopic, organismic, evolutionary, and structural. Its major characteristics are summarized in Figure 12.11. We shall then consider the characteristics of modern conflict theory as a whole.

---

[47]See, for example, F. J. Greenstein, "New Light on Changing American Values: A Forgotten Body of Survey Data," *Social Forces,* **43,** 1964, pp. 441–450.

FIGURE 12.11
THE STRUCTURE OF NATURALISTIC MODERN CONFLICT THEORY

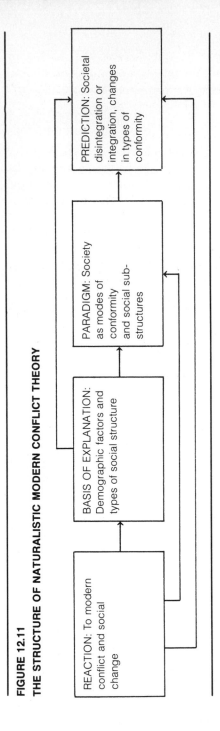

MODERN CONFLICT THEORY SUMMARIZED

In this chapter we defined modern conflict theory as the reaction of a group of intellectuals familiar with European sociological thought to the high levels of social and racial conflict in the United States, the repressive effects of bureaucratization and industrialization, and the application of reformist orientations to the modern problems of industrialization and urbanization. The result was a view of society as a systemic, evolving system of groups competing for resources and controlled by a particular kind of dominant elite. Various social and demographic conditions are seen to define the intensity, duration, and form of social conflict, while the social structure represents the type of domination present in the society at a particular stage of its evolution.

Our examination of Dahrendorf, Mills, Coser, and Riesman highlighted a number of commonalities: except for Dahrendorf, they were born in the early 1900s; they were influenced by European thinkers; all pursued academic careers but became involved in political, applied issues too; most observed social conflict within American society as it experienced high rates of industrialization and urbanization; and their intellectual interests have focused on conflict and domination within modern industrial society. Their backgrounds, careers, and interests have generally had much in common. Further, their paradigms possess a number of similar elements, as follows:

Aims   The sociological analysis of conflict and domination within contemporary industrial society.

Assumptions

1   Society represents a system of competing groups or interests.

2   Social or class conflict emerges under certain organizational or social conditions.

3   Industrialization contributes to capitalistic forms of domination, centralization, and elitism.

4   Social conflict emerges out of resource scarcity and monopolization.

5   Social conflict contributes to further societal evolution and adaptation.

245

Methodology   The application of earlier paradigms (e.g., Marx, Weber, and Simmel) to the analysis of modern conflict.

Typologies   Types of social structure and associated levels and types of social conflict.

From the above it can be seen that modern conflict theory represents a systemic, evolutionary, and radical reaction to contemporary forms of conflict and domination—theories developed by European-oriented intellectuals within the context of a conflict-ridden and exploitive culture. The continuity between earlier and modern conflict theory is clear here in the elaboration and further application of earlier Marxian thought. The major elements of this type of theory are summarized in Figure 12.12. We shall then, in the next chapter, proceed to an analysis of social-psychological theory.

EXERCISES

Consider the following social trends:

a   Increased unionization in American society

b   Increased minority-group reaction and attempts to develop minority power

c   Reaction to Watergate

d   Generational differences in social character within the United States

e   The effects of conflict on intergroup alliances (e.g., labor and politics, blacks and women).

Account for each trend, using the general explanations provided by Dahrendorf, Mills, Coser, and Riesman. Compare in detail the different types of explanation you develop, using each theorist. To what extent are they similar? Can you develop a general conflict-oriented explanation of each trend?

FIGURE 12.12
THE STRUCTURE OF MODERN CONFLICT THEORY

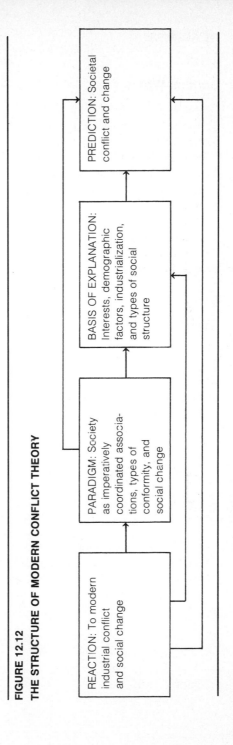

REACTION: To modern industrial conflict and social change

PARADIGM: Society as imperatively coordinated associations, types of conformity, and social change

BASIS OF EXPLANATION: Interests, demographic factors, industrialization, and types of social structure

PREDICTION: Societal conflict and change

READINGS

General Works

Denisoff, R. S. (ed.): *Sociology: Theories in Conflict,* Wadsworth, Belmont, Calif., 1972.

Martindale, D.: *The Nature and Types of Sociological Theory,* Houghton Mifflin, Boston, 1960, chaps. 8 and 15.

Timasheff, N. S.: *Sociological Theory, Its Nature and Growth,* 3d ed., Random House, New York, 1967, chap. 18.

Turner, J. H.: *The Structure of Sociological Theory,* Dorsey, Homewood, Ill., 1974, chaps. 5, 6, 7, and 8.

Specific Works by Theorists

Dahrendorf

Dahrendorf, R.: *Class and Class Conflict in Industrial Society,* Stanford University Press, Stanford, Calif., 1959.

Mills

Mills, C. W.: *The Power Elite,* Oxford University Press, New York, 1956.

————: *The Sociological Imagination,* Grove Press, New York, 1961.

————: *White Collar, The American Middle Classes,* Oxford University Press, New York, 1951.

Coser

Coser, L. A.: *Continuities in the Study of Social Conflict,* Free Press, New York, 1967.

————: *The Functions of Social Conflict,* Free Press, Chicago, 1956.

Riesman

Riesman, D.: *Individualism Reconsidered,* Doubleday, Garden City, N.Y., 1954.

———— *The Lonely Crowd,* Yale University Press, New Haven Conn., 1961.

13

SOCIAL-PSYCHOLOGICAL THEORY:

SOCIAL BEHAVIORISM CONTINUED

Although much of contemporary theory is macroscopic and deductive in form, the earlier social-behaviorist paradigm—with its American roots in the work of Mead, Cooley, and Sumner—has continued to have a major influence on modern sociology as the basis of the subfield called social psychology. Reflecting individualistic themes in American culture as well as more microscopic views of society inherent in the work of Weber and Mead, this particular paradigm is microscopic, inductive, process-oriented, and introspective in form—a strikingly different view from the more traditional macroscopic, deductive, structure-oriented, and objective structure-functionalist and conflict types.

In this chapter we shall delineate the major societal, intellectual, and biographical contexts under which this type of theory flourished and outline its major assumptions. We shall then discuss two major variants: the systemic and naturalistic types as contained in the work of four major theorists: Herbert Blumer, Erving Goffman, Peter Blau, and Harold Garfinkel. We shall also examine the general characteristics of this paradigm as a whole.

INTRODUCTION

The contemporary counterpart of earlier social behaviorism may be seen as the reaction of a particular group of intellectuals—in this case those familiar with and/or trained in Mead's "Chicago tradition"—in response to a number of specific conditions: the application of earlier individualistic conceptions of society to the contemporary scene, the strong emphasis on individualism inherent in the Protestant ethic (the basis of much American culture), the intellectual influence of European thinkers such as Durkheim and Weber, the "evolutionary optimism" of Darwin as applied to society, and the negative impact of modern industrialization and bureaucratization on the individual.

In general, then, the social-psychological paradigm may be viewed as the application of earlier notions of individualism and social evolution to events within contemporary society as they affect the individual. This approach views *society as located within the individual, particularly his or her self-concept; as dynamic and emergent through social exchange, interaction, and interpretation; and as being discovered through the processes of individual introspection and observation.* Emphasis is placed upon understanding the meaning of social phenomena, the sociological context of social interaction, the manner in which social structures are based upon exchange processes, and the manner in which social interaction is organized or made rational at the individual level in everyday life. The focus here is upon society as a dynamic and emerging system of interlinked and individual interpretations of reality, a system subject to constant change and reorganization. Rather than being an external system, essentially structural and somewhat static, society is located *within* the individual in his or her social interpretation of reality and is dynamic and process-oriented.

The various types of theory in social psychology elaborate a number of aspects of this paradigm—the symbolic aspects of interaction, its structure and content, its exchange basis, and the manner in which it is organized or made rational to the individual. In this manner the earlier social-behaviorist conceptualization of society is further applied and elaborated.

Social-psychological theory may also be classified into two major types: (1) the systemic, emphasizing the sociological aspects of the social self and interaction and analyzing their social contingencies; and (2) the naturalistic, viewing the foundation of interaction as located in the elements of the human constitution or nature. Thus Blumer and Goffman are concerned with the symbolic and structural aspects of interaction, while Blau sees social processes as rooted in primitive psychological processes, in particular attraction and goal-attainment drives, and Garfinkel on the other hand, views the basic motivation of a human being as "congruence with the moral order." The former two are more systemic, the latter two naturalistic. Once again, however, this difference is a matter of degree only, since all four theorists are primarily concerned with building sociological theories of interaction, and the naturalistic elements represent an extremely minor part of Blau and Garfinkel's work.

To summarize, social-psychological theory tends to represent the application of earlier notions of individualism and social evolution to events within contemporary society as they affect the individual. The major consequence is a type of theory which is microscopic, inductive, subjective, dynamic, and introspective, delineating the basis and contingencies of the social interaction process and varying as to whether its foundation is primarily systemic or naturalistic. This type of theorizing is summarized in Figure 13.1.

We turn first to discuss the systemic type of social-psychological theory as evident in the work of Blumer and Goffman.

FIGURE 13.1

MAJOR FACTORS BEHIND SOCIAL-PSYCHOLOGICAL THEORY

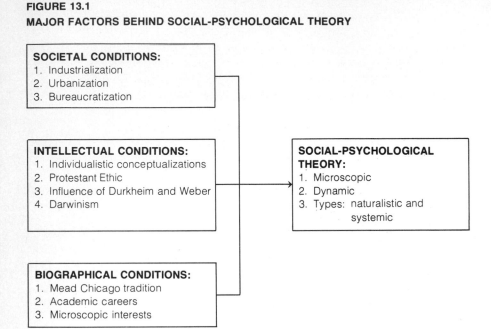

THE SYSTEMIC TYPE OF SOCIAL-PSYCHOLOGICAL THEORY

Blumer and Goffman describe the symbolic aspects of interaction and its structural contingencies. The former is well known for his development of *symbolic interactionism* and the latter for his *dramaturgical* model of interaction. Both are useful examples of the continuity between traditional and contemporary paradigms.

Herbert Blumer (1900)

Background   Blumer was educated at the University of Missouri, where he obtained his B.A. and M.A. degrees in 1921 and 1922 respectively. He then moved to the University of Chicago, where he experienced the strong influence of Mead and completed his Ph.D. in 1929. He stayed on in Chicago for some years, moving in the 1950s to Berkeley, where he has remained. His intellectual interests focus on social psychology, collective behavior, and mass communications. He is responsible for developing the term *symbolic interactionism* and has made major contributions to this particular type of theory in sociology. His works include numerous articles on race relations, collective behavior, and mass communications. The most authoritative collection of his work, however, is *Symbolic Interactionism, Perspective and Method* (1969); it is this work that concerns us in our present discussion.

Aims Blumer is concerned with developing a symbolic interactionist theory of society, *symbolic interaction* referring to "the peculiar and distinctive character of interaction as it takes place between human beings."[1] This peculiarity consists of the *reciprocal* and *symbolic interpretation* of each other's actions. Sociology, according to this perspective, is concerned with "the interpretive process by means of which human beings, individually and collectively, act in human society."[2] Such a paradigm conceptualizes society as a system of interpretive processes governing behavior.

Assumptions Building on the work of Mead, Blumer makes a number of basic assumptions concerning social reality, as follows:

1 "People, individually and collectively, are prepared to act on the basis of the meanings of the objects that comprise their world."[3] Behavior is based on social meanings accorded particular objects. These objects are of three major types: physical (e.g., trees), social (e.g., priests), and abstract (e.g., moral principles).[4]

2 Associations represent a "process in which . . . [people] . . . are making indications to one another and interpreting each other's indications";[5] i.e., human action is interpreted and constructed.

3 "Social acts . . . are constructed through a process in which the actors note, interpret, and assess the situations confronting them."[6] The human being is thus an acting organism with a self

[1]H. Blumer, *Symbolic Interactionism, Perspective and Method*, Prentice-Hall, Englewood Cliffs, N.J., 1969, pp. 78–79.
[2]Ibid., p. 89.
[3]Ibid., p. 50.
[4]Ibid., p. 10.
[5]Ibid., p. 50.
[6]Ibid., p. 50.

253

which participates in role taking.[7] The individual thus interacts with itself in the interpretive process.

4 Finally, "the complex interlinkages of acts that comprise organizations, institutions, division of labor, and networks of interdependency are moving and not static affairs."[8] Accordingly, societies or groups, since they *exist in interaction*, are dynamic and formative rather than static. As articulated lines of action,[9] they are neither preestablished nor do they possess an existence separate from that of their participants in interaction. On the other hand, the previous actions of these participants provide the background for any instance of joint action.[10]

To summarize, society consists of living lines of action, formed through the process of interpretive interaction which is guided by particular objects and defined by particular group contexts. According to this perspective, society represents a symbolic, interactive, interpretive process located within the individual; it is not a static, external system.

Methodology The above assumptions, according to Blumer, require a particular kind of methodology: the utilization of a more naturalistic type of inquiry (i.e., a method which goes "directly to the empirical social world" in contrast to predefined models), focusing on exploration and inspection, and the natural, ongoing character of the empirical world.[11] This approach emphasizes the need to place oneself in the role of the participant, take the dynamics of interaction seriously, develop "pictures" of social action (i.e., observe the process by which social action is constructed), and view institutions and groups dynamically (i.e., as arrangements of people linked in action).[12] Methodology appropriate to symbolic interactionism is empathetic, dynamic, and inductive in contrast to the artifically imposed, static, and deductive methods typical of traditional, "scientific" sociology. Such an approach, once again, represents a further elaboration and application of Mead's work.

[7] Ibid., p. 12.
[8] Ibid., p. 50.
[9] Ibid., p. 17.
[10] Ibid., p. 20.
[11] Ibid., p. 46.
[12] Ibid., pp. 47–60.

The Typology As in the case of social behaviorism typologies implicit in social-psychological theory are more models of social reality than types of social structure or society. In this respect Blumer's theory differs little: his typology of social reality is implicit in the assumptions discussed above. This model consists of the *individual* (his or her background, self-object, role taking), *objects* (physical, social, abstract), and *others* (their background, etc.), all of which represents an ongoing, dynamic, symbolic, interactive, and interpretive system located within the individuals concerned. Such a typology is summarized in Figure 13.2.

Summary and Conclusions Blumer's concept of society differs markedly from those of organic-structure-functionalists and conflict-radical theorists. Blumer sees society as consisting of living lines of action, formed through the process of interpretive interaction which is guided by particular objects and defined by particular group contexts. Society thus represents a *symbolic, interactive, interpretive process* located *within the individual*.

Such a perspective is bound to raise a number of critical issues:

1 To what extent, for example, is this a perspective or conceptual framework rather than a theory? In terms of an explanatory structure, it is clearly lacking.

FIGURE 13.2
BLUMER'S TYPOLOGY

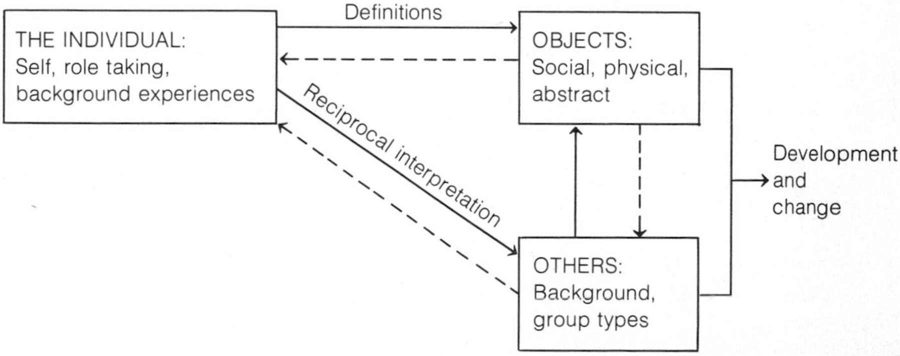

2   The extent to which Blumer moves significantly beyond the work of Mead represents another problem.

3   While rejecting structure functionalism and imposed definitions of social reality, one can argue that ultimately symbolic interactionism is systemic in form. Thus, while the *context* of interaction may vary, its structure or *form* is relatively uniform.

4   It can also be argued that naturalistic methods will eventually result in some kind of *imposed analysis* of any empirical situation—a problem which cannot be avoided.

Despite the above issues, Blumer has clearly made a major contribution to the development of an inductive, microscopic, and dynamic paradigm of society. His framework as a whole is summarized in Figure 13.3.

FIGURE 13.3
BLUMER'S THEORETICAL FRAMEWORK SUMMARIZED

BACKGROUND:
1   Educated at Chicago
2   Academic career at Berkeley
3   Interests in symbolic interactionism

AIMS:
Develop symbolic interactionist perspective—understanding of human interaction

ASSUMPTIONS:
1   Action on basis of meanings and objects
2   Action is interpreted and constructed
3   Action involves the self and role taking
4   Social organization is dynamic

METHODOLOGY:
Explanation, inspection, and application of Mead to analysis of social interaction

TYPOLOGY:
Model of social reality

ISSUES:
1   Lack of theory
2   Elaboration of Mead
3   Systemic form
4   Imposed analysis

Erving Goffman (1922)

Background   Goffman received his B.A. at the University of Toronto in 1945. He then moved to the University of Chicago, where he obtained his M.A. and Ph.D. in 1949 and 1953. Since then he has pursued an academic career at Berkeley and, more recently, at the University of Pennsylvania. His intellectual interests have been concentrated on developing a framework for the analysis of social interaction based on wide-ranging formal and informal observations of this process. His major publications include *The Presentation of Self in Everyday Life* (1959), *Asylums* (1961), and *Encounters* (1961). In this discussion we are particularly concerned with the first of these books, in which Goffman presents his dramaturgical model of interaction.

Aims   Goffman is primarily concerned with "the way in which the individual in ordinary work situations presents himself and his activity to others, the ways in which he guides and controls the impression they form of him, and the kinds of things he may and may not do while sustaining his performance before them."[13] He focuses on impression management in interaction, thereby complementing Blumer's emphasis on its symbolic aspects by examining the manner in which the actor seeks to maximize certain kinds of interpretations being made of his or her behavior. Once again, the focus is on microscopic aspects of social interaction.

Assumptions   Goffman makes a number of assumptions concerning the impression-management process, as follows:

1   Central to interaction are information sources or reciprocal images. Thus information about the individual defines the situation as it delineates the reciprocal role expectations involved.[14] Of central importance are the particular techniques individuals use to present themselves and the particular conditions under which these techniques came to be employed.

2   During interaction, a "performance" typically occurs: "the activity of a given participant on a given occasion which serves to

[13]E. Goffman, *The Presentation of Self in Everyday Life*, Doubleday, New York, 1959, p. xi.
[14]Ibid., p. 1.

influence in any way any of the other participants."[15] During such a performance, the individual may act out a part or routine—a preestablished pattern of action.[16]

3 This routine may become standardized in the form of a "front," "that part of the individual's performance which regularly functions in a general and fixed fashion to define the situation for those who observe the performance."[17] This front is influenced by the setting—the physical environment and the personal front—dress, age, sex, etc., appearance (indicators of the actor's status), and manner (indicators of oncoming behavior). In all this, consistency among these elements is expected.[18]

4 Furthermore, social fronts tend to become institutionalized, especially in reference to well-established roles.

5 Behavior within social fronts, on the other hand, may be subject to dramatization (e.g., when instant decisions are necessary) and idealization (e.g., behavior in reference to social stereotypes associated with a particular role).

6 Performances are obviously not isolated role behavior—they are interrelated with the behavior of others. When performers interlock and/or are interdependent, they form "teams" or sets of "individuals who cooperate in staging a single routine."[19] Team members are interdependent and, to a certain extent, "familiar" in their behavior toward one another.

7 Furthermore, team behavior takes place within specific regions—specific physical areas. Politeness and decorum typify behavior in the front region (the area to which the audience has access) while fatigue and informal behavior may occur in the back region (the area protected from audience observation).

To summarize, social interaction, particularly the normative or moral type,[20] is a function of impression management performed within particular fronts by performance teams and structured by particular regions. According to this type of analysis, in-

[15]Ibid., p. 15.
[16]Ibid., p. 16.
[17]Ibid., p. 22.
[18]For further elements such as "deference patterns," "status," and "role distance," see E. Goffman, *Encounters*, Bobbs-Merrill, Indianapolis, 1961.
[19]Goffman, *The Presentation of Self in Everyday life*, p. 79.
[20]Ibid., p. 241.

teraction is defined by the availability and exchange of certain kinds of information and is standardized by situational and role-related characteristics. Such a paradigm complements Blumer's approach by specifying some of the situational factors influencing the actual process of symbolic interaction.

Methodology   Goffman's methods consist of the informal analysis of varying types of everyday interaction by applying the dramaturgical or theatrical analogy; that is, he sees social interaction as conforming to what occurs on the stage. This is further elaborated by considering role-related aspects of the situation—concepts more typical of traditional role theory.[21] As with much of sociological theory, methods here consist of the application of other paradigms to the phenomena of interest.

The Typology   Like Blumer's, Goffman's theoretical typology consists of a particular model of social reality. This consists of the major factors defining social interaction: the *actor* with his conformity motivation, the *performance* or impression-management act, the *front*, and *performance teams* with their front and back regions. The individual is linked to the team through *interdependence* and *familiarity*. These elements represent the major factors or props in a theatrical or dramaturgical performance, i.e., social interaction. Such a model is summarized in Figure 13.4.

Summary and Conclusions   According to Goffman, social interaction is the result of impression management performed within particular fronts by individuals and performance teams—persons structured by particular regions. Interaction is further defined by the availability and exchange of certain kinds of information and is standardized by situational and role-related characteristics.

   This rather novel approach raises a number of obvious issues:

1   To what extent is the dramaturgical framework simply an analogy, a perspective rather than a theory?

2   Accordingly, to what extent does it simply *describe* rather than explain?

---

[21]For examples of this, see *Encounters*, in particular the essay "Fun in Games."   **259**

FIGURE 13.4
GOFFMAN'S TYPOLOGY

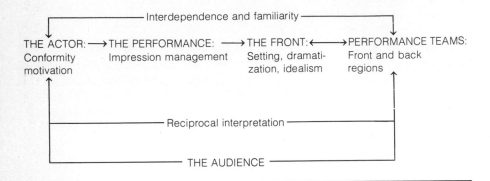

3   Since Goffman views all social interaction as impression management, what can we ever learn about an individual's "real" self, using his framework?

4   Finally, the extent to which his paradigm is based on informal, impressionistic data makes it problematic in general.

Despite the above problems, however, Goffman has made an important contribution to the detailed understanding of social interaction at the individual level. His framework as a whole is summarized in Figure 13.5.

THE SYSTEMIC TYPE OF SOCIAL-PSYCHOLOGICAL THEORY SUMMARIZED

In their development of a symbolic interactionist and dramaturgical approach to social phenomena, Blumer and Goffman reveal a number of commonalities insofar as they both:

1   Share Chicago and Berkeley academic backgrounds

2   Concentrate on the analysis of social interaction as the major focus of their theories

3   Focus on information exchange as the basis of social interaction

---

FIGURE 13.5
GOFFMAN'S THEORETICAL FRAMEWORK SUMMARIZED

BACKGROUND:
1   Educated at Toronto and Chicago
2   Academic career at Berkeley
3   Interests in social interaction

AIMS:
Analysis of self-presentation in social interaction

ASSUMPTIONS:
1   Importance of reciprocal images
2   Performance typically occurs
3   Development of fronts
4   Fronts become institutionalized
5   Dramatization and idealization of fronts
6   Performance teams
7   Team regions

METHODOLOGY:
Application of dramaturgical analogy to analysis of social interaction

TYPOLOGY:
Dramaturgical model of social interaction

ISSUES:
1   Lack of theory
2   Description rather than explanation
3   Lack of insight into real self
4   Impressionistic data base

---

4   Emphasize that social interpretation is a reciprocal process—i.e., a two-way process between actor and audience

5   Emphasize action as central to their frameworks

6   View social structure as interaction-based and therefore temporary and dynamic

7   Take a microscopic-inductive approach to the analysis of social reality

8   Advocate and use introspective-observational methods of data gathering and analysis

9   Delineate middle-range models of social reality   **261**

10 Raise issues concerning the type of theory they develop and its data base

In general, then, this type of theory is microscopic, systemic, and dynamic, representing the attempt to develop a view of social phenomena that reflects the interpretive process inherent in the dynamics of interaction. Its major characteristics are summarized in Figure 13.6. We shall now go on to consider its more naturalistic counterpart in contemporary theory.

THE NATURALISTIC TYPE OF SOCIAL-PSYCHOLOGICAL THEORY

This type of theory is as microscopic, inductive, and concerned with an internally oriented, introspective approach to social phenomena as its systemic equivalent. However, the work of Blau and Garfinkel may be viewed as more naturalistic insofar as Blau finds these phenomena to be rooted in primitive psychological processes and Garfinkel considers the individual's motivation to be congruent with the moral order. Both men, however, develop sociological theories of social reality, and—once again—this type of classification is a matter of *degree* rather than *kind*. In general, contemporary theory in sociology is predominantly *systemic*, with few naturalistic traces, as the model of "social humanity" has taken precedence over earlier views of the natural order. However, these traces do occur and require consideration. We turn, then, to a consideration of this kind of social-psychological theory.

Peter Blau (1918)

Background   Blau was born in Vienna and has pursued an extremely varied and distinguished academic career. He obtained his A.B. at Elmhurst College in 1942, an M.A. at Cambridge in 1950, and a Ph.D. at Columbia University in 1952. His professional career has consisted of professorships at the University of Chicago (1953–1970) and Columbia University, where he is at present. His major publications include *The Dynamics of Bureaucracy* (1955), *Exchange and Power in Social Life* (1964), and *The Structure of Organizations* (1971). In this discussion we are specifically concerned with his attempt to develop a general exchange theory of social life.

262

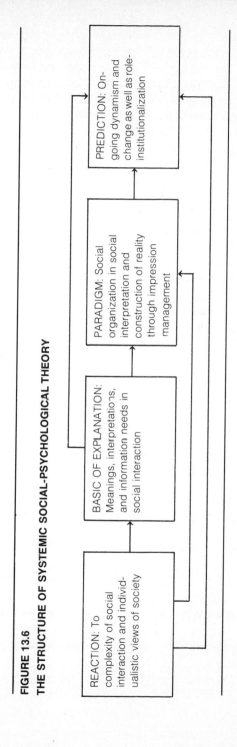

FIGURE 13.6
THE STRUCTURE OF SYSTEMIC SOCIAL-PSYCHOLOGICAL THEORY

REACTION: To complexity of social interaction and individ-ualistic views of society

BASIC OF EXPLANATION: Meanings, interpretations, and information needs in social interaction

PARADIGM: Social organization in social interpretation and construction of reality through impression management

PREDICTION: On-going dynamism and change as well as role-institutionalization

Aims Blau is primarily concerned with the analysis of social associations, of the processes governing them, and of the forms they assume.[22] Furthermore, he views the underlying process in such associations as social exchange, beginning at the individual or microscopic level and moving to the macroscopic. He attempts to develop a *general, inductive exchange theory of social structure*.

Assumptions Applying the exchange process to social organizations. Blau makes a number of major assumptions, as follows:

1 First, it is assumed that the more complex processes of social association evolve out of simple ones;[23] i.e., the emergence of social organization is an *inductive* process, beginning with microscopic processes.

2 Second, it is the forces of social attraction which stimulate exchange transactions. These forces—feelings of attraction and desires for various kinds of rewards—are rooted in humanity's primitive psychological processes.[24] Thus *attraction* and *reward motivation* give rise to the *exchange of resources*—the first step in the process of social association.

3 Once exchange takes place, the differentiation of status and power commences. Thus an individual who possesses resources that others need and who is not dependent on them in any way creates a situation in which their need-fulfillment desires command compliance with his or her wishes. In this manner, exchange gives rise to the differentiation of status and power.[25]

4 If the advantages of compliance outweigh the hardships, collective approval of the power situation tends to emerge, leading to consensus and its eventual legitimation. Thus legitimate authority becomes the basis of organization, resulting in the achievement of various objectives, organizational stability, and institutionalization of values, norms, principles, and knowledge transmission.[26]

5 While approval of power may develop on the one hand, there

[22]P. M. Blau, *Exchange and Power in Social Life*, Wiley, New York, 1964, p. 2.
[23]Ibid., "Introduction."
[24]Ibid., chaps. 1, 2, and 3.
[25]Ibid., chaps. 4 and 5.
[26]Ibid., chap. 8.

may also be individuals who feel exploited and who receive insufficient rewards. They may communicate their feelings of anger, frustration, and aggression to one another, resulting in collective disapproval of power and the emergence of opposition forces antagonistic to the group presently in power or in control of the situation.[27]

6 Consequently, while on the one hand the process of *reciprocity* in exchange may result in a balancing of forces and a strain toward equilibrium in relationships, disturbances of the reward/cost ratio may result in *imbalances* in relationships also, leading to opposition, conflict, and social change.[28]

7 As a result, the simultaneous operation of diverse balancing forces tends to produce imbalances in social life, resulting in an ongoing *dialectic* between reciprocity and imbalance—the basis of society's social *dynamics*. Exchange leads to both structure and process, statics and dynamics.[29]

To summarize, feelings of social attraction and desire for certain kinds of rewards result in exchange transactions; these, in turn, result in the differentiation of status and power along with its legitimation—the basis of social organization. Diverse reciprocity, however, also produces imbalances in the cost/reward ratio, resulting in an ongoing dialectic between reciprocity and imbalance—the basis of social dynamics. In this fashion Blau takes a microscopic process and traces its effects through the social system, resulting in an inductive, process-oriented theory of social structure.

Methodology Blau proceeds by delineating exchange processes and their effects at the microscopic level and then tracing the influences of these same processes through the group to the institutional and societal level of analysis. Such a method may be viewed as microscopic induction—the opposite of the Parsonian method in its attempt to build a general theory of society on the basis of limited propositions. Using such simplistic assumptions tends to result in the development of simplistic and general conclusions.

[27]Ibid., chap. 9.
[28]Ibid., chap. 11.
[29]Ibid., chap. 12.

The Typology   Like the others in this chapter, Blau's typology represents a model of social reality. This consists of the following elements: the *individual*, influenced by social attraction and reward motivation; the process of *social exchange*; the resultant *differentiation of status and power*; its *organization* and *legitimation* resulting in *equilibrium*; *imbalances* leading to *opposition and change*; and the resulting *dialectic* between *reciprocity* and *imbalance*, resulting in *social dynamics*. This inductive, process-oriented model of social reality is summarized in Figure 13.7.

Summary and Conclusions   In attempting to analyze the "processes that govern the associations among men as a prolegomenon of a theory of social structure,"[30] Blau concentrates on the social exchange process at the microscopic level as explaining certain subsequent processes: the differentiation of status and power, its organization and legitimation, its imbalance and the development of opposition, and the resultant dialectic between reciprocity and imbalance—the basis of social dynamics. Such an approach is microscopic, inductive, and process-oriented, resulting in a somewhat unique attempt to develop a general theory of social process and structure based on microscopic processes. Blau's work is bound to be controversial because:

1   While Blau is aware of the problems of tautology and reductionism,[31] the issue remains as to whether he has, in fact, dealt with these charges satisfactorily.

2   His framework may be viewed as too broad to be of specific use in understanding a *particular* society or social situation.

3   His notion of a "strain toward equilibrium" may be viewed as similar to the use of this concept in structure functionalism.

4   His discussions of the conditions leading to the emergence of opposition and change may be viewed as too broad.

Despite the above problems, Blau's work represents an important attempt to build an inductive theory of society based on microscopic processes. His framework as a whole is summarized in Figure 13.8.

[30]Ibid., p. xi.
[31]Ibid., "Introduction."

FIGURE 13.7
BLAU'S TYPOLOGY

THE INDIVIDUAL: ———→EXCHANGE PROCESS: ———→STATUS-POWER ———→ORGANIZATION, ———→IMBALANCE ———→DIALECTIC
Feelings of   Resource exchange   DIFFERENTIATION   LEGITIMATION,   AND   AND
attraction and   AND   OPPOSITION   CHANGE
reward motivation   EQUILIBRIUM

FIGURE 13.8
BLAU'S THEORETICAL FRAMEWORK SUMMARIZED

BACKGROUND:
1   Educated at Columbia University
2   Academic career at Chicago
3   Interests in organizational processes

AIMS:
Analyze social associations and governing processes

ASSUMPTIONS:
1   Complex processes of association evolve out of the simple
2   Social attraction stimulates exchange
3   Exchange results in status and power differentiation
4   Organization and legitimation of power may result
5   Collective disapproval and emergence of opposition may also result
6   Imbalances in relationships may thus lead to conflict
7   Ongoing dialectic between reciprocity and imbalance represents the basis of social
    dynamics

METHODOLOGY:
Application of exchange theory, using microscopic induction

TYPOLOGY:
Exchange model of social reality

ISSUES:
1   Tautology and reductionism
2   General and broad
3   Similarities to structure functionalism
4   Broad conditions of opposition and change

Harold Garfinkel (1917)

Background   Garfinkel was educated at the universities of New-
ark and North Carolina, completing his Ph.D. at Harvard under
Parsons in 1950. Since the 1960s he has been a professor of sociology at U.C.L.A. His intellectual interests focus on social organization, knowledge and science, and the distinctive subfield known
as ethnomethodology, to which he has contributed greatly. Much
of his work is contained in *Studies in Ethnomethodology* (1967),
the work we are concerned with here.

Aims   Garfinkel defines *ethnomethodology* as "the investigation
of the rational properties of indexical expressions and other prac-

tical actions as contingent ongoing accomplishments of organized artful practices of everyday life."[32] More simply stated, he is concerned with how, in everyday life and interaction, individuals rationalize or "make sense out of" social reality, particularly in their conversation and interaction. Social organization or the moral order exists *within interaction* in the way in which individuals *interpret reality*, make it rational, or make sense out of it. It is this process of "making sense out of" things—the interpretation of social reality—that Garfinkel is concerned with in his type of theory.

Such an approach differs radically from traditional sociology—which involves the imposition of predetermined concepts and definitions of reality onto empirical data. In contrast, ethnomethodology is concerned with the way in which the individuals (i.e., the data themselves) *create* social reality in social interaction. It is this *process of social interpretation*—the basis of social organization—as understood from the *participant's* point of view, that is central to Garfinkel's approach.

Assumptions   It is possible to abstract a number of central assumptions in Garfinkel's work, as follows:

1   He assumes that a moral order—a normatively valued social structure—exists; that it represents the basis of social organization and is also the subject matter of sociology.[33]

2   This moral order is accepted by and defines reality for its participants on an everyday basis.[34]

3   The moral order is "referred to" in organizations; i.e., it represents the basis for interpreting social reality.[35]

4   The individual's motivation is to be congruent with this moral order in interpreting social reality; i.e., he or she makes sense out of everyday actions by interpreting them in reference to this moral order. People thus attempt to fit their activities into this order so as to understand them or make them rational to themselves.[36]

---

[32]H. Garfinkel, *Studies in Ethnomethodology*, Prentice-Hall, Englewood Cliffs, N.J., 1967, p. 11.
[33]Ibid., pp. 34 and 93.
[34]Ibid., p. 34.
[35]Ibid., p. 93.
[36]Ibid., e.g., p. 60.

5 Furthermore, since this process of "interpretive rationality" occurs in all behavior, it is assumed that any social setting is self-organizing (i.e., all social situations organize themselves through the attempts of their members to develop rationality).

6 Such organization is dynamic, since it occurs in interaction.[37]

7 It is further assumed that it is this organizing process that constitutes social reality, in contrast to the *imposed* interpretation of scientists and traditional sociologists.[38]

8 Finally, following the work of Alfred Schutz, Garfinkel assumes that the rationalizing process consists of a number of distinct elements: "categorizing and comparing," "tolerable error" (i.e., accuracy), "search for means," "analysis of alternatives and consequences," "strategy," "concern for timing," "predictability," "rules of procedure," "choice," and "grounds of choice."[39] These are the processes the individual uses to achieve rationality or make sense out of everyday activity.

To summarize, the focus of sociology for Garfinkel is the "moral order" as it operates in the "organized practices of everyday life," in the individual's drive for rationality and congruence with this order, and in his or her interaction with others. Accordingly, social organization is dynamic and ongoing, representing negotiated order between interacting individuals as they constantly interpret and attempt to make sense out of everyday life.

Methodology Garfinkel's theoretical methodology consists primarily of applying Schutz's inventory of rationalities and model of social reality to sociology and sociological data. His empirical methods, on the other hand, involve the attempt to study the rationalization processes in a number of ways: the analysis of dialogue, case studies of particular types of people, experiments in which people are subjected to incongruent situations and their interpretations are observed, and situations in which distrust is assumed and the reactions of others are observed. All such methods are designed to highlight the manner in which the moral order operates in the individual's interpretation process as he or she strives for congruence and rationality. Examples of Garfinkel's

[37]See ibid., p. 3.
[38]See ibid., pp. 96–103.
[39]Ibid., chap. 8.

studies include the behavior of jurors, counselors, data coders, and researchers.

The Typology Garfinkel's model of social reality involves the *moral order*—the basis of social organization—operating through the individual's *drive for congruence* with it and for *rationality* in everyday activities. The result is that the *process of rationality* operates in interaction and in all social situations to produce *social organization*—a dynamic and ongoing state. Furthermore, the typical characteristics of rationality involve a number of basic elements as outlined by Schutz and discussed above. Such a model is summarized in Figure 13.9.

Summary and Conclusions For Garfinkel, sociology is the study of the moral order, operating through the organized practices of everyday life in the individual's drive for rationality and congruence with this order in his or her interaction with others. Accordingly, social organization is dynamic and ongoing, representing negotiated order between interacting individuals as they constantly interpret and attempt to make sense out of everyday life.

Such a paradigm has proved highly controversial and raises a number of distinct issues:

1 Ethnomethodology—in its emphasis upon a normatively valued moral order, congruence, and rationality—may, in a sense,

---

FIGURE 13.9
GARFINKEL'S TYPOLOGY

THE MORAL ORDER:⟶THE INDIVIDUAL:⟶RATIONALITY IN SOCIAL INTERACTION:

THE MORAL ORDER:	THE INDIVIDUAL:	RATIONALITY IN SOCIAL INTERACTION:
1. Institutionalized and absorbed	Drive for *congruence* with moral order and *rationality* in everyday life	1. Categorizing and comparing
2. Basis of social organization		2. Tolerable error
		3. Search for means
		4. Analysis of alternatives
		5. Strategy
		6. Timing
		7. Predictability
		8. Rules of procedure
		9. Choice
		10. Grounds of choice

be viewed as simply a different form of structure-functionalism in its systemic, macroscopic, and universalistic qualities.

2   Like symbolic interactionism, ethnomethodology is more of a perspective than a theory and reveals many theoretical gaps in its rather simplistic and mechanical model of social reality.

3   A further problem is the extent to which Garfinkel appears to neglect the structural context in which rationality emerges, i.e., the effect of varying group characteristics on this process.

4   Finally, the problem of microscopic reductionism, as in the case of Blau, also applies to ethnomethodology; i.e., all aspects of the social system become a function of the congruence-rationality process.

Despite such problems, Garfinkel has developed a dynamic and radical alternative to traditional theory, the importance of which is only beginning to achieve recognition within contemporary sociology. His framework as a whole is summarized in Figure 13.10.

THE NATURALISTIC TYPE OF SOCIAL-PSYCHOLOGICAL THEORY SUMMARIZED

Blau and Garfinkel reveal a number of similarities in that they both:

1   Study the basis of social organization

2   Delineate the basis of social organization as a particular process exchange or rationality

3   View social structure as dynamic and temporary

4   View social reality as internalized and microscopic

5   Develop process models of social reality

6   Use the method of microscopic induction

7   Apply nonsociological frameworks to the analysis of social organization

8   Raise the basic issues of reductionism and similarity to structure functionalism

FIGURE 13.10
GARFINKEL'S THEORETICAL FRAMEWORK SUMMARIZED

BACKGROUND:
1 Educated at Harvard
2 Academic career at U.C.L.A.
3 Interests in social organization

AIMS:
Understand rational properties of everyday life

ASSUMPTIONS:
1 A moral order exists
2 Moral order is accepted and defines reality
3 Moral order referred to in organization
4 Individual's motivation is congruence with the moral order
5 Any social setting is self-organizing
6 This organization is dynamic and occurs in interaction
7 This organizing process constitutes reality
8 Rationalizing process consists of ten typical processes

METHODOLOGY:
Application of Schutz's inventory of rationalities and model of social reality to sociological phenomena

TYPOLOGY:
Model of rationalizing process

ISSUES:
1 Similarity to structure functionalism
2 Lack of theory
3 Neglect of structural context
4 Problem of microscopic reductionism

This type of social-psychological theory, then, is microscopic, inductive, and dynamic. Its major characteristics are summarized in Figure 13.11. We shall now go on to delineate the characteristics of the social-psychological paradigm as a whole.

THE SOCIAL-PSYCHOLOGICAL PARADIGM SUMMARIZED

At the beginning of this chapter we portrayed this kind of theory as the reaction of a group of intellectuals familiar with the Chicago tradition to a number of conditions: application of earlier indi-

273

274

FIGURE 13.11

THE STRUCTURE OF NATURALISTIC SOCIAL-PYSCHOLOGICAL THEORY

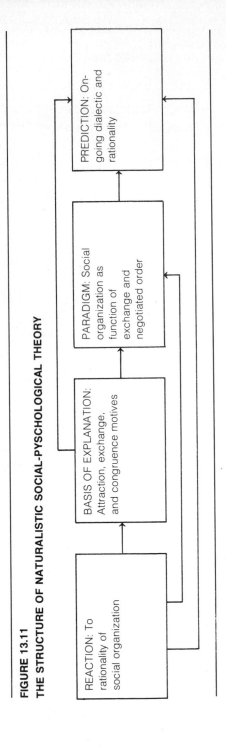

vidualistic conceptions of society to the contemporary scene, the strong emphasis on individualism inherent in the Protestant ethic, the intellectual influence of European thinkers such as Durkheim and Weber, the "evolutionary optimism" of Darwin, and the negative impact of modern industrialization and bureaucratization on the individual. The result was a view of society as located within the individual—in particular his or her self-concept, as dynamic and emergent through social exchange and interaction, and as discovered through the processes of individual introspection and observation.

Our examination of Blumer, Goffman, Blau, and Garfinkel has highlighted a number of broad similarities: with the exception of Blumer, these men were all born around 1920, all are concerned with the fields of social psychology and social organization, and all have completed major works on social structures and process at the microsopic or individual level. Their backgrounds, careers, and interests have thus had certain elements in common. Their paradigms also possess a number of similar elements as shown below.

Aims   The sociological analysis of social interaction.

Assumptions

1   Society is located within the individual's definition of social reality.

2   These definitions are dynamic and reciprocated within the process of social interaction.

3   Social interaction is defined by a number of situational conditions.

4   Social interaction leads to the emergence of dynamic and more complex linkages, associations, or forms of social organization.

5   Social interaction also possesses an underlying, self-organizing rationalizing force—the basis of general social organization.

Methodology   The application of earlier or nonsociological paradigms (e.g., Mead, Schutz, the dramaturgical analogy) to the analysis of social organization, using microscopic induction.

Typologies   Models of social reality.

From the above it is evident that social-psychological theory represents a microscopic, individualistic, internally oriented, symbolic, inductive, and dynamic reaction to the analysis of contemporary society; it is a theory developed within the context of a pragmatic and bureaucratic culture by intellectuals familar with Mead and the Chicago tradition. The continuity between earlier social-behaviorist and modern social-psychological theory is clear here in the elaboration and further application of earlier microscopic paradigms. The major elements of this type of theory are summarized in Figure 13.12. We shall proceed to Chapter 14 to view contemporary sociological theory as a whole.

EXERCISES

Consider the following situations:

a   Interaction between an auto salesman and his customer

b   Waiter-customer interaction in a restaurant

c   Waitress-customer interaction in a bar

d   A couple on their first date

e   Interaction between an employer and employee during a family dinner at the latter's home

Analyze each situation differently, using the frameworks provided by Blumer, Goffman, Blau, and Garfinkel. Compare in detail the different types of explanation you develop, applying each theorist. To what extent are they similar? Can you develop a general social-psychological explanation of each trend?

READINGS

General Works

Gouldner, A. W.: *The Coming Crisis of Western Sociology*, Avon, New York, 1970, chap. 10.
Turner, J. H.: *The Structure of Sociological Theory*, Dorsey, Homewood, Ill., 1974, chaps. 11, 15, and 17.

FIGURE 13.12

THE STRUCTURE OF SOCIAL-PSYCHOLOGICAL THEORY

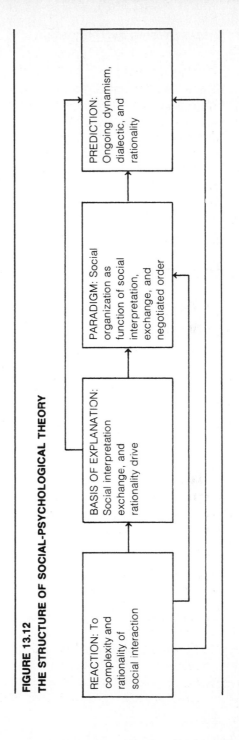

REACTION: To complexity and rationality of social interaction

BASIS OF EXPLANATION: Social interpretation exchange, and rationality drive

PARADIGM: Social organization as function of social interpretation, exchange, and negotiated order

PREDICTION: Ongoing dynamism, dialectic, and rationality

Specific Works by Theorists

Blumer

Blumer, H.: *Symbolic Interactionism, Perspective and Method*, Prentice-Hall, Englewood Cliffs, N.J., 1969.

Goffman

Goffman, E.: *Asylums*, Doubleday, Garden City, N.Y., 1961.
———: *Encounters*, Bobbs-Merrill, Indianapolis, 1961.
———: *The Presentation of Self in Everyday Life*, Doubleday, Garden City, N.Y., 1959.

Blau

Blau, P. M.: *Exchange and Power in Social Life*, Wiley, New York, 1964.

Garfinkel

Garfinkel, H.: *Studies in Ethnomethodology*, Prentice-Hall, Englewood Cliffs, N.J., 1967.

14

TOWARD A TYPOLOGY OF CONTEMPORARY SOCIOLOGICAL THEORIZING:

SUMMARY OF SECTION THREE

I n our analysis of contemporary sociological theory, we have made a number of major points, as follows:

1   We defined theory in American sociology as the application and development of European paradigms within the context of a materialistic, pragmatic, and utilitarian culture. Its continuity with traditional sociological theory was thus viewed as great, although its content is less idealistic and more empirically oriented.

2   Accordingly, the organic, conflict, and social-behaviorist paradigms are viewed as continuing in the form of structure functionalism, modern conflict theory, and social psychology.

3   We outlined the foundation of American sociological theory (1905–1918) as based in the work of Comte, Spencer, and Darwin; a belief in natural laws, progressive social change, social reformism, and an individualistic conception of society; a high percentage of individuals with theological and rural backgrounds; and a heavy emphasis on America's social problems in the wake of the society's post-Civil War industrial and urban development.

4   Accordingly, we defined American sociology as the response of conservative, middle-class intellectuals to America's social problems in the tradition of nineteenth-century European sociology.

5   We then delineated a number of stages in the development of contemporary theory: the *scientific stage* (1918–1935), in which it became deidealized, scientific, empirically oriented, professionalized, academically organized; the stage of *theory, research, and application* (1935–1954), marked by increasing utilitarianism, professionalism, and subfield proliferation; the *emergence of modern conflict theory* (1960s), that is, the development of radical and conflict theory in response to social and racial conflict and the negative effects of bureaucratization and industrialization; and, finally, the stage of *technology and modern systems theory* (1970s), or the application of cybernetics and systems theory to modern sociology in response to contemporary society's technological and economic needs.

6   From this we concluded that theorizing in American sociology represents the application of European philosophical ideas to the changing problems of a materialistic, pragmatic, and utilitarian society in which idealism has given way to empiricism and utilitarianism.

7 We then proceeded to describe three paradigms in contemporary theory: the structure functionalist, modern conflict, and the social-psychological.

8 Structure functionalism was viewed as a systemic, evolutionary, and homeostatic reaction to the needs of contemporary society, a theory developed by establishment-oriented intellectuals applying nineteenth-century European sociological thought within the context of a pragmatic and nonidealistic value system. Details of this paradigm as exemplified in the case of particular theorists are summarized in Figure 14.1. It can be seen that the naturalistic type represents the response of elitist intellectuals to systemic needs, using biological and cybernetic analogies and resulting in a naturalistic, organic approach to society. Etzioni and Tiryakian, on the other hand, react to these same problems from a more voluntaristic and phenomenological perspective, resulting in a more normative or systemic approach in the tradition of Durkheim and Tönnies. This paradigm as a whole, however, represents a systemic, evolutionary, and homeostatic reaction to the needs of contemporary society; it was developed by establishment-oriented intellectuals applying to organic analogy.

9 Modern conflict theory, on the other hand, was viewed as a systemic, evolutionary, and radical reaction to contemporary forms of conflict and domination; it was developed by European-oriented intellectuals within the context of a conflict-ridden and exploitive society. The continuity here between earlier and contemporary paradigms is evident, once again, in the elaboration and further application of earlier Marxian thought. The systemic approach exemplified in the work of Dahrendorf and Mills is summarized in Figure 14.2. It is evident that their theories may be seen as reactions to conflict and domination in the Marxian tradition—the tradition of Enlightenment idealism. Coser and Riesman, on the other hand, take a more functional and demographic approach, more in the naturalistic tradition, although only relatively speaking. Thus, modern conflict theory in general may be viewed as the response of European-oriented intellectuals to modern conflict and domination, applying both systemic and natural forms of explanation inherent in traditional conflict theory.

10 Third, social-psychological theory may be viewed as a microscopic, individualistic, internally oriented, symbolic, inductive, and dynamic reaction to the analysis of contemporary society, developed by intellectuals familiar with the Mead and Chicago

FIGURE 14.1

A SUMMARY OF THE STRUCTURE FUNCTIONALIST PARADIGM

TYPE	NATURALISTIC		SYSTEMIC	
THEORIST	PARSONS	BUCKLEY	ETZIONI	TIRYAKIAN
BACKGROUND	Trained in biology and familiar with Weber	Elitist education	Elitist education	Elitist education
AIMS	General theory of society	Apply modern systems theory to society	Develop a macrosociology	Develop a phenomenological theory of social order
ASSUMPTIONS	The social system exists	Society as an information system	Social system consists of control and cybernetic capacities	Social structure as phenomenal
METHODS	Historical deduction	Application of cybernetics	Application of voluntaristiccybernetorial approach to society	Application of phenomenology to society
TYPOLOGY	Stages of development	Systems model of society	Types of societies	Model of society
ISSUES	Application of the biological analogy	Application of the cybernetic analogy	Application of voluntaristiccybernetorial approach	Application of phenomenology

tradition within the context of a pragmatic and bureaucratic culture. Continuity between earlier social behaviorism and modern social psychology was clear in the elaboration and further application of earlier microscopic paradigms. Figure 14.3 reveals how the systemic type, as developed by Blumer and Goffman, represents an application and further elaboration of the Chicago-Mead model in response to the complexity and dynamism of social interaction.

        Blau and Garfinkel, on the other hand, with their Columbia

FIGURE 14.2
A SUMMARY OF THE MODERN CONFLICT PARADIGM

TYPE	SYSTEMIC		NATURALISTIC	
THEORIST	DAHRENDORF	MILLS	COSER	RIESMAN
BACKGROUND	European background and education	European familiarity and association with Gerth	Knowledge of Simmel and sociological theory	Varied education and career
AIMS	General theory of class conflict and social change	Application of sociological imagination to analysis of society	Analyze the social functions of conflict	Analyze changes in social character
ASSUMPTIONS	Coercion theory of society	Industrialization and rationalization lead to domination and alienation	Conflict may be functional	Demographic basis of conflict and conformity
METHODS	Application of Marx and Weber	Application of classic craftsmanship	Application of Simmel	Application of demographic and economic theory
TYPOLOGY	Model of class conflict	Types of social structure	Types of social structure	Types of social conformity
ISSUES	Synthesis of Marx and Weber	Subjective approach	Relationship to structure functionalism	Application of demographic factors

and Harvard backgrounds, take a more naturalistic approach in delineating the motivating phenomena with individuals as primary, resulting in frameworks which are somewhat similar in form to structure functionalism. Nevertheless, this type of paradigm as a whole may be viewed as the response of intellectuals familiar with the social-behaviorist tradition to the dynamism and complexity of social interaction, resulting in a kind of sociological theory which is microscopic, individualistic, internally oriented, symbolic, inductive, and dynamic.

283

CONCLUSIONS: TOWARD A MODEL OF CONTEMPORARY SOCIOLOGICAL THEORIZING

To emphasize the basis of our approach to theory again: sociological theory represents the reaction of a *particular* group of intellectuals to *particular* societal problems from the perspective of *particular* philosophical traditions, resulting in systemic conceptualizations of society which vary in level (macroscopic or microscopic) and *type of explanation* (i.e., naturalistic or systemic). In the case of contemporary theory, this model involves a number of distinct elements: the theorist's *background* (in particular, his educational training), his *philosophical viewpoint* (idealism, pragmatism, or naturalism); the predominant *societal problems* of the day (political-economic domination or the effects of industrialization); and the resultant *sociological paradigm* (structure functionalist, conflict, or social-psychological).

FIGURE 14.3
A SUMMARY OF THE SOCIAL-PSYCHOLOGICAL PARADIGM

TYPE	SYSTEMIC		NATURALISTIC	
THEORIST	BLUMER	GOFFMAN	BLAU	GARFINKEL
BACKGROUND	Chicago-Mead education	Chicago education	Columbia education and Chicago career	Harvard education under Parsons
AIMS	Symbolic interactionist understanding of human interaction	Analyze social interaction	Analyze microscopic basis of social associations	Analyze the rational properties of everyday life
ASSUMPTIONS	Action is interpreted and dynamic	Relevance of social information and impression management	Social exchange is the basis of social association and social structure	Rationalization process is basis of social organization
METHODS	Application of Mead	Dramaturgical analogy	Application of exchange theory	Application of Schutz
TYPOLOGY	Model of social reality	Dramaturgical model	Exchange model of society	Model of rationality
ISSUES	Lack of theory	Lack of theory	Reductionism	Reductionism

Once again, in broad and general terms, the model is assumed to operate as follows: educational background and philosophical viewpoint react to predominant societal problems to produce a systemic paradigm of society which differs in level and explanation. The elements of this model as applied to contemporary theory are summarized in Figure 14.4. From this it can be seen that structure functionalism is primarily a reaction of elitists and those familiar with biological and cybernetic analogies to political and economic problems within the tradition of European idealism and naturalism. Conflict theory is the reaction of those familiar with European thought to political and economic conflict and domination in the European traditions of idealism and naturalism; while social-psychological theory may be viewed as the reaction of elitists and those familiar with the Chicago-Mead tradition to the effects of industrialization from the perspective of European idealism and naturalism as well as American pragmatism.

Furthermore, the links between European naturalism and naturalistic sociological paradigms as well as the correlation between European idealism, American pragmatism, and more sociological types of explanation are also shown. While such a model is both *general* and *simplistic*, it highlights the manner in which contemporary theory represents *the systemic response of a particular group of intellectuals to the predominant societal problems and developments of the day*.

FIGURE 14.4
A MODEL OF CONTEMPORARY SOCIOLOGICAL THEORIZING

PARADIGM	GENERAL BACKGROUND	PHILOSOPHY	SOCIETAL PROBLEMS	EXPLANATION
STRUCTURE FUNCTIONALISM	Biological- cybernetic Elitist education	Naturalism Idealism	Political and economic Political and economic	Naturalistic Systemic
MODERN CONFLICT	European back- ground Varied and elitist background	Idealism Naturalism	Political and economic Political and economic	Systemic Naturalistic
SOCIAL- PSYCHOLOGICAL	Chicago-Mead Elitist education	Idealism Naturalism	Industrialization Industrialization	Systemic Naturalistic

Having analyzed the major types of traditional and contemporary sociological theory, we turn in Section Four to draw some major conclusions from this work concerning theory in general and sociological theory in particular. We shall also consider its development and future needs.

CONCLUSIONS

15

THE MAJOR CHARACTER-ISTICS OF SOCIOLOGICAL THEORY:

CONCLUSIONS

In this concluding section of our discussion we shall complete our analysis of sociological theory by summarizing the central problems of such theorizing and by drawing major conclusions regarding the major characteristics and needs of this type of theory.

CENTRAL PROBLEMS

In Chapter 1 we stated four major questions that are central to our analysis:

1 What is theory?

2 What is sociological theory?

3 What is traditional sociological theory?

4 What is contemporary sociological theory?

We shall now summarize our response to these major questions before drawing some general conclusions.

What Is Theory?

We defined *theorizing* as "the process by which individuals account for their physical and social environments within the context of a specific social setting." *Formal theory*, in particular, was viewed as "a set of abstract, logical propositions which attempts to explain relationships between phenomena and consists of eight structural elements: (1) a *paradigm*, (2) a set of *concepts*, (3) *logical relationships* between these concepts, (4) a set of operationalized *variables* and *indexes*, (5) a *methodology* designed to test these predicted relationships, (6) data *analysis*, (7) data *interpretation*, and (8) *evaluation* of the theory in light of all the above."

Furthermore, we distinguished between theories which are *formal*, explanatory, scientific, deductive, and objective and those which are more *informal*, descriptive, ideological, inductive, and intuitive. Finally, we attempted to show how theory is influenced by the particular societal, intellectual, and biographical *context* in which the theorist operates. In conclusion, theory is a *particular* definition of social and physical reality with a *particular* structure developed within a *particular* context.

What Is Sociological Theory?

Second, applying the above approach to sociology, we defined *sociological theory* as a "set of paradigms concerning society and social phenomena in reference to their separate societal reality, paradigms used to account for a society's social structure and internal social processes." We proceeded to discuss a continuum of views on theory ranging from the informal and artistic to the formal and scientific. Further, we described three major paradigms or "models of social reality" in sociological theory: the organic-structure-functional, the conflict-radical, and the social-behaviorist–social-psychological, viewing them as responses to political and economic change in Europe and the United States. This historical evolution also reveals a movement toward a scientific, microscopic, and sociological emphasis, in contrast to earlier philosophical, macroscopic, and naturalistic kinds of explanation. Finally, we attempted to show that sociological theory represents the reaction of a particular set of academics to society's perceived needs within the context of a particular set of intellectual values and societal experiences. Sociological theory is a dynamic, situational, and systemic reaction to perceived societal needs.

What Is Traditional Sociological Theory?

We described three major paradigms in traditional sociological theory: the organic, conflict, and social-behaviorist. The first represents the reaction, in the Enlightment tradition, of upper-class academics to political and economic problems of their day. These men conceptualized society as an organic, evolving system of norms and subsystems—a system reacting to natural laws, instincts, and society's division of labor system.

The conflict paradigm, in contrast, was seen generally as the reaction, in the tradition of Enlightenment philosophy and American pragmatism, of lower-class individuals to political oppression, conflict, and economic development—a reaction resulting in a materialistic-ecological approach to society as a system of competing groups.

Third, social behaviorism was defined as the reaction, in the spirit of Darwin, German idealism, and American pragmatism, of predominantly middle-class intellectuals to the problems of industrialization and urbanization. This reaction led to a microscopic conceptualization of society as a normative system of values, associations, and socialization based on society's demographic development and human instincts.

In this manner, *traditional theory represented the systemic reaction of intellectuals trained in Enlightenment naturalism and idealism to the political, social, and economic problems of the day. These reactions varied in their focus and ideological context, resulting in a set of paradigms concerning society and social phenomena in reference to their separate societal reality.*

What Is Contemporary Sociological Theory?

We concluded that theorizing in contemporary American sociology represents the application of European philosophical ideas to the changing problems of a materialistic, pragmatic, and utilitarian society in which idealism has given way to empiricism and utilitarianism. We delineated its three major paradigms as the structure functionalist, modern conflict, and social-psychological.

The first was viewed as a systemic evolutionary, and homeostatic reaction to the needs of contemporary society—a view developed by establishment-oriented intellectuals applying nineteenth-century European sociological thought within the context of a pragmatic and nonidealistic value system.

Modern conflict theory, on the other hand, was seen as a systemic, evolutionary, and radical reaction to contemporary forms of conflict and domination—a view developed by European-oriented intellectuals within the context of a conflict-ridden and exploitive society.

Third, social-psychological theory was viewed as a microscopic, individualistic, internally oriented, symbolic, inductive, and dynamic reaction to the analysis of contemporary society—a view developed within the context of a pragmatic and bureaucratic culture by intellectuals familiar with Mead and the Chicago tradition.

Contemporary theory, then, tends to represent the further application and elaboration of traditional paradigms within the context of a highly industrialized and utilitarian culture.

Having summarized our response to these central questions, we turn now to draw some major conclusions regarding sociological theory in general.

292

SOCIOLOGICAL THEORY AS A WHOLE: SOME CONCLUSIONS

In these final remarks, we shall attempt to assess some of this study's major implications for sociological theory as a whole with respect to its definition, major paradigms, characteristics, development, and future needs.

The Definition of Sociological Theory

Sociological theory is viewed primarily as a set of paradigms (i.e., models or definitions of reality) concerning society and social phenomena in reference to their separate societal reality. It has evolved out of Enlightenment naturalism and idealism and developed within the utilitarian context of American society. Sociological theory is thus a systemic, social reaction to perceived societal needs or problems, theory developed by particular intellectuals in specific social situations. Accordingly, it is dynamic, systemic, and reactive; however, despite variety in content and development, it remains a belief in society as a social system to be understood and explained for specific purposes within the Enlightenment tradition.

To summarize: *sociological theory represents the evolution and elaboration of a systemic model of social reality within the Enlightenment tradition in response to perceived societal problems and further elaborated within utilitarian American culture.*

The Major Paradigms of Sociological Theory

We have defined three major paradigms as the foundation of sociological theory: the organic-structure-functional, conflict-radical, and social-behaviorist–social-psychological. What are the general characteristics of these paradigms *as a whole?* An attempt is made to summarize them in Figure 15.1. While this typology is complex and compresses a great variety of information, a number of general trends are visible:

1 The organic-structure-functional paradigm tends to represent the application of naturalistic analogies to society by elitists, Enlightenment-educated intellectuals attempting to develop general

293

FIGURE 15.1
A SUMMARY OF MAJOR PARADIGMS IN SOCIOLOGICAL THEORY

PARADIGM	ORGANIC-STRUCTURE-FUNCTIONAL	CONFLICT-RADICAL	SOCIAL-BEHAVIORIST-SOCIAL PSYCHOLOGICAL
BACKGROUND	Elitist background. Enlightenment education with training in biology, physics	European education and Enlightenment idealism	Pragmatic—idealistic education
AIMS	Develop a general theory of society to maximize planning and control	Understand domination and conflict to maximize social change	Understand social action in order to understand society
ASSUMPTIONS	Application of naturalistic analogy to society	Society is system of competing elements and groups	Society exists at the microscopic level in the form of norms, values, social exchange
METHODS	Positivism and historical deduction	Dialectical materialism and historical induction	Interpretive and introspective
TYPOLOGY	Types of society and societal evolution	Types of social structure and stages of societal evolution and conflict	Types of microscopic social structure
ISSUES	Macroscopic reductionism	Macroscopic determinism and reductionism	Microscopic reductionism

theories of society that are intended to increase understanding and control. Their major methodology consists of historical deduction, their typologies delineate types of society, while the major issue they raise is the problem of macroscopic reductionism.

2   The conflict-radical paradigm consists of the application of Enlightenment idealism to the understanding of social conflict and change in order to maximize positive and radical social change. The methodology is primarily historical induction and the typologies delineate stages of conflict and types of society. These theories also raise the problem of macroscopic determinism and reductionism.

3   The social-behaviorist–social-psychological paradigm consists of the application of idealism and pragmatism to the understanding of social action and interaction. It views society as a microscopically based system of norms, values and social interpretations. Using interpretive understanding as a method, these theorists develop microscopic typologies of social action, raising the general problem of microscopic reductionism.

Looking at the three paradigms as a whole in general terms, it is possible to summarize sociological theory as the reaction of establishment intellectuals to societal problems in the tradition of naturalism, idealism, and pragmatism, resulting in the development of general and systemic theories of society (naturalistic or systemic, macroscopic or microscopic), using the methods of historical deduction and induction in which naturalistic, idealistic, and pragmatic paradigms are applied to society. Types of society or social structure are delineated, while problems of reductionism in the general application of these paradigms appear inevitable. In general, then, *sociological theory tends to be elitist, systemic, analogical, historical, typological, and reductionistic.*

The Major Characteristics of Sociological Theory
While we have outlined some of these characteristics above, we are specifically concerned here with characteristics of the major *assumptions* sociological theory makes. These may be summarized as follows: as a general paradigm, sociological theory tends to be:

1 *Systemic:* It perceives society and social phenomena as systems (i.e., integrated wholes) on either the microscopic or macroscopic level.

2 *Equilibrium-oriented:* It views society as either in equilibrium or moving through a number of evolutionary stages in which the system moves toward, achieves, and then moves away from equilibrium as part of the process of social dynamics.

3 *Functionalist:* Society and social phenomena are defined as the function of a number of underlying factors—examples are system problems, primary needs, residues, traits, and demographic pressures.

4 *Evolutionary:* Society is not viewed as static; rather, it is changing, dynamic, and evolving from one stage of economic development to the next, in particular from the pre- or nonindustrial to the capitalist and industrial.

5 *Naturalistic or systemic:* Its explanations are based on either naturalistic phenomena (i.e., characteristics of human nature) or the systemic and sociological, as we have attempted to show. The former type is founded on Enlightenment naturalism, the latter on Enlightenment idealism.

6 *Structure–process-oriented:* Sociological phenomena are conceptualized as bifurcated into social structure and social process, particularly within sociological typologies of society.

7 *Historical:* Historical induction and deduction constitute its main methods as it traces societal evolution and applies macroscopic assumptions to the individual level of analysis.

8 *Conservative:* In its emphasis upon societal and systemic priorities, in particular the orientation toward planning and control priorities inherent within the organic and structure-functionalist paradigms, sociological theory tends to be ideologically conservative in positing societal rather than individual needs as paramount in its models of humanity and society—an orientation further reinforced within the context of American society. While clearly this is not always the case, systemic conservatism represents a dominant emphasis in its development and continuing status.

9 *Utopian:* Sociological theory, in its ideological and evolutionary orientations, tends to be utopian in nature. That is, it projects some kind of social utopia (e.g., positivism, socialism, modernity) as desirable and the end-point of societal evolution. Many, if not all, of these utopias tend to be simplistic and authoritarian in form; nevertheless, they represent the logical projection, at least in the theorist's mind, of the basis of his theory.

10 *Analogical:* As we have seen, much of sociological theory consists of the application of nonsociological paradigms (e.g., biological, cybernetic, philosophical, or demographic) to the analysis of society. Its paradigmatic base is thus limited conceptually as intellectuals have developed sociological theory through their reaction to societal problems from the point of view of other philosophical perspectives.

To summarize once again: *sociological theory tends to represent the conservative application of systemic and nonsociological paradigms to societal problems, using historical induction and deduction.*

The Development of Sociological Theory

We have attempted to demonstrate the degree to which the foundation of sociology was contained in Enlightenment philosophy, particularly in naturalism and idealism. Furthermore, we portrayed contemporary American sociology as the application and development of European paradigms within the context of a materialistic, pragmatic, and utilitarian culture. We also noted that as this development took place, sociological theory developed from the philosophical, descriptive, macroscopic, and ideological to the more scientific, explanatory, microscopic, and "objective" in response to society's changing intellectual norms. To a large extent, then, *the development of sociological theory may be viewed as the systemic application of Enlightenment philosophy, in particular naturalism and idealism, to societal problems in the form of the sociological paradigm, further elaborated within the context of a pragmatic culture, evolving from the philosophical, descriptive, and macroscopic in form toward the scientific, explanatory, and microscopic.*

To summarize, sociological theory represents the evolution and elaboration of a systemic model of social reality within the Enlightenment tradition in response to perceived societal problems, a model further elaborated within utilitarian American culture. It tends to be systemic, equilibrium-oriented, functionalist, evolutionary, naturalistic and systemic, structure–process-oriented, historical, conservative, utopian, and analogical. Finally, it has evolved from the philosophical, descriptive, and macroscopic toward the scientific, explanatory, and microscopic.

Having drawn the above conclusions, we turn to the kinds of need within sociological theory that these conclusions imply.

Sociological Theory's Needs

From our discussion so far, it has been evident that sociological theory is limited in origin, development, ideology, form, and historical context. Thus, to a large extent, it represents the systemic reaction of Western philosophers to societal problems, in particular the effects of industrialization. Such a paradigm may be critiqued as elitist, conservative, and group-oriented, reflecting what Marcuse has termed "one-dimensional" thought—"a trend toward consummation of techological rationality and intensive efforts to contain this trend within the established institutions."[1] Sociological theory, in large measure, represents the imposition of a "technological utopia" on social reality, with the result that systemic, economic, and technological phenomena are its paramount criteria in theory development. Consequently, it tends to be systemic, materialistic, and group-oriented rather than spontaneous, humanistic, and individual-oriented (i.e., it is a materialistic, technological utopia, projected by a particular ethnocentric elite, and further developed by a pragmatic, cultural context).

In order to facilitate our discussion of needs and alternatives, the major characteristics and needs of sociological theory are summarized in Figure 15.2. We shall discuss each in turn.

Background   The social and educational background of theorists has been shown to be generally elitist and traditional. In contrast, there is an obvious need for a variety of socioeconomic backgrounds, educations, and values in order to broaden the origin and context of sociological theory.

Aims   The aims of sociological theory have, on the whole, been control-oriented and general. In contrast, theory could be more change-oriented and specific in reference to individual needs.

[1]H. Marcuse, *One-Dimensional Man*, Sphere, London, 1968, p. 30.

FIGURE 15.2
THE GENERAL CHARACTERISTICS AND NEEDS OF SOCIOLOGICAL THEORY

DIMENSION	CHARACTERISTICS	ALTERNATIVES
BACKGROUND	Elitist	Pluralist
	Traditional-elitist education	Broad education
AIMS	General	Specific
	Control-oriented	Change-oriented
ASSUMPTIONS	Limited analogies	Pluralistic analogies
	Bifurcation: macroscopic-microscopic	Synthesis: needs-structure
		Individualistic and inductive
	Systemic	Dynamic
	Equilibrium-oriented	Need-based
	Functionalistic	Change-oriented
	Evolutionary	Need-based
	Naturalistic-systemic	Synthesis: definitions of reality
	Structure process	Futuristic
	Historical	Radical
	Conservative	Open-ended
	Utopian	Need-based
	Analogical	
METHODOLOGY	Empirical	Critical, dialectic thought
	Historical deduction-induction	Need-based induction
TYPOLOGIES	Types of social structure	Relationship: human needs and social structure
ISSUES	Macroscopic, microscopic reductionism	Relationship: human needs and social structure

Assumptions The major assumptions of sociological theory have already been discussed above, underlining its systemic, functionalistic characteristics and its basis in very limited analogies or paradigms. In contrast, it is evident that sociological theory could be founded on a plurality of paradigms, based on human need, change-oriented, futuristic, and open-ended.

Methodology The methodology of sociological theory, founded on positivism or the scientific method, is primarily empirical (i.e., based on observation), historical, and deductive. Alternatives include a critical, value-based approach in contrast to the empirical and an emphasis on inductive "explanations" based on what human needs are defined to be.

Typologies Accordingly, resultant typologies, instead of delineating types of social structure, would focus on the structural implications (i.e., types of utopia) of particular value systems (i.e., assumptions concerning human needs).

Issues Resultant issues would consist not of the problems of reductionism but the relationship between particular value systems and the types of social system they imply.

In general, then, we are arguing for a plurality of need-based, critical, and dynamic sociological paradigms based on a variety of value systems and for an intellectual response to a wide range of human needs. Such alternatives, in fact, are crucial to the future development of sociology in general, since if they are not developed, sociological theory will continue to serve elitist-systemic interests and reflect limited and conservative value systems, moving sociology toward an intellectual dead end. It is crucial, therefore, that future theorizing be diversified both in form and content if sociology is to make a vital contribution to societal development.

EXERCISES

1 Analyze the *ideological* implications of the three major paradigms in sociological theory. What models of humanity and society do they imply?

2 Discuss the *practical* implications of the three paradigms in reference to some major societal problems.

3 Select some nonsociological paradigms (e.g., existentialism, Christianity, Buddhism) and assess their sociological implications (i.e., their models of humanity and society). How do they differ from those in sociological theory?

READINGS

Gouldner, A. W.: *The Coming Crisis of Western Sociology,* Avon, New York, 1970, chap. 13.

Larson, C. J.: *Major Themes in Sociological Theory,* McKay, New York, 1973, chap. 7.

Marcuse, H.: *One Dimensional Man,* Sphere, London, 1968, chaps. 5, 6, and 7.

Martindale, D.: *The Nature and Types of Sociological Theory,* Houghton Mifflin, Boston, 1960, chap. 20.

Timasheff, N. S.: *Sociological Theory, Its Nature and Growth,* 3d ed., Random House, New York, 1967, chap. 22.

Turner, J. H.: *The Structure of Sociological Theory,* Dorsey, Homewood, Ill., chap. 17.

SELECTED
BIBLIOGRAPHY

GENERAL WORKS

Berger, J., et al.: *Sociological Theories in Progress*, vol. 1, Houghton Mifflin, Boston, 1966.

————: *Sociological Theories in Progress,* vol. 2, Houghton Mifflin, Boston, 1972.

Coser, L. A., and B. Rosenberg: *Sociological Theory,* 3d ed., Macmillan, New York, 1969.

Klapp, O. E.: *Models of Social Order,* National Press, Palo Alto, Calif., 1973.

Larson, C. J.: *Major Themes in Sociological Theory,* McKay, New York, 1973.

MacIntyre, Alasdair, and Dorothy Emmet: *Sociological Theory and Philosophical Analysis,* Macmillan, New York, 1970.

Martindale, D.: *The Nature and Types of Sociological Theory,* Houghton Mifflin, Boston, 1960.

Timasheff, N. S.: *Sociological Theory: Its Nature and Growth,* Random House, New York, 1966.

SPECIFIC THEORISTS

Blau

Blau, Peter M.: *Bureaucracy in Modern Society,* Random House, New York, 1956.

————: *Dynamics of Bureaucracy: A Study of Interpersonal Relationships in Two Government Agencies,* 2d ed., University of Chicago Press, Chicago, 1963.

————: *Exchange and Power in Social Life,* Wiley, New York, 1964.

———— and Otis D. Duncan: *American Occupational Structure,* Wiley, New York, 1967.

————: *The Dynamics of Bureaucracy,* rev. ed., University of Chicago Press, Chicago, 1973.

————: *The Organization of Academic Work,* Wiley, New York, 1973.

Blumer

Blumer, Herbert: *Appraisal of Thomas and Znaniecki's The Polish*

Peasant in Europe and America, Social Science Research, New York, 1939.

———— *Symbolic Interactionism: Perspective and Method,* Prentice-Hall, Englewood Cliffs, N.J., 1969.

———— et al.: *Movies, Delinquency, and Crime,* Patterson Smith, Montclair, N.J., 1973.

Buckley

Buckley, Walter: *Sociology and Modern Systems Theory,* Prentice-Hall, Englewood Cliffs, N.J., 1967.

———— (ed.): *Modern Systems Research for the Behaviorist Scientist,* Aldine, Chicago, 1968.

Comte

Comte, A.: *General View of Positivism,* Speller, New York, 1957.

————: *System of Positive Polity,* B. Franklin, New York, 1968 (4 vols.).

————: *Introduction to Positive Philosophy,* Frederick Ferre (ed.), Bobbs-Merrill, Indianapolis, 1970.

————: *A General View of Positivism,* Ann Greer (ed.), Wm. C. Brown, Dubuque, Iowa, 1972.

Coser

Coser, L.: *Functions of Social Conflict,* Free Press, Chicago, 1956.

————: *Men of Ideas,* Free Press, New York, 1965.

———— (ed.): *George Simmel,* Prentice-Hall, Englewood Cliffs, N.J., 1965.

————: *Continuities in the Study of Social Conflict,* Free Press, New York, 1967.

————: *Sociology through Literature,* 2d ed., Prentice-Hall, Englewood Cliffs, N.J., 1972.

————: *The Greedy Society,* Free Press, New York, 1974.

Dahrendorf

Dahrendorf, Ralf: *Class and Class Conflict in Industrial Society,* Standord University Press, Stanford, Calif., 1959.

————: *Essays in the Theory of Society,* Stanford University Press, Stanford, Calif., 1969.

————: *Society and Democracy in Germany,* Doubleday, Garden City, N.Y., 1969.

Durkheim

Durkheim, Emile: *Division of Labor in Society,* Free Press, Glencoe, Ill., 1947.

————: *Rules of Sociological Method,* Free Press, Glencoe, Ill., 1950.

————: *Suicide,* Free Press, Glencoe, Ill., 1951.

————: *Sociology and Philosophy,* Free Press, Glencoe, Ill., 1953.

————: *Elementary Forms of the Religious Life,* Joseph W. Swain (trans.), Free Press, Chicago, 1954.

————: *Education and Sociology,* Free Press, Chicago, 1956.

————: *Moral Education,* Free Press, New York, 1961.

————' *Socialism,* Macmillan, New York, 1962.

————: *Elementary Forms of the Religious Life,* Humanities, New York, 1964.

————: *On Morality and Society,* University of Chicago Press, Chicago, 1973.

Etzioni

Etzioni, Amitai: *Modern Organizations,* Prentice-Hall, Englewood Cliffs, N.J., 1964.

————: *Active Society,* Free Press, New York, 1968.

————: *Readings on Modern Organizations,* Prentice-Hall, Englewood Cliffs, N.J., 1969.

————: *Sociological Reader on Complex Organizations,* 2d ed., Holt, New York, 1969.

————: *Comparative Analysis of Complex Organizations,* Free Press, New York, 1971.

Garfinkel

Garfinkel, Harold: *Studies in Ethnomethodology,* Prentice-Hall, Englewood Cliffs, N.J., 1967.

Goffman

Goffman, Erving: *Presentation of Self in Everyday life,* Doubleday, Garden City, N.Y., 1959.
———: *Asylums: Essays on the Social Situation of Mental Patients and Other Inmates,* Doubleday, Garden City, N.Y., 1961.
———: *Encounters: Two Studies in the Sociology of Interaction,* Bobbs-Merrill, Indianapolis, 1961.
———: *Behavior in Public Places: Notes on the Social Organization of Gatherings,* Free Press, New York, 1963.
———: *Stigma: Notes on the Management of Spoiled Identity,* Prentice-Hall, Englewood Cliffs, N.J., 1963.
———: *Interaction Ritual: Essays on Face-To-Face Behavior,* Doubleday, Garden City, N.Y., 1967.
———: *Relations in Public,* Harper & Row, New York, 1972.

Marx

Marx, Karl: *Early Writings,* McGraw-Hill, New York, 1963.
———: *Selected Writings in Sociology and Social Philosophy,* T. B. Bottomore (ed.), McGraw-Hill, New York, 1964.
———: *Capital,* Frederick Engels (ed.), International Publishers, New York, 1967 (3 vols.).
———: *Communist Manifesto,* J. H. Laski (ed.), Pantheon, New York, 1967.
———: *Writings of the Young Marx on Philosophy and Society,* Loyd D. Easton and Kurt H. Guddat (trans.), Doubleday, Garden City, N.Y., 1967.
———: *Economic and Philosophical Manuscripts of 1844,* Dirk J. Struik (ed.), Martin Milligan (trans.), International Publishers, New York, 1971.
———: *Karl Marx on America and the Civil War,* Saul K. Padover (ed.), McGraw-Hill, New York, 1973.
———: *Karl Marx on Society and Social Change: With Selections by Friedrich Engels,* University of Chicago Press, Chicago, 1973.

Mead

Mead, George H.: *Mind, Self and Society: From the Standpoint of a Social Behaviorist,* Charles W. Morris (ed.), University of Chicago Press, Chicago, 1934.

————: *Movements of Thought in the Nineteenth Century,* Merritt H. Moore (ed.), University of Chicago Press, Chicago, 1936.
————: *Philosophy of the Present,* Arthur E. Murphy (ed.), Open Court, La Salle, Ill., 1959.
————: *George Herbert Mead on Social Psychology,* Anselm Strauss, (ed.), University of Chicago Press, Chicago, 1964.
————: *Philosophy of the Act,* Charles W. Morris (ed.), University of Chicago Press, Chicago, 1972.

Mills

Mills, C. Wright: *Power Elite,* Oxford University Press, Fair Lawn, N.J., 1956.
————: *White Collar: American Middle Classes,* Oxford University Press, Fair Lawn, N.J., 1956.
————: *Sociological Imagination,* Oxford University Press, Fair Lawn, N.J., 1959.
————: *Images of Man,* Braziller, New York, 1960.
————: *Power, Politics, and People,* Irving L. Horowitz (ed.), Oxford University Press, Fair Lawn, N.J., 1963.
————: *Sociology and Pragmatism: The Higher Learning in America,* Irving L. Horowitz (ed.), Oxford University Press, Fair Lawn, N.J., 1964.

Pareto

Pareto, Vilfredo: *Mind and Society: A Treatise on General Sociology,* Dover, New York, 1935.
————: *Rise and Fall of Elites,* Bedminster, Totowa, N.J., 1968.
————: *Manual of Political Economy,* Alfred N. Page (ed.), Ann Schweir (trans.), Kelley, Clifton, N.J., 1969.

Park

Park, Robert E.: *Robert E. Park on Social Control and Collective Behavior: Selected Papers,* Ralph H. Turner (ed.), University of Chicago Press, Chicago, 1967.
————: *Human Communities,* Free Press, Glencoe, Ill., 1952.
————: *Society,* Free Press, Chicago, 1955.
————: *Introduction to the Science of Sociology,* 3d ed., M. Janowitz (ed.), University of Chicago Press, Chicago, 1969.

Parsons

Parsons, Talcott: *Structure of Social Action,* Free Press, Glencoe, Ill., 1949.

———: *Social System,* Free Press, Glencoe, Ill., 1951.

——— and Edward A. Shils (eds.): *Toward a General Theory of Action,* Harvard University Press, Cambridge, Mass., 1951.

——— et al.: *Family, Socialization and Interaction Process,* Free Press, Chicago, 1955.

——— and Neil J. Smelser: *Economy and Society: A Study in the Integration of Economic and Social Theory,* Free Press, New York, 1957.

———: *Structure and Process in Modern Societies,* Free Press, New York, 1960.

———: *Social Structure and Personality,* Free Press, New York, 1964.

——— (ed.): *Theories of Society,* Free Press, New York, 1965.

———: *Societies: Evolutionary and Comparative Perspectives,* Prentice-Hall, Englewood Cliffs, N.J., 1966.

———: *Sociological Theory and Modern Society,* Free Press, New York, 1967.

———: *Politics and Social Structure,* Free Press, New York, 1969.

———: *The System of Modern Societies,* Prentice-Hall, Englewood Cliffs, N.J., 1971.

——— and Victor Lidz: *Readings on Premodern Societies*, Prentice-Hall, Englewood Cliffs, N.J., 1972.

——— and Gerald Platt: *The American University,* Harvard University Press, Cambridge, Mass., 1973.

Riesman

Riesman, David: *Individualism Reconsidered and Other Essays*, Free Press, Glencoe, Ill., 1954.

——— and Nathan Glazer: *Faces in the Crowd: Individual Studies in Character and Politics*, rev. ed., Yale University Press, New Haven, Conn., 1964.

———: *The Lonely Crowd: A Study of the Changing American Character,* rev. ed., Yale University Press, New Haven, Conn., 1969.

——— et al.: *Academic Values and Mass Education: The Early Years of Oakland and Monteith,* Doubleday, Garden City, N.Y., 1970.

Simmel

Simmel, Georg: *Conflict and the Web of Group Affiliations,* Free
Press, Glenecoe, Ill., 1955.
————: *Georg Simmel on Individuality and Social Forms,* Donald
N. Levine (ed.), University of Chicago Press, Chicago, 1971.

Spencer

Spencer, Herbert: *Social Statistics*, Kelley, Clifton, N.J., 1851.
————: *Principles of Sociology,* Greenwood, Westport, Conn.,
1880–1897.
————: *Study of Sociology,* University of Michigan Press, Ann Ar-
bor, Mich., 1961.
————: *Education: Intellectual, Moral and Physical,* Littlefield, Totowa, N.J., 1963.
————: *Evolution of Society,* Robert L. Carneiro (ed.), University
of Chicago Press, Chicago, 1967.
————: *Man versus the State,* Donald Macrae (ed.), Penguin, Bal-
timore, 1970
————: *Herbert Spencer on Social Evolution,* J. D. Peel (ed.), University of Chicago Press, Chicago, 1972.

Sumner

Sumner, William G.: *Challenge of Facts and Other Essays,* AMS
Press, New York, 1914.
————: *Forgotten Man and Other Essays,* A. G. Keller (ed.), Books
for Libraries, Freeport, N.Y., 1919.
————: *Essays of William Graham Sumner,* Albert G. Keller and
Maurice R. Davie (eds.), Shoe String, Hamden, Conn., 1969
(2 vols.).
————: *Sumner Today: Selected Essays,* Maurice R. Davie (ed.),
Greenwood, Westport, Conn., 1971.

Tiryakian

Tiryakin, Edward A.: *Sociological Theory, Values, and Sociocul-
tural Change,* Free Press, New York, 1962.
————: *Phenomenon of Sociology: A Reader in the Sociology of
Sociology,* Appleton Century Crofts, New York, 1971.

Tönnies

Tönnies, Ferdinand: *Community and Society: Gemeinschaft and Gesellschaft,* Charles P. Loomis (trans.), Michigan State University Press, Lansing, Mich., 1957.
————: *Custom,* Free Press, New York, 1961.

Veblen

Veblen, Thorstein: *Theory of the Leisure Class,* Kelley, New York, 1899.
————: *Theory of Business Enterprise,* Kelley, New York, 1904.
————: *Instinct of Workmanship,* rev. ed., Kelley, New York, 1918.
————: *Vested Interests,* Kelley, New York, 1920.
————: *Essays in Our Changing Order,* Leon Ardzrooni (ed.), Kelley, New York, 1934.
————: *Higher Learning in America,* Hill and Wang, New York, 1957.

Weber

Weber, Max: *The Protestant Ethic and the Spirit of Capitalism,* Scribner, New York, 1930.
————: *From Max Weber: Essays in Sociology,* Hans H. Gerth and C. Wright Mills (trans.), Oxford University Press, Fair Lawn, N.J., 1946.
————: *Theory of Social and Economic Organization,* Talcott Parsons (trans.), Free Press, Glencoe, Ill., 1947.
————: *Max Weber on Methodology of the Social Sciences,* Free Press, Glencoe, Ill., 1949.
————: *Ancient Judaism,* Free Press, Glencoe, Ill., 1952.
————: *Max Weber on Law in Economy and Society,* Edward Shils and Max Rheinstein (trans.), B. Y. Edward (ed.), Harvard University Press, Cambridge, Mass., 1954.
————: *City,* Free Press, New York, 1958.
————: *Basic Concepts in Sociology,* H. P. Secher (trans.), Greenwood, Westport, Conn., 1962.
————: *Sociology of Religion,* Ephraim Fischoffs (trans.), Beacon Press, Boston, 1964.
————: *Economy and Society: An Outline of Interpretive Sociology,* 4th ed., Guenther Roth and Claus Wittich (eds.), E. Fischoff et al. (trans.), Bedminister, Totowa, N.J., 1968 (3 vols.).

311

NAME INDEX

Andreski, S., 97
Aron, R., 96, 130, 165

Barnes, H. E., 45
Becker, H., 45, 65
Bendix, R., 167
Berger, J., 304
Bernard, J., 180n., 188
Bernard, L. L., 180n., 188
Blalock, H. M., 11n., 12, 19n., 23, 28n.
Blau, P., 262, 264–267, 278, 284, 304–305
Blumer, H., 252–255, 278, 284, 305
Boskoff, A., 45
Bottomore, T. B., 105n., 132, 307
Buckley, W., 37n., 197–201, 218, 282, 305

Cantor, N. F., 65
Carneiro, R. L., 97

Cassirer, E., 65
Catlin, G. E. G., 42n.
Catton, W. R., 36n., 45
Collins, R., 8
Comte, A., 70–73, 96, 171, 305
Coser, L., 32, 96, 130, 165, 234–237, 248, 283, 304, 305

Dahrendorf, R., 32, 224–227, 248, 283, 306
Davie, M. R., 158n., 167, 310
Denisoff, R. S., 248
Duncan, O. D., 304
Durkheim, E., 31, 42n., 43, 82–87, 97, 171, 306

Easton, L. D., 307
Edward, B. Y., 311
Emmer, D., 304
Engles, F., 132, 307

313

SUBJECT INDEX

Structure functionalist paradigm,
  summary of, 282

Theological paradigm, 55
Theorizing:
  biographical conditions of, 21
  defined, 5
  intellectual conditions of, 20–21
  a model of, 47–49
  societal conditions of, 20
  and sociological theory, 5

Theory:
  defined, 10–16
  formal type of, 12–16
  major types of, 16–17
Theory construction, process of,
  18–19
Traditional sociological theory,
  51–65
  defined, 291–292
  a typology of, 169–175
Typology, defined, 10